PARIS

The Virago Woman's
Travel Guide

Virago "a woman
of great stature,
strength & courage "

VIRAGO WOMAN'S TRAVEL GUIDE TO
PARIS

CATHERINE CULLEN

Ulysses Press

Published by: Ulysses Press
3286 Adeline Street Suite 1
Berkeley, CA 94703

First published by Virago Press Limited 1993
United Kingdom

Library of Congress Catalog Card Number 93-60070

ISBN 0-915233-89-4
Printed in the U.S.A. by the George Banta Company

10 9 8 7 6 5 4 3 2 1

Executive Editor: *Ray Riegert*
Editorial Director: *Leslie Henriques*
Managing Editor: *Claire Chun*
U.S. Editor: *Sayre Van Young*
Editorial Associates: *Per Casey, Andrea Orvik, Lee Micheaux, Kimberly Kradel, William Kiester*
Virago Cover Design: *The Senate*
U.S. Cover Design: *Bonnie Smetts Design*
Interior Design: *Per Casey*
Index: *Sayre Van Young*

Distributed in the United States by Publishers Group West, in Canada by Raincoast Books.

DISCLAIMER: The author and publisher have made every effort to ensure the accuracy of information contained in *The Virago Woman's Guide to Paris*, but can accept no liability for any loss, injury or inconvenience sustained by any traveler as a result of information or advice contained in this guide.

Printed on recycled paper

ACKNOWLEDGMENTS

For all their help and advice I wish to thank Miranda Davies, Leah Price and Geraldine Ward, as well as Nathalie Bonnin and Beatrice Pire for giving me a hand with the research.

Catherine Cullen, Paris, 1993

Many thanks to Lucy Drew for help with nightlife listings and Julian Jackson for accommodation and sharing his knowledge of French history.

Jackie Holmes, London, 1993

CONTENTS

INTRODUCTION

The city of can-can girls, catwalks and Coco Chanel, Paris has long enjoyed a reputation as Europe's capital of fun, fashion and romance. Whether your idea of a good time is designer window shopping, dawdling in sidewalk cafés, devouring art, strolling along the Seine, watching Parisians pose, or indulging in some of the world's best cuisine, Paris will not disappoint. Its beauty is legendary – and intoxicating: stand at any time of the day or night on one of the elegant bridges arched over the Seine and soak in the glories that surround you: the monumental Notre Dame on the Ile de la Cité, once Paris's center of political and religious life, on the Right Bank Georges Haussmann's grand boulevards, designed to pay homage to commerce in the Second Empire, or the leafy *quais* of the Left Bank, long the heart of intellectual and radical life.

It's a compact city, best seen on foot, not only because most sights are in walking distance of one another, but because of the myriad pleasures of its street life. There are magnificent vistas on both banks, markets and delicatessens where the produce is arranged with skills a still-life artist would die for, lovers embracing against photogenic cityscapes, and aromas wafting from patisseries and boulangeries guaranteed to make even a post-prandial stomach water. Take Paris slowly, and sidetrack at whim – this way you'll get the most out of the city, stumbling across vignettes of life ranging from the clichéd (fire jugglers outside the Pompidou, Gauloise-smoking concierges, baguette-carrying bicyclists) to the unexpected. But don't neglect its museums whose collections are among the finest in the world.

Its history is an especially rich and intriguing one for women: the great *salons* of the seventeenth and eighteenth centuries gave women an intellectual influence and freedom; in the nineteenth century, for the bohemian and the *flâneuse* pleasure and revolution were a seductive mix; in the mid-twentieth century, Paris spelled freedom for Simone de Beauvoir who set the agenda for contemporary feminism in her exhilarating *The Second Sex*.

Paris is strikingly cosmopolitan: the nineteenth-century mass immigration from the French provinces (one out of every six inhabitants of France is Parisian) was followed by the arrival of Eastern European emigrés at the beginning of this century and later by those from the ex-French colonies. It's also long been a haven for refugees and dissidents, as well as droves of American and British artists and writers seeking intellectual stimulation, sexual freedom and simply *la bonne vie*. (Deciding whether to flee Paris during World War II, Gertrude Stein is reputed to have said to Alice B. Toklas, "I *am* fussy about my food. Let's not leave.")

Today you can taste food and hear music from all over the world: there are North African, Cambodian, Lebanese and Eastern European restaurants; Russian and Turkish tea houses; while the live music available ranges from gigs by visiting U.S. and British bands to the refreshing sounds of French Caribbean zouk and Algerian rai. It's also considered by many to be the film capital of the world.

Despite this exotic veneer, late twentieth-century immigration has been far from glamorous. Members of France's ex-colonies – in north and west Africa, the Caribbean and southeast Asia – have flooded into the city since the 1950s, prepared to do unappealing jobs for pitiable wages and to live in the areas of the city shunned by Parisians. Now, with unemployment rising, they are viewed by many French as stealing their work – hence an insidious increase in racism.

Paris is very much a modern city beset by twentieth-century problems. It is France's most important center of industry, banking and commerce, and has a population of eight million. Unemployment is high, homelessness is on the increase, traffic jams are endemic, and green space is limited.

However, although it would be crass to ignore these distressing aspects, Paris remains a glorious spectacle of a city, perfect for either a long sojourn or short break.

PRACTICALITIES

WHEN TO GO

 **P**aris is special at *any* time. The climate is fairly predictable, with fewer days weighed down by gloomy skies, and walking around is always a pleasure, even in winter when temperatures can drop below freezing and bitter winds may sweep the streets.

Visitors flock to the city all year round, but September and October are surprisingly busy months, partly due to trade fairs, so take extra care to book a hotel room well in advance. Autumn and spring – the most magical seasons – are often mild and sunny, while high summer, besides attracting the biggest tourist crowds, tends to be hot and quite possibly humid. The one advantage of visiting at this time – more specifically mid-July to the end of August – is the mass exodus of Parisians, who pack their bags and leave the city for their annual vacation. Your favorite bakery will be closed, as will other shops, bars and restaurants, but at least you'll find many fewer traffic jams, easy parking and room to breathe in the Metro.

FESTIVALS AND EVENTS

Paris is never short of cultural events. The *Festival d'Automne*, lasting three months from October, includes concerts, theater and ballet, overlapping with a yearly celebration of international dance. Summer, though less prolific, brings the Quartier d'Eté festival, created in 1990 to liven up the city's sleepier months and again featuring a mixture of music, theater and dance.

CALENDAR OF EVENTS

JANUARY

06 Epiphany or *Fête des Rois* – religious festival when people eat a special almond cake, the *galette des rois*, in which a charm is hidden. Whoever finds the charm dons a crown and is king.

MARCH

An *International Festival of Women's Films* takes place every year in Sceaux, outside Paris. Information from the Center d'Action Culturelle "Les Gemeaux" (tel. 46 60 05 64).

During the first week, hundreds of farmers gather with their livestock for the immensely popular *Salon de l'Agriculture* at the Parc des Expositions de Paris, Porte de Versailles.

APRIL

01 April Fool's Day, known as *Poisson d'Avril*, provides another chance for bakers to show their skills by producing an endless variety of bread, pastry and chocolate fish.

Mid-month sees the annual Paris running marathon.

MAY

01 Labor Day is a public holiday, celebrated by trade-union marches and various other events.

A puppet festival, *Les Semaines de la Marionette à Paris*, takes place around Beaubourg during the last two weeks.

JUNE

Mid-June to mid-July sees the *Festival de la Butte Montmartre*, *Festival du Marais* and *Festival "Foire St-Germain,"* each marked by theater, dance, music and other local celebrations.

21 The *Fête de la Musique* brings out every kind of musician on to the streets, into parks and cafés, to demonstrate their skills.

The last Saturday heralds a huge Gay Pride march, starting at 2 p.m. from the Place de la Bastille.

JULY

14 Bastille Day – national holiday marked by fireworks and occasional dancing in the streets.

AUGUST

15 *Fête de l'Assomption* at Notre Dame.

SEPTEMBER

The *Fête de l'Humanité*, a popular three-day cultural event organized by the French Communist Party, takes place around mid-month.

OCTOBER

The *Festival d'Automne*, combining dance, theater and classical music, lasts until December.

Festival International de Danse de Paris – celebration of ballet in all its forms lasting through to the end of November.

DECEMBER

24 Christmas Mass at Notre Dame.

GETTING THERE

Paris by Air

The first thing you need is a good travel agent – if you don't have one, ask your friends for references. If you're a student or under 26 years of age, companies like Student Travel Association (STA) and Council Travel are helpful. STA's main phone number is 213-934-8722 and they have offices in cities throughout the United States. The main number for Council Travel is 212-661-1414.

Most of the major carriers in the U.S. and Canada offer frequent flights year round to both Roissy-Charles de Gaulle and Orly airports in Paris. Have your travel agent shop around for the best prices and be sure to ask about consolidated bookings; these are essentially wholesale tickets and can save travelers vast amounts.

The cost of a roundtrip flight from North America varies greatly and depends on the point of disembarkation and time of the year. During the low season, or winter, there are fares as low as US$400 from both the East and West Coast. During the shoulder seasons the fares are greater at about US$650 from the East Coast and US$850 from the West Coast. The summer is, of course, the most expensive time of the year to travel to Paris. A high season ticket will cost about US$750 from the East Coast and US$950 from the West Coast. These prices are based, however, on the cheaper and more restricted fares. If you can't book well in advance and be flexible in the length of your stay, your tickets will cost even more.

As a general rule, children under two cost ten percent of the ticket price while those between two and twelve cost 65 percent.

Also keep in mind that the lowest fares generally have the strictest cancellation penalties. If your plans are in doubt, it may be a good idea to pay a higher fare that comes with lower penalties for canceling or rescheduling. For more information see the section on trip cancellation insurance.

USEFUL NUMBERS

American Airlines	U.S. 800-433-7300	Paris 42 89 05 22
Air France	U.S. 800-237-2747	Paris 45 35 61 61
British Air	U.S. 800-247-9297	Paris 47 78 14 14
Air Canada	U.S. 800-776-3000	Paris 42 18 19 20
Delta	U.S. 800-221-1212	Paris 47 68 92 92
United Airlines	U.S. 800-241-6522	Paris 48 97 82 82
Eurrail	U.S. 800-848-7245	Paris 40 19 19 88
Council Travel	U.S. 212-661-1414	Paris 46 34 13 04
STA	U.S. 800-777-0112	

When traveling with a baby, especially if you're breastfeeding, it's worth asking upon check-in for a seat next to another woman. Some airlines and flights are equipped with infant seats; ask your travel agent or an airline representative to see if one is available. If not, certain children's car seats can also be used in plane seats and will make your child safer and more comfortable; however, you will have to pay a fare for the child. The Federal Aviation Administration (202-367-3479) offers a free booklet on child safety seats for planes. Finally, if you're over 28 weeks pregnant, certain airlines will refuse to carry you. Ask when you book.

The least expensive way to get to Paris is to have a travel agent shop the major carriers like Air France, Delta and TWA, or wholesalers (known in the trade as consolidators). Many discount tickets are advertised in the Sunday travel sections of major daily newspapers such as the *New York Times*, *Chicago Tribune*, *Los Angeles Times* and *San Francisco Examiner*.

Packages

Many tour operators offer well-priced group and independent tours. Look for tours that match your special interests. Ask the operator to provide information on the group makeup. Does the company specialize in single or senior tours? Is the daily itinerary compatible with your special interests? If you're traveling with a group, how much time is available for sightseeing on your own? Before booking, you might want to call other women who have toured with the company. When selecting a package, be sure to get details about the hotels and locations.

A smattering of tour companies with packages to Paris include: Brendan Tours (800-421-8446), Cityrama (800-225-2595), Five Star Touring (212-818-9140) or In Quest of the Classics (800-221-5246, or in California 800-227-1393).

REGULATIONS

Passports and Permits

At the time of writing, U.S. and Canadian citizens need a passport but no visa to enter France. If you don't already have one, and you are a U.S. citizen, passports can be applied for at U.S. Passport Agency offices, county courts and designated post offices. Apply well in advance of your travel date; if possible as much as five weeks. An adult passport, good for ten years, costs US$65; a child's (under 18) is good for five years and costs US$40. Call your local post office for more information.

For Canadian citizens, there are 25 passport offices serving the major cities of your country. For information call 819-994-3500. If you don't live in a serviced city, you can apply through the mail by writing to: Passport Office, Department of External Affairs, Ottawa, Canada, K1A OG3. A five-year Canadian passport costs CA$35. Again, apply well in advance.

Upon entry you are entitled to stay for a period of up to ninety days (renewable by hopping over the border for a day trip and making sure your passport is stamped on re-entry). Obtaining a work permit, however, is the equivalent of a non-American trying to obtain a Green Card. One way around this is to enroll as a student, at which point you're entitled to a student permit, allowing you to work for a limited number of hours during vacation periods. Further details can be obtained from the Ministry for Labor – Foreign Workers Section, tel. 45 31 10 03. Alternatively, for students there's an exchange agreement between the French and U.S. governments, administered by the Council on International Educational Exchange (tel. New York 212-661-1414; Paris 46 34 13 04), whereby students can obtain a three-month full-time work permit, but neither is a permanent solution.

Insurance

It's a good idea to buy trip cancellation insurance; it typically costs about $5.50 per $100 of coverage. Travel Guard International (800-782-5151) offers such a program. In addition to refunds for reasons such as illness, the company offers a policy that will refund up to half your cancellation penalty if you decide not to go for any reason. You can also purchase lost luggage insurance from this company, but first see if this risk is covered by your homeowner's or renter's policy.

Your own health insurance may reimburse you for the cost of medical emergencies in France. You may also supplement it with a medical evacuation insurance policy. There are several American companies offering a program that will refer you to an English-speaking hospital and, if necessary, pay for an evacuation to a medical center in the United States. Try Worldwide Assistance for information (800-368-7878).

If you are a member, or would like to become one, the International Association for Medical Assistance (716-754-4883) can supply the names of French physicians trained to American standards.

MONEY

Currency

Currency in France is the *franc*, which divides into 100 *centimes*. Currently the exchange rate hovers around 5F to the U.S. dollar and 4F to the Canadian dollar.

Changing Money

The number of banks and *bureaux de change* scattered all over the city make changing money easy, though you're definitely advised to arrive with at least some French cash, especially late at night. Provided you have your passport, traveler's checks don't pose any problem. Rates of exchange and commissions vary from bank to bank; the best deal is with the Banque Nationale de Paris (BNP). The most reliable private offices are Chequepoint and Change.

Banks are generally open 9 a.m.–4.30 p.m. or 5 p.m. Monday to Friday, and close on weekends. Visa card holders, provided you know your secret PIN number, can withdraw French money from any outside cash machine, usually open 24 hours. The hotline for stolen cards is 47 77 11 90.

Most exchange *bureaux* operate 9 a.m.–6 p.m. Monday to Saturday, except for Roissy and Orly airports (daily 7 a.m.–11 p.m.) and the Gare du Lyon and Gare du Nord (daily 8 a.m.–9 p.m.).

DENOMINATIONS

COINS		BILLS
5 centime	1 franc	20 franc
10 centime	2 franc	50 franc
20 centime	5 franc	100 franc
50 centime	10 franc	500 franc

COST OF LIVING

Paris is not outrageously expensive, especially if you avoid touristy restaurants and the temptation of extravagant clothes shopping or buying endless drinks in fashionable bars. Also, especially when it comes to food, you tend to get quality for your money. Starting with a low budget, the following paragraph gives you an idea of what a day in Paris can cost.

A room without bathroom, picnic breakfast and lunch bought from the local market and bakery, and dinner in an inexpensive restaurant takes you up to 300 to 350F a day. This doesn't include the inevitable cups of tea and coffee, the price of which can be exorbitant (from 6F at the counter to 25F at a table or on the *terrasse*). For an average-priced day allow 600 to 700F for a room with bathroom, lunch and breakfast in a café, finishing with dinner in a middle-range restaurant. Finally, if you can afford to go whole hog, there are numerous five-star luxury hotels and restaurants in Paris, where rooms tend to start at around 1000F for a double with bath, and a meal for one can cost the same again. By the time you've visited a few designer boutiques and been to a concert at the Opéra Bastille, the sky's the limit.

INFORMATION

The French Tourist Board delights in promoting and extolling the virtues of France. Write or call the French Government Tourist Information (628 Fifth Avenue, New York, New York 10020, 212-757-1125; or 9454 Wilshire Boulevard, Suite 303, Beverly Hills, California 90212, 310-271-6665). There also offices at 645 North Michigan Avenue, Suite 630, Chicago, Illinois 60611, 312-337-6301 or 2305 Cedar Springs Road, Suite 205, Dallas, Texas 75201, 214-720-4010. You could also try calling 900-990-0040 (50 cents per minute), another French Tourist Board information line.

Staff at the Paris branch (127 avenue des Champs Elysées, 75008 (tel. 47 23 61 72, open Monday–Saturday 9 a.m.–8/10 p.m; Sunday 9 a.m.–6/8 p.m.) are generally helpful and will answer your questions in English, as well as plying you with hundreds of glossy brochures and leaflets packed with information. There are also branches at the Gares de l'Est, Austerlitz, Lyon and du Nord. Alternatively, you can get tourist information in English over the phone by dialing 47 20 88 89.

Maps

A pocket-book A–Z like *Leconte* or *Paris Eclair*, divided into *arrondissements* and including a street index and bus routes, is invaluable for navigating Paris.

Having said that, this must be one of the easiest cities in the world to find your way around, both because the center is small and because it's so logically divided into *arrondissements*. Look at a full-sized map and you'll see that they follow each other sequentially in a clockwise spiral, taking the Louvre as the epicenter in the first *arrondissement*, and going out to the twentieth. The most comprehensive map is probably the Michelin N. 10 1:10, available in the basement of the department store Printemps – which, incidentally, hands out a small free map that shows the main monuments drawn in relief.

What's On

Paris is particularly good at disseminating information. Residents are bombarded by any number of free newspapers covering what is happening in their *quartier* – anything from theater, to jazz, art exhibitions and antique fairs. Equally, you can learn a lot by merely keeping your eyes open in the Metro, where the billboards are frequently changed, and in bars and cafés, which traditionally advertise on behalf of local galleries. Otherwise the Parisian bible is *Pariscope* (3F) or its poorer cousin and rival, *Officiel des Spectacles* (2F). These small pocket-sized publications contain all the listings for theaters, cinemas, concerts, museums, monuments, sports facilities, restaurants and clubs. *Pariscope* also has a children's section. This guide is an absolute must for film enthusiasts, as it lists all the 300-plus films showing in Paris at any given moment ("v.o." indicates that the film is shown in the language of its country of origin, with subtitles in French) by genre, and by cinema, plus a critique on the latest releases. In addition, it carries opening times and addresses of just about anything you might want to visit, and telephone numbers to call for further information. It comes out on Wednesdays, and is available at any newsstand.

For information directed at women, *Lesbia* is a lesbian magazine (again available at most newsstands), with comprehensive women's listings, as well as features, reviews and personal ads. *Paris Féministe* (see Maison des Femmes) also carries listings of events and groups for women in Paris.

COMMUNICATIONS

Mailing

The French post office [*La Poste*] serves so many functions that simply sending a letter or buying a stamp can be a nightmare, especially if you're in a rush. Offices have separate windows for – among other things – telegrams, long-distance calls, an express mail system called *chronopost*, numerous savings accounts, retirement plans and housing funds, as well as paying bills, so if you want to buy a stamp or send a package, make sure you are in the right line [*Envoi de lettres et paquets, timbres* or *Toutes Opérations*]. Opening hours are generally 8 a.m.–7 p.m. weekdays; 8 a.m.–noon Saturday.

Visitors with no fixed address can receive mail for a small fee at any chosen post office, provided it's clearly marked with your surname in capital letters and the words "poste restante." A passport is needed to prove your identity.

USEFUL POSTAL ADDRESSES

Main post office: 52 rue du Louvre, 75001 (tel. 42 33 71 60).
Open 24 hours a day.
71 avenue des Champs Elysées, 75008 (tel. 43 59 55 18).
Open 8 a.m. – 10 p.m. Monday-Saturday; 10 a.m. – noon, 2–8 p.m. Sunday.
You can also buy stamps at any *Tabac*, and mail letters and postcards in the yellow letterboxes scattered liberally all over the city.

Phoning

International calls can be made from any public telephone. Coin boxes have been entirely phased out in Paris (except in cafés, where you have to have a drink first if you want to use the phone), so you'll need to invest in a phonecard [*télécarte*], available from newsstands, *Tabacs* or post offices in multiples of 50 and 120 units.

Parisian numbers and those in the suburbs close to Paris begin with a 4. To call other parts of France, you will need to dial a 16 before the number. To reach Paris from outside the city you will have to dial 16-1 and then the number you are trying to reach. To call abroad, dial 9, wait for the tone, dial 33 and the country code (U.S. is 11, Canada is 1), then the number. For Directory Assistance dial 12.

MEDIA

Television

The best thing about French TV is the films, for which you're better off going to a movie theater. Otherwise the rather unappetizing selection of programs tends to fall into the categories of hackneyed human interest/social conscience, self-congratulatory talkshows, or self-conscious arts review programs. French television's loss seems to be the cinema's gain.

Radio

For English-language radio programs, tune into the faithful BBC World Service on 463m or between 21m and 31m short wave. France Inter (FM 87.8) is a program devoted exclusively to news coverage, while Radio Classique 24 (FM 10.1) provides undiluted classical music with very little talking.

Newspapers and magazines

You'll find most English-language newspapers in Paris on the day they come out, among them *The European* and the *International Herald Tribune*, all available from the larger kiosks located in the most touristy areas like the first, sixth and eighth *arrondissements*.

France's most respected national newspaper is *Le Monde*. Established in 1944, it prides itself on weighty journalism with no concessions to the lighter side of life, written in a very correct, sometimes elaborately constructed French that can be difficult to follow. *Le Figaro*, while older, is a little less dry and has a magazine called *Figaro Madame*, devoted to fashion and shopping features. Altogether a better bet is the trendy tabloid-shaped, slightly left-of-center *Libération*, written in a more colloquial, more readable French, and with plenty of arts coverage.

Party organs include the Communist *L'Humanité*, founded by the Socialist Jean-Jaurès, and *Minute*, a rag in every sense of the word, which belongs to the National Front. *Le Canard Enchainé* is the French equivalent of Britain's *Private Eye*, and probably equally unintelligible to foreigners.

Weekly news magazines of the *Time/Newsweek* variety include *Le Nouvel Observateur*, a serious, glossy current affairs magazine that leans towards the Left, and its rival, *L'Express* – in much the same genre, but leaning the other way. The traditional French gossip magazine is *Paris Match*, though it poses as something more serious.

Apart from the usual range of monthlies like *Elle*, *Cosmopolitan* and *Marie-Claire* (all of which now have their English-speaking counterparts), *Biba* is a women's magazine that profiles a different selection of notable women every month. *Lesbia* is the most widely available gay women's monthly magazine; although it's aimed specifically at lesbians, it has plenty of information of interest to feminists. *Anima* is a glossy magazine specifically aimed at black women.

LANGUAGE

English-speakers in particular have a reputation with the French for not making the effort to learn the language. That said, the theory that the French really appreciate your efforts is not necessarily best tested in Paris, where the most fluent foreigner can be reduced to pulp by the look of blank incomprehension from the woman behind the counter as she utters an incredulous *"Comment?"* Don't be disheartened. If you barely speak a word, in a city as cosmopolitan as Paris there will always be someone on hand to help out. Equally, if you have an urge to dust off your schoolgirl French or practice your teach-yourself-French course, so long as it is not in a crowded bakery with a line stretching out of the door, or Printemps on the first day of the sales, you're likely to obtain a smile for your efforts. Saying *"Bonjour,"* as is the custom, when you walk into a shop, and *"Au revoir"* when you leave will take you halfway there.

For those who want to brush up on their language beforehand, teach-yourself courses with realistic recorded conversations are good for getting your ear accustomed to and prepared for set situations. A dictionary is useful in theory, but by the time you have found all the words necessary to construct your phrase the opportunity to use it has been lost along with the patience of the person you are attempting to communicate with. It's much better to arm yourself with a phrase book. Business travelers who don't want the effort of taking a course are well served by the *French Businessmate* (Richard Drew Publishing), a handy pocket dictionary which plows steadily from A to Z, taking advantage of M to include a menu reader to guide you round some of the worst pitfalls of French cuisine, and W for wine to make some helpful suggestions. With some additional travel tips thrown in – for instance, under S for shake it you're reminded that it's customary to shake hands on being introduced to someone for the first time, and again on taking your leave – you could find worse ways of spending your money.

French is a minefield of masculine and feminine, and whether you should use the formal *vous* form or the informal *tu* form is always an important decision. As a rule of thumb, if you use *vous* [*vouvoyer*] with everyone until they use the *tu* form [*tutoyer*] with you, you will avoid either appearing over familiar or giving offense. Keeping to *vous* can also help to maintain your distance when a man is becoming too friendly.

Lastly, remember that women over thirty are usually referred to as *Madame*, partly as a form of respect. If you are (or look as if you are) younger, expect to be addressed as *Mademoiselle*.

Pronunciation

Let's face it: it is virtually impossible to speak French like a French person. It's surprising, however, how a comparatively small mispronunciation can render you totally incomprehensible, so here are a few tips.

Consonants at the ends of words are silent unless followed by a vowel, when the first word is run into the second – e.g., *pas encore* becomes *pazonkor*. Otherwise, consonants are similar to English ones, except that:

> ch is pronounced sh (*chou* is pronounced shoe)
> c is pronounced s (cerise is pronounced *serrease*)
> h is silent (*hôtel* is pronounced *oh!-tel*)
> there is no difference between th and t (*thé* is pronounced *tay*)
> ll comes out as a y sound (*grillée* is pronounced *greeyay*)
> w practically does not exist
> r is like clearing your throat as you speak

LANGUAGE

PRACTICALITIES

BASICS

DAILY LIVING

Hello/Good morning	Bonjour
Good afternoon/evening (used as hello and goodbye)	Bonsoir
Goodbye	Au revoir
Hi/'Bye (informal)	Salut
Yes	Oui
No	Non
That's fine/Okay	D'accord
That's great	Très bien
Please	S'il vous plaît
Thank you	Merci
How are you?	Comment ça va?
Fine, thanks	Ça va bien, merci
Do you speak English?	Parlez vous Anglais?
I don't speak French	Je ne parle pas Français
I don't understand	Je ne comprends pas
I don't know	Je ne sais pas
Excuse me	Pardon (when you want to get past)
Excuse me	S'il vous plaît, Madame (when you want to ask the waitress/store clerk/police-woman a question)
May I?	Je peux?
Sorry	Pardon (when you have bumped into someone). *Je suis désolée* (when you have stepped on their toe). *Je suis navrée* (when you have spilt your coffee over the cashmere coat of your chic parisienne neighbor in the café)
Morning	Matin
Afternoon	Après-midi
Evening	Soi (Soirée as in an evening out)
This evening	Ce soir
Night	Nuit
Today	Aujourd'hui
Tomorrow	Demain
Day after tomorrow	Après-demain
Next week	La semaine prochaine
Last week	La semaine dernière
Yesterday	Hier
Now	Maintenant
Immediately	Immédiatement
Ready	Prêt(e)
Are you ready?	Vous êtes prêt(e)?
Wait	Attendez
Here	Ici or Tenez (when you're handing something to someone)

There	Là
Everywhere	Partout
Good	Bon(ne)
Bad	Mauvais(e)
Very good	Très bon(ne)
Terrible	Affreux/Affreuse
Big	Grand(e)
Small	Petit(e)
Cheap	Bon marché
Expensive	Chèr(e)
Early	Tôt
Late	Tard (to be late: être en retard)
Near	Près
Far	Loin
Is it far from here?	Est-ce que c'est loin d'ici?
Free/vacant	Libre
Free/without charge	Gratuit(e)
Occupied/busy	Prise (a chair)/Occupé (telephone)
With	Avec
Without	Sans
More	Encore
A bit more	Un peu plus
Less	Moins
Enough	Assez
Hot	Chaud(e)
Cold	Froid(e)
Open	Ouvert(e)
Closed	Fermé(e)
Entrance	Entrée
Exit	Sortie
Toilet	Toilette
Push	Poussez
Pull	Tirez

The simplest way to ask a question is to use an interrogative tone of voice, e.g:

How do we get to the Louvre?	S'il vous plaît, pour aller au Louvre?

(literally translated: Please, to go to the Louvre?)

QUESTION WORDS

Where?	Où?
Where is?	Où est/se trouve…?
Where are?	Où sont?
What?	Comment?
Who?	Qui?
When?	Quand?
How?	Comment?
How much?	Combien?

A polite and easy way to ask a question is to preface your statement with "S'il vous plaît," as in:

Where is the bakery?	S'il vous plaît, la boulangerie?
Metro station	Station de métro
Supermarket	Supermarché

Drugstore	Pharmacie
Railway station	Gare (it's as well to state which main-line station: e.g., Gare du Nord)

STREET DIRECTIONS

Left	Gauche
Right	Droit(e)
Straight ahead	Tout droit
On the corner	Au coin
Opposite	En face (de)

HOTELS

A tip, when you're asking for a room: if you ask for "côté cour" it means you are asking not to overlook the road, thus avoiding the traffic noise. They should give you a room overlooking the central courtyard, which will be quiet.

Do you have a room?	Avez-vous une chambre?
for one/two people	pour une/deux personne(s)
for one/two nights	pour une/deux nuit(s)
with a shower	avec douche
with a bath	avec salle de bains
Can I see it?	Je peux la voir?
Do you have a crib?	Avez-vous un lit d'enfant?
Is breakfast included?	Est ce que le petit-déjeuner est compris?
Do you accept credit cards?	Vous acceptez la carte de crédit?

USING PUBLIC TRANSPORTATION

Timetable	Horaire
Weekdays	Jours ouvrables
Holidays	Jours fériés
A ticket please	Un billet s'il vous plaît
Return ticket	Billet aller-retour
The bus stop	L'arrêt de l'autobus
What time is the next bus for...?	A quelle heure passera le prochain bus pour...?
Do you go to Opéra?	Vous allez vers Opéra?
Can you tell me when to get off?	Pouvez-vous m'indiquer l'arret? (there is no guarantee that he will; better to make your destination known to elderly passengers who will take great joy in making sure you get to your destination)
Thief	Voleur

IN A CAFÉ OR RESTAURANT

A table for two please	Une table pour une/deux personne(s) s'il vous plaît
Can I have the menu please?	La carte s'il vous plaît?

L
A
N
G
U
A
G
E

I'd like...	Je voudrais...
A carafe of house white/red	Une carafe de vin blanc/rouge
A jug of water	Une carafe d'eau
The bill please	S'il vous plaît, l'addition/la note
Is service included?	Le service est-il compris?
Can I telephone from here?	Est-ce que je peux téléphoner s'il vous plaît?
Where are the toilets?	S'il vous plaît, les toilettes?
Out of order	Hors service
Weekly closing day	Fermeture hebdomadaire
Closed for annual holidays	Fermeture annuelle

WHEN PESTERED

Enough!	Ça suffit
Stop it!	Arrêtez!
I'm in a hurry	Je suis pressée
I'm waiting for my husband	J'attends mon mari
When asked for a cigarette	
I don't smoke!	Je ne fume pas!

EMERGENCY SITUATIONS

Leave me alone (aggressive)	Fichez-mois la paix
Please help me	Aidez-moi s'il vous plaît
Help!	Au secours!
Please call a doctor	Appelez un médecin s'il vous plaît
I have a stomach/headache	J'ai mal au ventre/à là tête
I am ill	Je suis malade
Someone has stolen my bag/wallet	On m'a volé mon sac/porte-monnaie
I have been raped	J'ai été violée (careful – J'ai été volée means "I have been robbed")

NUMBERS

zero	zéro
one	un/une
two	deux
three	trois
four	quatre
five	cinq
six	six
seven	sept
eight	huit
nine	neuf
ten	dix
eleven	onze
twelve	douze
thirteen	treize
fourteen	quatorze
fifteen	quinze
sixteen	seize

seventeen	dix-sept
eighteen	dix-huit
nineteen	dix-neuf
twenty	vingt
twenty-one	vingt et un
twenty-two	vingt-deux
twenty-three	vingt-trois
twenty-four	vingt-quatre
twenty-five	vingt-cinq
twenty-six	vingt-six
twenty-seven	vingt-sept
twenty-eight	vingt-huit
twenty-nine	vingt-neuf
thirty	trente
forty	quarante
fifty	cinquante
sixty	soixante
seventy	soixante-dix
eighty	quatre-vingt(s)
ninety	quatre-vingt-dix
hundred	cent
a hundred and one	cent un
two hundred	deux cents
two hundred and one	deux cent un
three hundred	trois cents
four hundred	quartre cents
five hundred	cinq cents
six hundred	six cents
seven hundred	sept cents
eight hundred	huit cents
nine hundred	neuf cents
thousand	mille
two thousand	deux mille

SEASONS, MONTHS, DAYS AND TIME

year	an, année
month	mois
week	semaine
day	jour
next	prochain(e)
last	dernier (dernière)
spring	printemps
summer	été
autumn	automne
winter	hiver
January	janvier
February	février
March	mars
April	avril
May	mai

June	juin
July	juillet
August	août
September	septembre
October	octobre
November	novembre
December	décembre
Monday	lundi
Tuesday	mardi
Wednesday	mercredi
Thursday	jeudi
Friday	vendredi
Saturday	samedi
Sunday	dimanche
What time is it?	Quelle heure est-il?
Have you got the time?	Vous avez l'heure?
I make it ...	D'après ma montre il est ...
It's one o'clock	Il est une heure
It's noon/midnight	Il est midi/minuit
It's two o'clock	Il est deux heures
It's five past two	Il est deux heures cinq
It's ten to three	Il est trois heures moins dix
It's half-past two	Il est deux heures et demie
It's quarter past two	Il est deux heures et quart
It's quarter to three	Il est trois heures moins quart
It's just after two	Il est deux heures passées
It's nearly three	Il est presque trois heures
What's the date today?	Quelle est la date d'aujourd'hui?
Today's the twelfth	Aujourd'hui nous sommes le 12

USEFUL EXPRESSIONS

I don't feel well	Je ne me sens pas bien
I feel sick/nauseous	J'ai envie de vomir
I've got a headache	J'ai mal à la tête
I've got a pain in my stomach	J'ai mal au ventre
I've got a sore throat	J'ai mal à la gorge
A cough	Une toux
I've got a cold	Je suis enrhumée
diarrhea	la diarrhée
indigestion	l'indigestion
the Pill	la pilule
the morning-after Pill	la pilule du lendemain
tablets	des médicaments
syrup	du sirop
antibiotics	les antibiotiques

POLICE AND CRIME

There are several types of police (popularly known as *les flics*) in France: *agents de police* employed by the Ministry of the Interior, *gendarmes* linked to the Ministry of Defense, and the *CRS*. The last, representing the elite of the French police force, are troubleshooting thugs who ride around in gray-green armored vans, looking about as friendly as your average serial killer. They're in charge of national security; one of their primary functions is to enforce and maintain order in the case of public unrest, riots or protests – a role which makes them particularly unpopular.

Paris is not a particularly dangerous city, but it obviously pays to listen to your instincts and use common sense. In addition, there are a few rules worth respecting. Always keep an eye on your personal belongings, separate your money and your passport, and try not to get on the Metro with a camera bag, video recorder and in-flight bag emblazoned with the emblem of your tour company, slung about your neck – you'll be an instant target for pickpockets. Some big stations, like Châtelet-Les-Halles, should be avoided late at night, as they're renowned for drug-dealing, as should areas like Pigalle, especially alone. Otherwise, certain suburbs present much more of a nighttime threat than anywhere in central Paris, but there's probably little reason for you to venture that far.

EMERGENCIES

Police tel. 17
Ambulance tel. 15
Fire tel. 18
SOS Help – tel. 47 23 80 80 – is an English-language helpline, open 3–11 p.m. daily.

Despite these spots to avoid, crime statistics are relatively low in Paris. In 1992 about 300 homicides were committed in the greater Paris area, considerably lower than in London or New York. Most crimes are directed towards personal property: between four and six cases of pickpocketing a month are reported. Such incidents, usually directed at tourists and the elderly, tend to take place in the Metro, in flea markets, and around the most crowded monuments. Take care, and you shouldn't be bothered.

Drivers suffer so many break-ins that, as in New York and Rome, almost everyone has removable radios and tape players. Luggage and portable stereos are tempting for thieves, especially in a foreign car, so try not to leave anything valuable in sight.

If you need to report a theft, go either to the Gendarmerie or the Police Nationale. Provided you get on the right side of them, they can be polite and helpful enough, but no more. It is as well to adopt your most respectful manner, as this small concession to their vanity will pay dividends in ensuring that the inevitable paperwork is dispatched with a minimum of fuss and some attempt at efficiency.

Take care to observe the speed limits in towns (50km/h), as the police could impose a hefty on-the-spot fine, payable immediately. Pleading foreign ignorance does not help. Finally, drug smuggling and possession is strictly forbidden in France. The police view the matter very seriously, and possession of a few grams of marijuana is sufficient to get you flung in jail.

SEXUAL HARASSMENT

As women, we're conditioned to accept boundaries in relation to our safety: we avoid wandering alone in parts of our cities at night, and brace ourselves for remarks and jeers when passing groups of men. Dress and behavior are considered open to unasked-for comment. And we feel doubly cautious about accepting or asking for help from male strangers. At home we learn to live within these limitations and to rely on certain instincts, based on familiarity with our own particular culture and territory. Abroad it is different. The risks may be no greater – they may even be less – but without the back-up of that instinctive knowledge we're more likely to feel more threatened or exposed than we do on home ground.

SEXUAL CRIME
In the event of rape, the police are less geared to dealing with the emotional effects than they are in the U.S. There's no rape crisis center, but there is a hotline which you can call for advice and information: Viols Femmes Informations, 4 Square St. Irénée, 75011 (tel. 05 05 95 95). There are also several women's refuges for victims of all male abuse, which will at least provide a sympathetic ear and all-women environment, albeit in French. Phone SOS Femmes Alternatives (45 85 11 37) or the Maison des Femmes (43 48 24 91).

In Paris, as anywhere, it's impossible to avoid sexual harassment altogether. However, the more you know about the city and about French attitudes and codes of behavior, the more confident – and therefore safe – you'll feel about what to do and where to go. As a rule, Frenchmen aren't shy with women. They genuinely enjoy their company, although seduction will probably never be too far from their minds – to them it's all part of the communication process, rejection included.

How bothered you are by sexual harassment is partly a matter of definition. If you consider that simply being looked at amounts to an affront, you'll be permanently harassed in Paris. Appearance is of paramount importance in this stylish city, and the attention it draws, from and towards both men and women, is an unavoidable hazard. It's true, however, that – at least compared to sober Anglo-Saxons –

Frenchmen tend to be more pushy, and are more likely to try and strike up a conversation in a bar or even in the street. This can clearly be annoying, if not disconcerting, but the point to remember is that you have the choice. If you don't wish to respond, then don't – you're unlikely to be bothered further. If you do respond, be prepared for the man to make his intentions reasonably clear quite quickly. Frenchmen aren't macho in the same way as Italians, but they have enough of a Latin temperament to make coming on to women almost a point of honor. Obviously, unless your safety feels threatened, it doesn't pay to show anger or be too aggressive, as hurt male pride could well make things worse. Generally speaking, the best line of defense is indifference. These encounters are usually harmless and, providing you avoid the areas pinpointed throughout this book, there's really little to be anxious about.

There is, however, a specific type of creep to watch out for whom the French call *les dragueurs*. Like their Greek or Roman equivalents, these are men of all ages, often from the outer suburbs, who hang around the main tourist areas to "cruise" for foreign women. Having managed to catch your eye, the *dragueur* will smile, greet, and very probably follow you, uttering banal compliments and even launching into a speech about "love at first sight." Again, it's best to ignore him completely, and if you are going to lose your temper, make sure there are plenty of people around.

If you're approached in a café, accepting a drink is likely to be interpreted as an invitation. Should the man be persistent, try saying "*J'attends mon ami*" (I'm waiting for my boyfriend), or "*S'il vous plaît, laissez moi tranquille*" (Please leave me alone), having already practiced your pronunciation.

Dress

One of your first decisions is whether you want to emphasize that you're a tourist or whether you want to take on one of the many Parisian modes of dress. Sneakers, a dangling camera and a visible fannypack are liable to give the game away, but if that's how you feel most comfortable, then go ahead – you won't be exactly mobbed because of it. Despite the city's overriding reputation for classic chic, nothing in the way of dress is strictly forbidden or taboo. On the contrary, innovation, even a mild eccentricity in clothing, is positively applauded, and you'll see every kind of fashion on the streets and in the Metro: from the all-black "gamine" look complete with Doctor Martens, to the PVC miniskirted vamps with leather jackets and peaked caps *à la* Brigitte Bardot who tend to hang around Beaubourg. Very short skirts and low-necked tops are likely to attract admiring glances – or more.

Be prepared for topless advertising. The French are generally less inhibited about sex than other nations, and puritanical attitudes (often laced with hypocrisy) tend to be reserved for very strict

Catholics. Witness the fact that a politician has only to be discovered with a new mistress for his rating in the polls to soar immediately. If you're going out or if you're invited somewhere, dress well: French people generally try to make an effort when they go out socially.

HEALTH AND SEX

Except for emergency cases, all charges for medicine and/or hospital or doctor's visits have to be paid upfront. You're well advised to take out adequate health insurance before you leave so that you're not stuck having to pay for treatment.

With luck, if you're ill you can avoid the system altogether by simply going to a *pharmacie*. Pharmacists are well-equipped and knowledgeable, and may well be able to recommend something to clear up the problem. In addition, they are obliged to give first aid on request, though for a fee, and will always provide the address of the nearest doctor or advise where to go for treatment such as X-rays or blood tests. If you need a doctor, be sure to ask for a *médecin conventionné* – in other words, someone who'll charge the fees dictated by the social security system; otherwise you might find yourself being overcharged. The regular fee for a consultation is around 110–130F. Hotels may have house physicians or be able to refer you to a doctor. You can also call the American Hospital (46 41 25 25) for referrals.

Contraception and Safe Sex

Condoms [*préservatifs*] and other forms of contraception are available from any pharmacy, as are tampons [*tampons*] and sanitary towels [*serviettes hygiéniques*], much cheaper in supermarkets. You will need a prescription for the Pill, a diaphragm or the morning-after Pill, which is readily available in France. The RU 486 (abortion pill) is not available over the counter; you must first go to a hospital for tests.

Safe sex is beginning to pierce the consciousness of the French, but perhaps to a lesser extent than in Britain and America. At the beginning the French approach was not to scare people with AIDS but to convey the message that condoms should be seen as a "natural" element in lovemaking. Now that Paris has become the AIDS capital of Europe, with more recorded HIV infection than any other major city, the government is trying to concentrate on information about AIDS, and is showing ads for the use of condoms. But although some dispensers have been set up in the Metro and outside pharmacies, it still appears that safe sex is not yet a reflex in France. Indeed, there are currently estimated to be around 200,000 HIV-positive people in the country, and 20,250 cases of AIDS, of which, according to the statistics, 50.5% are homosexuals, 21.7% are drug addicts and 11.7% are heterosexuals. Following a scandal some years ago about contaminated blood being used in transfusions (the effects of which are still dreadfully present), donated blood now undergoes strictly controlled tests.

Home pregnancy tests are easily available in pharmacies; ask for *un test de grossesse*. As with any home kit, if the results are positive it's better to go and see a doctor for a confirmation, because such kits can give erroneous results. If it's negative, the instructions generally inform you to repeat the test five to seven days later to make sure you are not pregnant. Abortions have been legal in France since 1975.

WOMEN AND FEMINISM

Many of the feminist themes that emerged in France at the dawn of the twentieth century had already been expressed by outstanding women at various times since the Middle Ages. In the fourteenth century, Christine de Pisan became one of the first to claim that the differences between men and women stemmed more from education than from nature; Louise Labbé and Marie de Gourney, in the fifteenth, protested against the "civil death" of women locked in their homes and unable to participate in economic and political life; and during the French Revolution, for the first time, women demonstrating against an increase in the price of bread began to claim political rights. They formed political clubs of their own, wrote in newspapers, demanded education for girls and reform of the marriage laws. In 1791 Olympe de Gouges wrote the Declaration of the Rights of Woman.

Not much later, other memorable women such as Flora Tristan and Jeanne Deroin were vigorously upholding the links between

---

AIDS INFORMATION

Aids Hotline (toll-free number) 05 36 66 36
English-speaking association for HIV-positive people: FAACTS:
tel. 45 50 26 49 (Thursday afternoons only)

HIV tests are free and anonymous in the following places:
Center Medico-Social
218 rue de Belleville, 75020 Metro Télégraphe.
tel. 47 97 40 49
Center SIDAG, 3 rue de Ridder, 75015.
Metro Plaisance
tel. 45 43 85 78
Free anonymous treatments for sexually transmitted diseases are offered by the
Institut Prophylactique. 36 rue d'Assas, 75006.
tel. 42 22 32 06

women's liberation and the rights of the working class. In the words of Flora Tristan: "The most oppressed man can oppress someone else – his wife. She is the proletarian's proletarian." The nineteenth century saw an increasing involvement of women in revolutionary social movements – including, during the 1848 Revolution, the foundation of a daily feminist newspaper. By the end of the nineteenth century, however, the women's movement was seriously threatened by a now familiar polemic, mainly instigated by socialist men, accusing feminism of being a bourgeois aberration and feminists the enemies of socialism.

What came to be identified as feminism by 1914 was philanthropic and reformist, with over 123 feminist organizations working to make republican society more comfortable for women of all classes. As many as thirty-five women's newspapers were produced between 1875 and 1914, representing the entire spectrum of women's interests. The most prestigious and ambitious of these was *La Fronde*, founded by Marguerite Durand and run entirely by women. The two most heated issues were the constant question of women's allegiance to class or to sex, and women's suffrage.

French women finally obtained the right to vote in 1944, when they were allowed, for the first time, to participate in political life as members and candidates within political parties. This was not – and is still not – without its problems. Even Simone de Beauvoir did not see a need for women's emancipation outside the agenda of the Left. By the 1960s, women's political involvement had diversified and feminism, too, split into different strands. Many of the ideas and practices that appeared in the *Mouvement de Libération des Femmes* (MLF) towards the end of the decade were part of the more general political thinking of the post-'68 "revolutionary" groups, very much influenced first by Marxism, then in the early 1980s by psychoanalysis. After years of bitter fighting, the law legalizing abortion (defended by Simone Veil) was finally adopted only in 1975.

WOMEN'S ORGANIZATIONS/INFORMATION

Maison des Femmes, 8 Cité Prost, off rue Chanzy 75011, tel. 43 48 24 91
Feminist, lesbian, anti-racist and battered women's groups all meet here.

Centre Audio Visuel Simone de Beauvoir, Palais de Tokyo, 2 rue de la Manutention, 75016, tel. 47 23 67 48
Includes screening of audiovisual works by women and about women.

Bibliothèque Marguerite Durand, 79 rue Nationale, 75013, open Tuesday–Saturday 2–6 p.m.
Feminist library where you can consult, among others, ARCL (Archives Recherches et Cultures Lesbiennes), a directory of feminist and lesbian addresses in France.

SOS Femmes Alternatives, tel. 43 48 24 91
Helpline for victims of sexual violence.

WOMEN AND FEMINISM

Today feminism in France seems to have moved on, broken by internal quarrels, splits and a more general disaffection for the very term "feminist," especially among young women. Bookshops and papers have folded, International Women's Day is barely commemorated, and a handful of women's services, such as the Paris women's helpline *SOS Femmes Alternatives*, are at pains to survive. The specificity of French feminist theory comes from the specificity of French culture, again triggered by the role played by Marxism and psychoanalysis in the past two decades, and it seems inevitable that the way feminism develops in France will depend very much on the political and social evolution of the whole country through the 1990s.

DIRECTORY

AIRLINE OFFICES
    Air Canada, tel. 42 18 19 20
    Air France, tel. 45 35 61 61
    American Airlines, tel. 42 89 05 22
    British Air, tel. 47 78 14 14
    Delta, tel. 47 68 92 92
    United Airlines, tel. 48 97 82 82

AIRPORTS
    Roissy-Charles de Gaulle, tel. 48 62 22 80
    Orly, tel. 49 75 15 15

BIKE RENTAL
    Paris by Cycle, 99 rue La Jonquière, 75017, tel. 42 63 36 63
    Paris Cycles, Rond-Point d'Acclimation, 75116, tel. 47 47 76 50

BUS, METRO AND RER INFORMATION
    RATP, tel. 43 46 14 14

CAR PARKING
    This list is by no means exhaustive, but covers most of the main sites. For further information, tel. 43 46 98 30, 9 a.m.–5 p.m. Monday–Friday. Bring your car into Paris only if it's absolutely necessary; the efficiency of public transportation and the agony of trying to park make it wise to leave your vehicle at the périphérique.
    Parking Concorde: place de la Concorde, 75001
    Parking Saint-Honoré: 58 place du Marché Saint-Honoré, 75001
    Parking Notre Dame: Parvis du Notre Dame, 75004 (i.e., under the terrace in front of the church)
    Parking St-Germain: 169 boulevard St-Germain, 75006
    Parking Tour Eiffel: place Joffre, 75007
    Parking George V: 101 avenue des Champs Elysées, 75008
    Parking Opéra: 4 rue Chaussée d'Antin, 75009
    Parking Tour Montparnasse: 17 rue de l'Arrivee, 75015

CAR REPAIR

Allô Assistance, 4 rue Nicolas-Charlet, 75015, tel. 43 06 39 16
ASD Auto Secours Dépannage, tel. 48 58 11 33
Both operate throughout France on a 24-hour basis

DENTISTS

American Hospital Service Dentaire (tel. 46 41 27 81) maintains a list of dentists, all of whom speak English.

DRY CLEANING

Dry cleaners go under the name of "Pressing" or "Tenturier." There is bound to be one close to your hotel, so ask at the desk. If all else fails, these two are reasonably central:
Pressing Renova, 35 rue des Archives, 75004, tel. 42 72 73 32
Luxury up-scale service, e.g., ballgowns, furs:
Pouyanne, 28 Franklin D. Roosevelt, 75008, tel. 43 59 03 47

EMBASSIES AND CONSULATES

Canada, 35 avenue Montaigne, 75008, tel. 47 23 01 01
USA, 2 avenue Gabriel, 75008, tel. 42 96 12 02

EMERGENCY SERVICES

Police tel. 17
Fire tel. 18
Ambulance tel. 15

EXPATRIATE PARIS

WICE, 20 boulevard du Montparnasse, 75015, tel. 45 66 75 50

FINDING AN APARTMENT/JOB

American Church, 65 quai d'Orsay, 75007, tel. 47 05 07 99. Excellent noticeboard with accommodations and jobs. Competition is fierce; new advertisements go up every day at 10 a.m.
France USA, 3 la Rochelle, 75014, tel. 45 38 56 57. Consult the noticeboard, or get a copy of their free magazine, fortnightly on Wednesday, crammed full of useful information for English-speakers including jobs, accommodations, services and personals.
Carrières et Emplois is a newspaper that comes out every Wednesday and is dedicated exclusively to advertisements for jobs, categorized by field. Available from any newsstand.

FLOWERS

Marché aux Fleurs, place Louis-Lépine, Ile de la Cité, 75004. Metro Cité. Open 8 a.m.–4 p.m. Monday-Saturday
Interflora, Les Jardins d'Apollon, 76 rue La Fayette, 75009, tel. 47 70 41 68
Monceau Fleurs, 92 boulevard Malesherbes, 75008, tel. 45 63 88 23
84 boulevard Raspail, 75006, tel. 45 48 70 01
2 quai Celestins, 75004, tel. 42 72 24 86
The Monceau chain is about a third cheaper than any other flower shop.

GYM

Gymnase Club is a chain of 14 well-equipped, well-run clubs, complete with sauna, jacuzzi, etc. There is a minimum age of 18 and no maximum. The atmosphere is relaxed; the teachers are friendly and helpful. A ticket for a month costs 850F, or buy a book of 10 tickets for the same price – all classes included. Most gyms are open 7 a.m.–10 p.m. weekdays, 9 a.m.–7 p.m. Saturday, 9 a.m.–5 p.m. Sunday. For further information contact Gymnase Club Palais Royal. 147*bis* rue Saint-Honoré, 75001, tel. 40 20 03 03, or Porte Maillot, 17 rue du Débarcadère, 75017, tel. 45 74 58 49. The managers speak English.

HEALTHCARE

Ambulance

Assistance Publique, tel. 43 78 26 26

Emergencies

SOS Médecins, tel. 43 37 77 77 (24 hours)

AUMP (Paris Medical Emergencies Association),

tel. 48 28 40 04

American Hospital

63 boulevard Victor Hugo, 92200 Neuilly-sur-Seine,

tel. 46 41 25 25

Outpatient clinic (Emergency Unit), recorded information in English

Dr. Hubert Gamon, 20 rue Cler, 75007, tel. 45 55 79 91

Dr. Stephen Wilson, 44 avenue Segur, 75015, tel. 45 67 26 53

Pharmacies

Dhéry, 84 avenue des Champs Elysées, 75008

Metro Charles-de-Gaulle-Etoile,

tel. 45 62 02 41. Open 24 hours a day

Anglo-American Pharmacy

Pharmacie Swann, 6 rue de Castiglione, 75001. Metro Tuileries,

tel. 42 60 72 96

British and American Pharmacy,

1 rue Auber, 75009. Metro Auber,

tel. 47 42 49 40

HELPLINES

AA: Alcooliques Anonymes, 3 rue Frédéric Sauton, 75005, tel. 43 25 75 00, 24 hours

AIDS Hotline: Free advice on 45 82 93 39 9 a.m.–5 p.m. Monday-Friday, 9 a.m.–12 p.m. Saturday.

Drugs: S.O.S. Drogue International, 27 rue Plantes, 75014, tel. 45 39 78 88

Rape Crisis Hotline: (toll free) 05 05 95 95

KINDERGARTENS AND SCHOOLS

Le Petit Cours (2–11 years, bilingual), 104 rue Ordener, 75018, tel. 46 06 80 33

International School of Paris, 7 rue Chardin, 75016, tel. 45 27 50 01

Ecole Active Bilingue, 6 avenue Van Dyck, 75008, tel. 46 22 14 24

LAUNDRIES

There are laundrettes in every *arrondissement*. For the nearest, go to the post office and consult the computerized telephone directory (MINITEL) under "Laverie." Most require two 10F pieces to operate the washing machine, and your own soap.

Laverie Beaubourg, 28 rue Beaubourg, 75003
Laverie Self-Service Monceau, 9 rue Treilhard, 75008
Laverie du Temple, 27 rue Vieille du Temple, 75004

LOST PROPERTY

Préfecture de Police Objets Trouves, 36 rue Morillons, 75015

MOPED/SCOOTER RENTAL

Mega Scooter, 10 rue Paul Bert, 75011, tel. 43 48 63 08
Scoot'heure, 6 rue d'Arras, 75005, tel. 43 25 69 25
Helmets are obligatory in France.

PACKING

phrasebook
student ID card (reductions almost everywhere)
a corkscrew/Swiss army knife (for those picnics of red wine, cheese and a *baguette*)
a small backpack to carry the day's necessities
plug adaptor
contact lens solution (very expensive in Paris)

SWIMMING POOLS

See *Pariscope* for a complete list. Centrally located pools include:
Piscine des Halles, Level – 3 Forum des Halles, 75001, tel. 42 36 98 44: large pool.
Piscine St. Merri, 18 rue de Renard, 75004, tel. 42 72 29 45: small pool just behind the Pompidou Center.
Piscine de Pontoise, 19 rue de Pontoise 75005 tel. 43 54 82 45: nude swimming Monday and Thursday evenings 8 p.m.–10 p.m.
Piscine Jean-Taris, 16 rue de Thoin, 75005, tel. 43 25 54 03: electronic purification, not chlorine. Small pool for children.
Open air:
Piscine de Plein Air du Parc de Sceaux, 148 avenue du General de Gaulle, 92160 Antony, tel. 46 60 75 30: slightly out of Paris, reached by RER; four pools with a grassy area where you can sunbathe and picnic.

TOILETS

Most of the big department stores like Galeries Lafayette, Printemps, or Bon Marché, have lavatory facilities. Otherwise, watch for the public cubicles.

TRAIN INFORMATION

SNCF, tel. 45 82 50 50

ORIENTATION

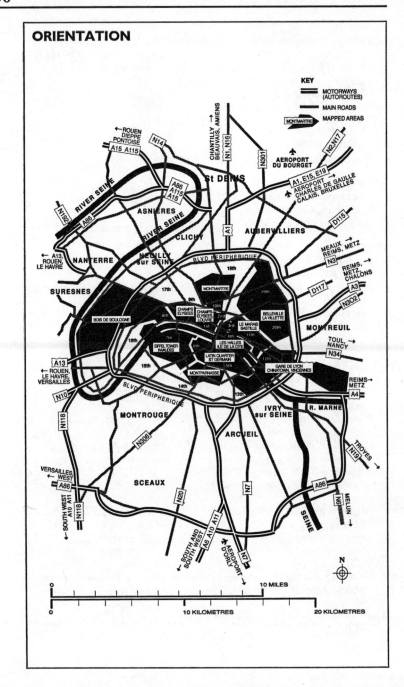

KEY
MOTORWAYS (AUTOROUTES)
MAIN ROADS
MONTMARTRE MAPPED AREAS

← ROUEN DIEPPE PONTOISE
A15 A115
N14
CHANTILLY BEAUVAIS, AMIENS →
N1, N16
N301
N2 N17
AEROPORT DU BOURGET
A1, E15, E19
AEROPORT CHARLES DE GAULLE CALAIS, BRUXELLES
A86 A115 A15
St DENIS
N192
D115
ASNIÈRES
RIVER SEINE
RIVER SEINE
A86
CLICHY
AUBERVILLIERS
MEAUX REIMS, METZ →
N3
REIMS, METZ, CHALONS →
← A13 ROUEN, LE HAVRE
NANTERRE
NEUILLY sur SEINE
A1
D117
A3
N302
BLVD PERIPHERIQUE
18th
SURESNES
17th
9th
MONTMARTRE
19th
MONTREUIL
BOIS DE BOULOGNE
8th
CHAMPS ELYSEES
CHAMPS ELYSEES LOUVRE
10th
2nd
3rd
1st
BELLEVILLE LA VILLETTE
20th
18th
7th
EIFFEL TOWER INVALIDES
LE MARAIS BASTILLE
4th
11th
TOUL, NANCY →
N34
LES HALLES ILE DE LA CITE
6th
LATIN QUARTER ST GERMAIN
15th
5th
12th
A13 ROUEN, LE HAVRE, VERSAILLES
MONTPARNASSE
GARE DE LYON CHINATOWN, VINCENNES
REIMS METZ →
A4
BLVD PERIPHERIQUE
14th
13th
N10
IVRY sur SEINE
R. MARNE
N118
MONTROUGE
ARCUEIL
N306
TROYES N19 →
VERSAILLES, WEST
A86
SCEAUX
N20
N7
A86
SEINE
SOUTH WEST A10 A11
N118
SOUTH AND SOUTH WEST A6 A10 A11
AEROPORT D'ORLY
N7
MELUN N6
N

10 MILES

0

0   10 KILOMETRES   20 KILOMETRES

THE GUIDE

Paris is a compact city – only forty minutes' Metro ride from one end to the other, and two hours across on foot. It's a wonderful city to walk in: dense, crowded, animated and sprinkled with cafés where you can stop off for a drink or a meal at any time of day. There aren't many parks or green spaces; the streets are what count, and of course, the bridges over the Seine which lend such a magical quality to the city in the early-morning or evening light.

Since 1860, Paris has been divided into twenty *arrondissements* (administrative sections), each divided into four *quartiers.* If you look at a map, you'll see how the *arrondissements* begin with the Louvre/Opéra area and spiral out like a snail's shell in a clockwise direction, thus explaining the apparent illogic of having the fourth next to the twelfth, the seventh next to the fifteenth, and so on. Having grasped this and taken in the gentle curve of the river between Left and Right banks, you should have few problems finding your way around. Note that the last one or two numbers of any Paris zip code, included with the addresses in this book, indicate the *arrondissement*: i.e. 75001 to 75020.

You could fill your days with sightseeing, from the monumental grandeur of the Arc de Triomphe through a wealth of museums, churches, galleries and architectural innovations, old and new. Or simply wander the streets in search of female echoes of the capital's rich historic, literary and artistic past. But Paris is also alive with shops, restaurants, clubs, movie theaters, bars and cafés, almost all of which provide good quality for the price you pay.

The cafés are good for all seasons: in winter, when it's wet and grey and the atmosphere inside is lively and warm, and in the spring and summer when the tables are out and you can settle down to people-watching. Life goes on in cafés of all kinds, from the vast yuppie emporiums of Les Halles to the small dingy places in the outer *arrondissements*. People come here to write books, love letters and postcards, to sleep, flirt, quarrel, discuss politics and complain drunkenly about the hardships of life, the loss of a job, or the depar-

THE GUIDE

ture of a lifelong partner. With the exception of heavily touristy areas like the Champs Elysées, you can sit in most cafés for literally *hours* without being frowned upon. Waiters can be offhand or even bad-tempered, in true Parisian style, but generally speaking they won't push you to consume or move on.

ARRIVAL

Paris has two main international airports: Roissy Charles de Gaulle to the northeast and Orly to the south.

From Charles de Gaulle

By train: the cheapest and quickest way into the city center is to take the free airport *navette* to the railway station (Gare SNCF), where you catch the Parisian express suburban network train RER to the Gare du Nord, leaving every 15 minutes from 5 a.m. to 11:15 p.m. (journey time approximately 35 minutes). From here you transfer to the Metro.

By bus: The Air France bus leaves every 15 minutes, from the terminal and deposits you either at Porte Maillot, next to the Metro stop to the west of the city, or by the Arc de Triomphe at the end of the Champs Elysées. Buses run from 5:45 a.m. to 11 p.m.

By taxi: Expect to pay 150F to 200F into central Paris, plus an extra charge for luggage. The trip takes about 45 minutes.

From Orly

By train: Orly is connected to central Paris by a bus–rail link. Orly–Rail – part of the RER network which takes you to the Gare d'Austerlitz and other stops that intersect with the Metro system. Departure every 15 minutes from 5:30 a.m. to 11:30 p.m.

By bus: Air France bus goes to the Gare des Invalides in the seventh *arrondissement*. Orlybus takes you to Denfert-Rochereau Metro in the fourteenth. Departure every 10 to 15 minutes, 6 a.m. to 11 p.m.

By taxi: Takes about 35 minutes and costs between 100F and 150 F.

Arriving by Train

If you cross the Channel by sea, the train comes into the Gare du Nord (tel. 42 80 03 03) from Boulogne or Calais, and Gare St-Lazare (tel. 43 38 52 29) from Dieppe and the Normandy coast. All Paris's six main-line stations are on the Metro and are equipped with cafés, *bureaux de change* and banks. The Gare du Nord also has a tourist information office. The central number for all SNCF information is 45 82 50 50.

Arriving by Bus

Nearly all international buses to Paris come into the Gare Routière Internationale, a grand name for a squat, depressing-looking building in a rather undesirable *quartier*. Not a good place to hang around late at night. Luckily there is a taxi stand right opposite the bus station, so get off quickly and grab a cab. If you can't afford a taxi, join others emptying off the bus and swarm with them to the nearby Metro station, where you can get a train direct to the center. Be warned: the underground corridors giving access to the platform are longish, and can make you feel a little uneasy if you're alone.

GETTING AROUND

Paris has an excellent public transportation system – efficient, well-run, well-lit, well-marked and easy to navigate. Compared to London's Underground, the distance between stations is small and you'll probably feel safer at night. At night, lots of people use the Metro until it stops running at 12:45 a.m. Buses are also very frequent. Most day buses start at about 6 a.m. finishing around 8:30 p.m. but there are night buses from 1:30 to 5:30 a.m. on ten main routes (tel. RATP, 43 46 14 14, for information).

Buses are preferable to the Metro provided you're not in a hurry. Besides offering the cheapest sightseeing tour of Paris, they seem to attract a nicer, less pushy, more courteous sort of person. Each bus stop displays a map outlining the route of every bus that stops there, duplicated on board with the major stops clearly labeled, which makes it easy to keep an eye on where you are going. Be sure to signal to the driver if you're waiting alone at a bus stop, since they don't stop automatically. Also, unless it's already illuminated, be sure to press the sign saying "Arrêt demandé" shortly before the stop where you want to get off.

Tickets

The same tickets are valid for both bus and Metro, plus the RER where it's within the confines of the city. You can buy either a single ticket (on the bus or in the station), a cheaper *carnet de dix* (ten tickets) or, if you are staying any length of time, a pass. Weekly and monthly passes require a photo. The day pass, allowing unlimited travel throughout the day, and special tourist passes of three and five days respectively, rarely seem to work out any cheaper.

Night Travel

It's best to be accompanied at night on the Metro, more for peace of mind than anything else. Most central stations feel pretty safe, and it's only as the train approaches the *périphérique* and the pas-

METRO & RER

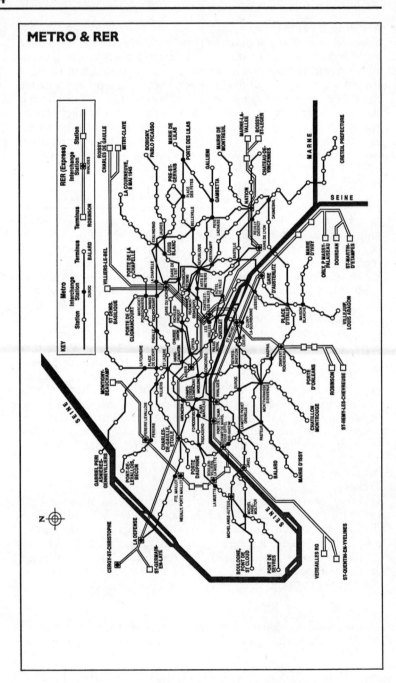

sengers thin out that there's any reason to be nervous. A few spots to avoid are Les Halles and the northern section of the Metro map from place de Clichy round to Belleville, especially Barbes Rochechouart, Pigalle and Strasbourg St-Denis. Also beware if you are staying with a well-heeled friend in the sixteenth. People here don't seem to use the Metro at night, so you might be one of the few getting off late, and the streets – particularly avenue Foch – tend to attract dodgy characters.

If you're in doubt, taxis are plentiful and reasonably cheap – 50F or less should get you around the center – and most drivers seem to know where they are going. Make sure the meter works when you get in, and check your change before leaving. If you are getting out in a dark street and the inside light doesn't come on until you open the door, the taxi driver might take the opportunity to slip you a couple of low-denomination coins instead of higher ones. In the event of any problems, note down the taxi's registration number, helpfully marked on one of the rear side windows, and report him to the Préfecture, which issues his license (phone number also displayed). Taxi stands are liberally scattered around Paris; one recommended number is Taxis Bleus (49 36 10 10).

GETTING AROUND

LANDMARKS
AND
MONUMENTS

On either bank of the Seine, peppering the first, seventh and eighth *arrondissements* are some of the city's most famous – and instantly recognizable – sites. For this is the Paris of postcards and souvenirs, and the over-familiarity of monuments, like the Eiffel Tower, the Champs Elysées and Arc de Triomphe, can lend an air of kitschy surreality to the area.

So how best to get about? As far as transportation goes, the only advantage of the Metro is speed. Far more rewarding are the efficient green and grey buses, which allow you to enjoy dramatic perspectives like the view up or down the Champs Elysées or along avenue de l'Opéra with the great green-domed building looming ahead. But though it involves trudging down some long, heavily trafficked boulevards, it pays to explore as much as possible on foot. This is how you'll bump into the sites that DON'T make it on to the souvenir ashtrays: the beautiful fountain outside the Comédie Française or that hidden bistro, located in a tiny courtyard off rue Richelieu, where waitresses dash across the cobblestoned alley with steaming plates of *pot au feu*. And it's the only way to take in the beauty of the river and its marvellous bridges or to explore *les passages*, the beautiful glass-roofed shopping arcades where you can buy souvenirs without feeling you have "tourist" written all over you.

No matter how many allegorical female figures you discover, the Arc de Triomphe, Les Invalides, L'Ecole Militaire and the Champ de Mars may well leave you saturated with tributes to great men, not to mention all things military. But don't despair. There are plenty of antidotes: the Louvre, the Musée d'Orsay, Pont Alexandre III, and the Rodin Museum not only show exhibits of the female form at its most beautiful, but celebrate the work of several great women artists – Elisabeth Vigée-Lebrun, Rosa Bonheur and Camille Claudel.

There's probably no better way to start your journey than by wandering down one of the most famous avenues in the world, the Champs Elysées, named after the place in Hell where, in Latin and Greek mythology, the souls of virtuous men and heroes sojourned. When they named the avenue they did not, perhaps, foresee the number of virtuous women and heroines who, throughout the history of Paris, would also have cause to take this route.

THE BRIDGES OF PARIS

The Seine has always been inextricably linked with the history of Paris. The Parisii and the Lutecians relied on it to provide water and protection, and as the main route by which essential supplies were brought into the capital. For centuries things remained the same – the river was seen not from an aesthetic but merely a utilitarian point of view. Initially there were no bridges, and the river was crossed by boat; then during the Middle Ages, bridges started to be constructed, but they were made of wood, so they were frequently washed away, knocked down by boats, or destroyed to repel the threat of invasion. Crammed with houses and shops, they were a thriving hub of commerce and a popular place to wander. Under Henry IV in the sixteenth century things started to change – he opened up the view of the river by forbidding the construction of houses on the bridges. In the seventeenth century, with growing interest in the river and evolving construction techniques, a total of seven bridges were built, including three of the Pont Neuf, the Pont Marie and the Pont Royal.

In the nineteenth century, new building developments – the creation of a suspension bridge, the use of metal structures and the invention of steel – meant that no fewer than twenty-one new bridges were built, and old ones were reconstructed.

PONT ALEXANDRE III

From the humblest to the most exalted: where the Pont des Arts is probably the simplest and most unadorned, this bridge is probably the most glitzy.

Named after the Tsar Alexander III, who laid the first stone, the bridge was built in only two years, between 1898 and 1900, and inaugurated at the time of the Universal Exhibition. Constructed entirely of metal, it represents an impressive feat of engineering, since the engineers, Résal and Alby, were instructed that the bridge should in no way block the perspective of Les Invalides from the Champs Elysées, and that it should not have several arches, since this would obstruct river traffic. The result is one massive arch which spans the river gracefully, with ornamental statues at the four corners that act as counterweights. The bridge is liberally draped in female forms, representing France at various stages of its history, and also Art, Commerce, Industry and Science – all of them guarded by appropriately ferocious-looking lions. The keystones on either side of the bridge are decorated by groups of nymphs: one bearing the arms of Paris, and the other those of Russia. The dazzling gilding, which is positively blinding in bright sunlight, was the result of the same golden paintbrush that touched the dome of Les Invalides in the year of the bicentennial celebrations. In a few years it should have weathered a bit. This magnificent king of bridges is finally topped off by picturesque candelabra-style lamps which, when you see them lit at night, cause one of those rushes of blood to the head that remind you how glad you are to be in such an enchanting city.

LANDMARKS AND MONUMENTS

ALONG THE CHAMPS ELYSÉES

The Champs Elysées is the most photographed stretch of the Triumphal Way, an endless ribbon of cars that sweep under more arches and past more monuments than exist in the rest of Paris put together. This grand perspective is the pride of the French state, stretching nine kilometers from the Louvre via the place de la Concorde and the Arc de Triomphe, to the Parisian engineering feat of the late twentieth century – the equally grandiose Grande Arche in the corporate complex of La Défense, with its skyscraping temples to multinational petroleum, micro-electronics and car companies.

ARC DE TRIOMPHE
Place Charles de Gaulle. Metro Charles de Gaulle–Etoile.
Open daily 10 a.m.–5 p.m.; closed Tuesday and public holidays.

This monument, almost as synonymous with Paris as the Eiffel Tower, was begun in 1806 at the instigation of Napoleon I, who had originally wanted a triumphal arch built near the former Bastille. But Napoleon met his downfall before the Arc was completed, and had to content himself with a life-sized wood and canvas model on the occasion of his marriage in 1810 to Marie-Louise, daughter of the Emperor of Austria. Eventually completed in 1836 at the request of Louis-Philippe, it remains a superb example of Empire architecture and, not least – like so much of monumental Paris – a powerful celebration of the allegorical female form. Among the sculptures and bas-reliefs that decorate the arch, take time to gaze at Rude's celebrated *La Marseillaise*, named after the marching song of the Revolution. A winged Victory, held aloft by a staggering group of heroically naked soldiers, she leaps out triumphantly, sword in hand, towards the distant place de la Concorde in violent celebration of her country's military might.

THE MARRIAGE OF NAPOLEON AND EMPRESS MARIE-LOUISE

In April 1810, a few months after divorcing Josephine, Napoleon prepared to marry nineteen-year-old Marie-Louise, the eldest daughter of the Emperor of Austria. Her strict upbringing – she was never allowed to see a male animal, and all references to sexual intercourse were cut out of the books she read – had left her in complete ignorance of sex, so what she made of her new husband, who boasted that she was the first virgin he had ever deflowered, is anyone's guess. Napoleon, however, was keen to make a good impression, and even allowed his sister Pauline to give him waltzing lessons (to little avail). She did, however, succeed in persuading him to get a better tailor. "Your clothes never fit properly," she complained, "and why are you so obstinate about not wearing suspenders? Your breeches always look as if they are falling down."

CHAMPS ELYSÉES

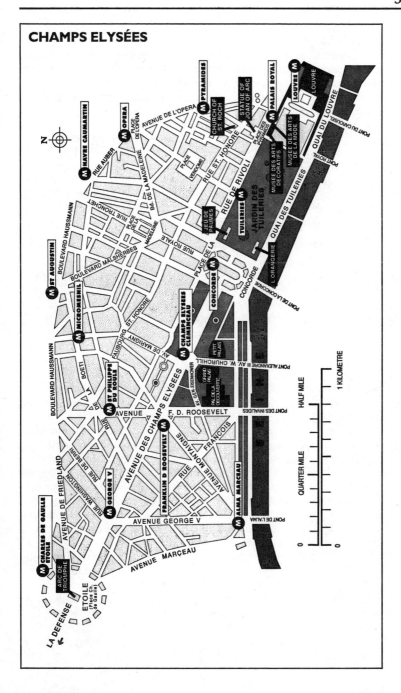

The giant arch, standing in the center of the city's most chaotic roundabout, is best appreciated from a distance, as you approach along the Champs Elysées. Inside is a small museum containing documents and drawings relating to its history, but it is more exciting to take the lift up and admire the view from the top of Haussmann's place de l'Etoile, around which cars spin giddily like Matchbox toys, to peel off down the elegant tree-lined avenues that fan out star-like in all directions.

Beneath the arch marked by an eternally burning flame lies the Tomb of the Unknown Soldier, a symbolic victim of the First World War, where General de Gaulle came to pay his respects on August 26 1944, the day after the Liberation of Paris. More recently, in 1970, a group of women placed a garland under the Arc de Triomphe, with the inscription: "Someone is more unknown than the Unknown Soldier: his wife."

THE CHAMPS ELYSÉES

"The Champs Elysées are too straight and too proper for a walk," wrote one journalist in the 1780s. With the series of extensions that have gradually prolonged the Triumphal Way as far as the modern development of La Défense, the Champs Elysées is even straighter and less attractive to walk down today. Work is in progress to create more pedestrian space, laid out with plants and shrubs, and a vast underground parking garage, but for the moment this is car territory, despite the massive crowds who stroll along the avenue on Sunday afternoons. The best way to tackle it is to take the Balabus which runs in the summer from Gare de Lyon to La Défense, and allows you to get on and off as often as you like without buying another ticket. This special service was introduced to show off what the advertisements insist is "the most beautiful route in the world." From the Arc de Triomphe to the Rond-Point, a smaller roundabout dotted with fountains, the avenue is lined with shops, up-scale arcades, cafés, movie theaters, airline offices and banks. Yet it's not just a mecca for tourists; the Champs Elysées is a busy business, banking and trading area with a particularly high concentration of television and film producers and directors. Fouquet's, a famous café on the corner of the Avenue George V, is one of their favorite haunts – you can tell from the prices.

Heading down the Champs Elysées from the Arc de Triomphe, you will come across the famous (now rather seedy) Lido cabaret, several brightly lit shopping arcades, including a huge Virgin Megastore, some flashy theaters and a few big hotels such as the Astoria Carlton, superseded only by the world-famous George V to your left on the extremely chic avenue of the same name. In keeping with this moneyed atmosphere, several huge, glistening car showrooms draw clusters of wistful spectators, especially men and their sons, come to inspect the latest Renault model or the top-of-the-range Alfa Romeos captured behind the spotless glass.

As the name Elysian Fields suggests, the avenue was once rather different. In the eighteenth century, puppet theaters, open-air restaurants and lemonade vendors (girls of dubious repute, much featured in popular songs) made it a place of pleasure, while the plentiful trees provided a bucolic backdrop and a convenient screen for illicit adventures. Cows were still grazing in the fields, and only six houses stood here when Napoleon decided to create the Triumphal Way. In the end he never experienced the elation of parading along his chosen route, and all that passed under the Arc de Triomphe were his ashes – watched by a crowd of 100,000 – on their way from exile in St. Helena to the Invalides.

Number 25 was built in the mid-nineteenth century by the intriguing courtesan, La Païva, who had used first prostitution and then marriage to the Portuguese Marquis de Païva, as stepping stones from a Moscow slum to the elegant Champs. The Hôtel Päiva, financed in part by her Prussian lover, Henckel von Donnersmark, became a meeting place for Prussian spies. Indeed, when the Prussian army marched into Paris in 1871, the Hôtel Päiva was the only grand house permitted to remain open. The next year her husband committed suicide, and she married Von Donnersmark whose wedding gift – former Empress Eugenie's diamond necklace – may have been some compensation for the fact that she was hissed at whenever she appeared in public. Eventually in 1878 she was banished from France, and went to live with Donnersmark in his castle. Traumatized by her declining beauty she shattered the Venetian mirror in her bedroom. Donnersmark, however, remained so enchanted by her that when she died, at the age of sixty-five, he had her body preserved in alcohol.

In 1989, the Champs Elysées relived some of its former glory with a sumptuous international celebration for the bicentennial of the Revolution. Watched by TV viewers throughout the world, President Mitterrand sat under a massive red, white and blue awning erected in the place de la Concorde; representatives of every branch of the armed forces paraded by on foot, in tanks, in helicopters and in jets; and following up was a series of gaudily theatrical and at times surreal floats – the creation of Jean-Paul Goode, the *enfant terrible* of Paris designers – accompanied by lasers, music, and, finally, Jessye Norman singing "La Marseillaise." The spectacle took all day, and the noise, lights, crowds and rejoicing carried on far into the night.

Halfway down towards the place de la Concorde, at Rond-Point, the shops and showrooms give way to row upon row of chestnut trees. Leading off the place Clemenceau is the avenue Winston Churchill, from where you will see, poking above the trees, the roofs of the Grand and Petit Palais, built for the Paris Exhibition of 1900.

Grand Palais

Avenue General Eisenhower 75008. Metro Champs Elysées–Clemenceau. Tel. 42 89 54 10. Open daily 10 a.m.–8 p.m.; Wednesday 10 p.m.

The Grand Palais, topped by a steel and glass dome in elegant Art Nouveau style, was intended as the Republic's monument to French art. After the highly elaborate exterior, complete with colonnade, bas-reliefs and friezes depicting every conceivable allegory of Art, it is a relief to be inside. Now used for temporary exhibitions of crowd-drawing artists it also hosts the superb annual modern art fair in October, known as the FIAC.

The west wing is occupied by Paris's original science museum, the Palais de la Découverte, founded in 1937 and devoted to scientific discoveries. Although it's been largely superseded by the Cité des Sciences et de l'Industrie, it's still popular with children, with a great Planetarium and plenty of scope for interaction, including a chance to experiment with static electricity that literally makes your hair stand on end.

Petit Palais

Avenue Winston Churchill. Metro Champs Elysées–Clemenceau. Tel. 42 65 12 73. Open 10 a.m.–5:40 p.m. every day except Monday and public holidays.

The Petit Palais opposite is equally flamboyant, entered through an ornately sculpted confection of fruit, flowers and animals flanked by a grand colonnade of Ionic columns. The museum houses an impressive permanent collection of paintings, notably Courbet's *Le Sommeil* and Bonnard's *Nu dans le bain* as well as paintings by Pissarro, Monet and Cézanne. There's also an unremarkable assortment of sculpture, furniture and decorative art from the Middle Ages to the nineteenth century.

PLACE DE LA CONCORDE

Back on the Champs Elysées it's a short walk to the place de la Concorde, a square which has seen more than its fair share of blood. Designed in the mid-eighteenth century as an octagon bordered by a dry moat, tragedy first hit in 1770 when the marriage of Marie-Antoinette to the then Dauphin was celebrated with a fireworks display. The crowd, presumably unused to pyrotechnics, panicked, and in the resultant chaos 133 people were crushed to death in the moat. Twenty-two years later, people gathered for a rather different reason – to topple the central statue of Louis XV. The following year the guillotine was set up, and by 1795, over 1300 people had met their end beneath its ruthless blade. Among them were Charlotte Corday, Madame Roland, Marie-Antoinette, Madame du Barry, and finally Robespierre himself.

WOMEN IN THE REVOLUTION

The French Revolution of 1789 gave women, for the first time, the possibility of joining in the political fray on an equal footing with men. Many women came to prominence in these turbulent years: Madame de Staël, who argued for a constitutional monarchy in France and allied herself with her lovers Narbonne and Talleyrand; Madame Roland, whose Republican zeal and hatred of the monarchy inspired the Girondins and who went to the scaffold uttering those famous words, "O Liberty, what crimes are committed in thy name!" Théroigne de Méricourt who, dressed in scarlet, rode into battle with the mob; and Charlotte Corday, a young girl prepared to sacrifice herself for her cause by carrying out the cold-blooded assassination of Marat.

In 1789 Olympe de Gouges, French feminist writer, published her *Declaration of the Rights of Woman* in response to the *Declaration of the Rights of Man*, in the hopes that women would take their place in the revolutionary shake-up and in the new order that was to result. It was, after all, the women who marched to Versailles in 1789 against the King. Patriotic women's clubs sprang up, the most influential of which was the Républicaines Révolutionnaires led by Claire Lacombe; there were also clubs where women were admitted on an equal basis with men and allowed freely to air their views on current political debates. But the honeymoon period was short lived. By 1793, Condorcet, who had championed women's rights calling for equal education for all, had been toppled, Olympe de Gouges, having pronounced boldly that women had an equal right for their voices to be heard since they had an equal right to mount the scaffold, ended up being executed herself – the consequence of writing an insulting letter to Robespierre after the arrest of Louis XVI.

The *place* is now best seen at night with its postcard-perfect views in every direction: between replicas of the Marly Horses, which once graced Louis XIV's extravagant chateau at Marly, up to the Arc de Triomphe; across the Seine to the neoclassical National Assembly; north to the Madeleine, framed by the neoclassical colonnades of the Hôtel Crillon and Hôtel de la Marine; and through the rows of trees along the Tuileries, illuminated by the soft light of electric bulbs in the former gas lamps. Louise-Philippe added the Egyptian obelisk in 1836, a gift from the viceroy of Egypt. This was a suitably uncontroversial alternative both to the plaster Liberty statue to which Manon Roland cried, "O Liberty, what crimes are committed in thy name!" a moment before her execution, and to the statue of Louis XV which it had replaced.

Far more striking than the obelisk are the eight monumental statues of women, mounted on individual pavilions around the square. In a show of French unity, each of these stern matrons represents a regional capital, and some – perhaps unflatteringly – were modeled on well-known women of the time. For instance, the figure of Strasbourg, hand on hip, is a portrait of Victor Hugo's lover Juliette Drouot, while Lille is thought to have been inspired by Marie-Antoinette d'Ensignies, wife of the city's Chief Inspector of Police.

LANDMARKS AND MONUMENTS

FROM THE TUILERIES TO THE LOUVRE

Leaving the place de la Concorde by the northwestern corner, you'll come upon rue de Rivoli, bordered on one side by the Tuileries Gardens and on the other by an arcade, topped off by a line-up of elegant façades. One of Paris's major shopping streets, it's home to two of the city's longest established department stores– Bazar de l'Hôtel de Ville and La Samaritaine – along with a well-stocked W.H. Smith with a tearoom upstairs. Various small streets lead off the rue de Rivoli into attractive squares.

Jardin des Tuileries

Metro Concorde–Tuileries.
Open 6:30 a.m.–8 p.m. October–April; 10:45 p.m. May;
10 p.m. June–August; 9 p.m. September.

In most Parisian parks, sitting alone is seen as an invitation for a pick-up, and you should be on your guard. In the Tuileries, it's a tradition. The historian Taine described it as "an open-air drawing room" and throughout the eighteenth and nineteenth centuries its gravel paths were one of the few public places where respectable young women could allow themselves a bit of flirting. Public, however, did not mean open to all; there was a rule that poorly dressed people or those bearing bundles must be turned away at the gate. If you don't want to be bothered you *could* make for the area around the Orangerie – a resort of cruising gays.

MADAME ROLAND (1754–93)

Madame Roland was a fervent republican, and one of the most outspoken women of the Revolution. She was, however, no supporter of women's rights, and once wrote: "It often angers me to see women disputing privileges which ill befit them . . . However gifted they may be in some respects, they should never show their learning in public."

In her *salon* in rue Guénégaud she gathered together leading male political figures, among them Robespierre, Brissot, Pétion and Buzot, all of whom were violently opposed to any attempts to reconcile the Revolution and the monarchy. She rejoiced in the events of 1789, and by August 1790 she was openly campaigning for the abolition of the monarchy. It was at this time that her *salons* reached their zenith, attended by all the most powerful men. However, with the growing split between rival left-wing factions – namely the Girondins and the Montagnards – her power began to fade. Madame Roland's husband, twenty years her senior, whom she had pushed into politics, abandoned his position in the Ministry of the Interior when he realized that his wife was in love with Buzot. In 1793 she herself was arrested and eventually imprisoned in the Conciergerie, where she managed to write her memoirs before being executed on November 8 of the same year.

THE TUILERIES & THE LOUVRE

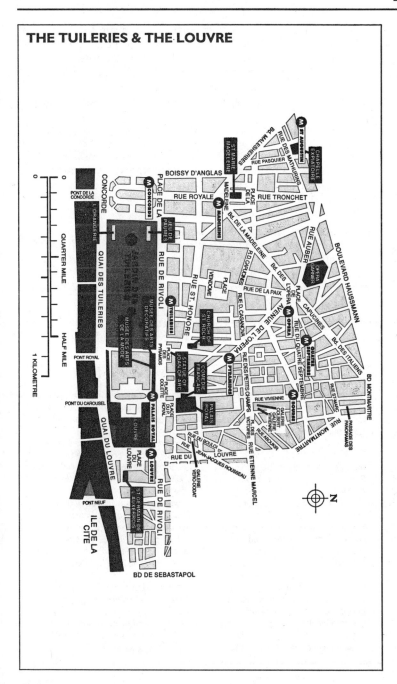

LANDMARKS AND MONUMENTS

It was Catherine de' Medici, eager to re-create the fashion of outdoor promenades from her native Italy, who began the gardens, though today's layout bears little resemblance to Catherine's original design. The long perspectives and symmetrical groves reveal the hand of Louis XIV's favorite gardener, Le Nôtre. "Many talk with distaste of the straight lines, the clipped trees, the formal flower-beds," wrote Mrs. Frances Trollope (mother of Anthony) in 1836, "nay, some will even abuse the venerable orange-trees themselves, because they grow in square boxes, and do not wave their boughs in the breeze like so many ragged willow-trees. But I should think it was as reasonable to quarrel with Westminster Abbey because it did not look like a Grecian temple, as to find fault with the Gardens of the Tuileries because they are arranged like French pleasure-grounds, and not like an English park."

The Jeu de Paume and The Orangerie

Jeu de Paume: Place de la Concorde. Metro Concorde. Tel. 47 03 12 50. Open Tuesday 12 p.m.–9:30 p.m., Wednesday–Friday 12 p.m.–7 p.m., Saturday and Sunday 10 a.m.–7 p.m; closed Monday. Orangerie: Place de la Concorde. Metro Concorde. Tel: 42 97 48 16. Open daily 9:45 a.m.–5:15 p.m.; closed Tuesday.

At the Place de la Concorde end of the Tuileries Gardens stand two large pavilions. The Jeu de Paume was originally built by Henri IV

CATHERINE DE' MEDICI (1519–89)

Catherine de' Medici belonged to the junior branch of the illustrious Medici family in Florence, and inherited (and largely deserved) her clan's reputation for political ambition and perfidiousness, as well as aesthetic refinement, and generous patronage of the arts.

She married the future king of France, Henri II, in 1553, and remained in his shadow during his lifetime while he openly showed his preference for his mistress, Diane de Poitiers. However, in a country torn apart by the Wars of Religion, her appointment as Regent of the kingdom on her husband's death enabled her to display her political gifts to the full.

At first, she attempted to implement a policy of reconciliation with an "Edict of Tolerance" and the "Peace of Amboise" granted to the Protestant Huguenots in 1563. But she soon opted for the overriding interests of the royal family and endeavored to consolidate the legitimacy of her sons, who successively ruled France as Charles IX, François II and Henri III. This entailed the elimination of the Protestant party, to which end she gave her passive consent to the Saint Bartholemew Massacre on August 24, 1572. Her lack of moral scruples in the conduct of her policies earned her a reputation as a treacherous witch. Conscious that as a woman she had to play things carefully in order to be taken seriously, she adopted as her emblem and rôle model, the ancient Greek sea captain, Artemisia, a highly successful military tactician, known for her loyalty to her late husband, although she later threw herself off a cliff for unrequited love. Catherine was made of tougher stuff.

as a games room for his son to play *paume*, a form of indoor tennis reminiscent of squash. Eventually the game lost its popularity and in the early twentieth century the building was turned into an art gallery, made famous in 1947 for housing Paris's Impressionist collections, moved in 1986 to the Musée d'Orsay. The inside of the Jeu de Paume has since been gutted and remodeled to accommodate short-term exhibitions by contemporary artists.

The Orangerie, across the garden on the side nearest the Seine, houses the Walter–Guillaume Collection, a permanent exhibition of exceptional works from the Impressionists to the 1930s. Paul Guillaume opened his own gallery at the age of twenty-three. An enlightened pioneer in the field of modern art, he started with avant-garde Russian painters such as Natalia Goncharova, and subsequently championed the cause of young unknowns such as Utrillo and Soutine.

After his death in 1934 his widow Domenica continued to add to his valuable collection with the help of her second husband, Jean Walter, an architect. The whole lot was donated to the Louvre in 1977, with instructions that the works should be kept and shown together – thanks to which the Orangerie now holds a palatable collection of masterpieces by Cézanne, Picasso, Renoir, Rousseau, Utrillo, Derain and Modigliani. Best of all are huge, mesmerizing canvases from Monet's Water Lilies series, a gift by the artist to the state installed here under his very specific instructions.

On the other side of the Tuileries Gardens, if you head east across the place du Carousel, you come to the Louvre.

THE LOUVRE

34–6 quai du Louvre, 75001. Tel. 40 20 50 50. Metro Louvre–Rivoli/Palais Royal–Musée du Louvre. Main Entrance: Pyramid. Museum hours: 9 a.m.–6 p.m. Evening opening hours until 10 p.m. Monday (Sully and Denon wings alternately) and Wednesday (the whole museum). Closed Tuesday.

  Audioguides available in six languages at the rental counters located in the Napoleon Hall, on the Mezzanine level (under the Pyramid).

From Fortified Castle to Museum   Eight centuries ago, King Philippe-Auguste, worried about the possibility of invasion, set about building a huge fortress on the Right Bank of the Seine. For over four hundred years this fortified castle was home for generations of French monarchs; then, in 1527, François I decided to modernize it and create a Renaissance-style château to house his collection of Italian Renaissance art, including Leonardo da Vinci's *Mona Lisa*. Nothing remains of the old fortress today except a wall of the medieval dungeon, while above ground, successive monarchs have gradually added to the palace throughout the years. Catherine de' Medici even built a second palace, the Palais des Tuileries – destroyed by fire in 1871 – next door to the Palais du Louvre, declaring that the Louvre wasn't comfortable enough.

When, between 1678 and 1680, Louis XIV decided to move the court to Versailles, the Louvre was given to the Academies of Art – the fruition of an idea first conceived by Henri IV, who wanted all the artists and craftsmen working for the Court to be lodged in the Louvre. This was to their advantage, since the King effectively paid for the rent and upkeep of the apartments, which – not surprisingly – were in great demand. During the reign of Louis XIV many well-known painters, sculptors and cabinet-makers installed themselves in the palace until it gradually became a kind of free-for-all; rough-and-ready cabarets opened in the *Cour carrée*, and rows of prostitutes would come to entertain the motley population.

Louis XV took no further interest in the Louvre, and would have sold it to a demolition company had it not been for the intervention of his mistress Madame de Pompadour's brother, the Marquis de Marigny. Napoleon III contributed greatly to its extension with the inauguration, in 1857, of the *nouveau Louvre* with six new pavilions (Turgot, Richelieu, Colbert, Mollien, Denon and Daru). The decision to open the Louvre to the public as a museum was one of the direct consequences of the French Revolution since, royalty having been abolished, it was felt that the people had the right to see the sculptures which were part of their national heritage. The *Grande Galerie* was opened to the public in 1793 and, from 1803, the Napoleon Museum – as it was known – was considered the most prestigious museum in the world. After Napoleon's defeat in 1815, most of the treasures gathered during his conquests had to be returned to their owners.

Le Grand Louvre Despite a steady increase in the Louvre collections since early this century, the decision to modernize it and create new galleries was not taken until 1981. The task finally fell

---

NATALIA GONCHAROVA (1881–1962)

Born into an artistic family of impoverished Russian aristocrats, Goncharova left her home for Moscow in 1892 to study painting. Together with Mikhail Larionov, who she was to marry many years later at the age of seventy-four, she founded the Rayonnist movement, one of the earliest developments in abstract art. Their paintings were shown at all the Post-Impressionist and Futurist exhibitions – first in Russia, then later in London and Paris, which she eventually made her home.

Inspired by both Fauvist and Cubist aesthetics, combined with her country's traditional techniques, Goncharova's style combines raw color with primitive forms. This suited her second career as a set designer; she worked on Rimsky-Korsakov's *Le Coq d'Or* and Diaghilev's *Ballets Russes*.

to the Sino-American architect Ieoh Ming Pei, whose instructions were to create a series of new rooms under the *Cour Napoléon*, to contain all the infrastructure needed to run the museum, and to come up with a scheme for the main entrance. The inspired idea of creating the dramatic glass Pyramid was adopted to give light and height to what might have seemed a rather dark bunker-like construction. It has the added advantage of making the main entrance to the Louvre very easy to find. From here escalators lead down into the Napoleon Hall, to a public reception area equipped with information desk, lavatories, post office, café, ice-cream bar, restaurant, *bureau de change*, bookshop, and a gift shop selling reproduction statues, postcards and souvenirs.

Whether you like it or loathe it – and it tends to provoke strong reactions – the decision to allow the construction of the Pyramid was both daring and controversial, the type of move we have come to expect from the French who, under President François Mitterrand, have long supported modern innovative architecture, as shown by the Arche de La Défense and the new Opéra, not to mention the new National Library under construction. You have to admire their courage. The building of the Pyramid was greeted with some suspicion, fueled by rumors that expert mountaineers were needed to clean every one of its individual triangular windows. Whether or not this is true, the Pyramid does tend to look a little smoky in daylight, as though it could do with a polish. Like so many of the city's grand sites, it looks best at night when, illuminated against the outline of the museum buildings, it glows benevolently like some kind of magic crystal embedded in the concrete, tempting you into the bowels of the earth to discover the incredible wealth of riches that the Louvre has in store.

The Museum You'd be daft – or masochistic – to attempt to see the whole of the Louvre in a single day. Even limiting yourself to the "highlights" is tiring, while the art collection alone merits several visits. List your priorities before you go, get hold of a plan in the reception area, and above all, wear your comfiest shoes. The museum is divided into three areas: the Richelieu Wing on the rue de Rivoli side; Denon, on the river side, and Sully, at the end. Each area is divided into numbered sections; the number is displayed at the entrance to the rooms, and spread over three floors.

Due to the reorganization and the opening of the Richelieu Wing in 1993, the works on display may vary at different times. Below is a rudimentary outline of some of the treasures awaiting you.

Greek, Etruscan and Roman Antiquities *(Denon ground floor, 2, 3, 4, 5. First floor, 3; Sully ground floor, 8, 7, first floor, 8).* In the Greek section, the crowd will guide you to the famous *Venus* *de Milo*, discovered by a farmer in 1820 on the island of Milos and purchased for King Louis-Philippe. The arms – missing today – were carved separately, and the body is formed of two pieces (the head and torso, and the draped legs). The statue, dating from the end of the second century bc, is a perfect representation of classical art. No one knows who sculpted her, or how her arms were originally positioned. It's worth standing for a few minutes to observe its powerful naturalism, the contrast between the details of the drapery and the smoothness of the torso, and the slightly twisted movement of the body that animates this remarkable sculpture.

Among the examples of Greek sculpture from the archaic (seventh to sixth centuries bc) period, look especially for the *Hera of Samos*: dressed in a chiton (tunic) and a himation (cloak) with a wedding veil, she is the wife of Zeus and patroness of marriage and fertility. From the sixth century bc the *Rampin* (or *Triumphant*) *Horseman* is a masterpiece of precision and grace in the Attic style: note the special smile (sculptors of the period had not yet figured out how to create glum faces) and the delicate curls in the hair and beard. Have a look, too, at the cartoonish *Lady of Auxerre* with a neat dreadlock wig and improbably huge hands, thought to be one of the oldest Greek statues found to date.

As you leave the Greek section in Room 4, you will see the most famous work of the Etruscan civilization: the *Caere Sarcophagus* (530–510 bc). The Etruscans (of still uncertain origin) lived in central Italy, and came into contact with the Greek colonies settled in southern Italy towards the eighth century bc. The Greeks were shocked by the Etruscans' hedonistic lifestyle and the fact that women were permitted to dine alongside the men. This terracotta sarcophagus would have done nothing to allay their prejudices – it represents a couple banqueting in bed. The most minute details of their clothing, the way their hair is dressed, their ornaments, their cushion and their bed are all exactly rendered.

From here, on your left, you will walk through Anne d'Autriche's summer-time suite to the Roman antiquities. These include attractive mosaics from a Lebanese church, as well as jewels, ceramics, ivories and other treasures.

Egyptian Antiquities *(Sully ground floor, 7, 6, 5; first floor, 6, 7, 8)*. This collection of jewelry, sarcophagi, figurines and statues was among the museum's original exhibits, and remains one of the finest and richest in the world. Major pieces include two giant sphinxes from the burial chamber of Ramses III, as well as the pink granite *Tanis Sphinx* and the *Mastaba Akhethetep*, a funerary chapel for nobles of the Old Empire. In the same room is the *Gebel-el Arak* knife, one of the most ancient of all known Egyptian reliefs, with a carved land-and-water battle scene, the concubines of the dead, ivory statuettes, two lions and several ivory pieces from a game.

The stele of Princess Nefertiti, with its well-preserved colors and delicate carvings, is a good example of funerary art during the Fifth Dynasty, and the painted bas-relief from a pillar of the tomb of Sethi I in the Valley of the Kings shows Hattor, goddess of death and rebirth, allowing the King to touch her magic collar.

Sculptures *(Denon ground floor, 7, 8, 9, 10, 5).* These rooms cover the entire development of sculpture in France from its beginnings to the end of the nineteenth century, as well as Italian sculpture from the eleventh century to the eighteenth. Probably the least visited part of the museum, it's by no means the least interesting.

Art from great cathedrals includes a statue of *Sainte Geneviève* which previously decorated the portal of the church of Sainte-Geneviève de Paris. On each side of the saint, an angel and a devil recall the miracle of the candle, a famous episode from the legend of the Patroness of Paris (c. 1230). Have a look, too, at the beautiful *Christ Head* from L'Hôtel Dieu de Tonnerre (c. 1300) and statues representing *The Virgin and Child* from all over France, especially the *Virgin with Child* from the Château de Conasnon, and the one from Ecouen (sixteenth century). There are also some fine examples of garden statuary – look at the figure of Diana leaning on a stag from the Château d'Anet.

In the eighteenth-century section, don't miss Pigalle's *Madame Pompadour en amitié.* Finished in 1758, this group, also known as Love and Friendship, represents Madame de Pompadour as Friendship, a euphemistic reference to her relationship with the King. Another famous garden statue is of Marie-Adelaïde of Savoie, Duchesse of Burgundy, represented in a youthful allegory sculpted in 1708 for the Duke of Antin's gardens. Last – but not least – is the Pigalle's *Voltaire nu,* most unusual for its time. The statue was intended as a gesture of homage to Voltaire – who did not, however, appreciate being "disguised as a monkey."

Applied Arts *(Sully, first floor, 8, 5, 4, 3, 2, 1; Denon).* Situated in the magnificent Apollo Gallery, this department houses a collection of diverse objets d'art and beautifully crafted pieces of furniture from a number of periods. Most popular is the royal collection, which includes acres of tapestries, a mosaic table from the Richelieu Castle, and of course the Crown Jewels, including the Regent, a 137-carat diamond.

The Paintings *(Sully and Denon, first and second floors).* This section is probably the richest in the museum. It is also the most tiring, because there are so many masterpieces that demand your attention, so allow plenty of time. If you're seriously interested in art, consider making two or three trips.

The majority of the masterpieces – representing the French, Italian, Spanish, Dutch, Flemish, German and English schools – are situated in the gigantic quarter-of-a-mile-long Grande Galerie. You'll quickly notice that until you reach the eighteenth-century collection, all the artists are men. Don't let this deceive you into thinking that there were no female painters between the fifteenth century and the eighteenth; the Louvre owns some twenty paintings by women of the period – Constance Mayer, Jeanne Philiberte Ledoux, Antoinette Hautebourt Lescot, Suzanne Roslin – but they are simply not on display. Some are being restored, but the rest can be counted among the thousands of paintings awaiting their turn to be viewed.

French School *(Sully, second floor, 1, 2, 3, 4). Fourteenth to sixteenth century:* In the fifteenth-century paintings women were represented as obedient wives, pious mothers, or dignified gentlewomen. Their resigned, often sad faces were beautifully painted by the great Flemish School: Van Eyck, Van der Weyden and Bouts and Metsys, to name but a few. Most often, the only visible parts of their bodies are their faces and hands, and they never seem to smile. A portrait of *Anne de Beaujeu* and her daughter *Suzanne* were part of a triptych by Jean Hey, the rest of which has now disappeared. It is amusing to see Suzanne's little hands clasped in the position of one at prayer, while her face bears the unmistakable expression of a sulking child.

With the advent of the Renaissance, a great deal of the attention hitherto directed towards the divine world focused on men and women, and an outstanding school of portrait painting began to flourish in France. Featuring painters like François Clouet, Jean Clouet, Jean Cousin, and Pierre Dumoustier, this school originated from the time when François I decided to establish his court at Fontainebleau and, from 1430 onwards, commissioned a large number of Italian, French and Flemish artists to decorate the new additions to the castle. The resulting "School of Fontainebleau" embraces a huge collection of graceful, often erotic subjects, with little concern for proportions, in a two-dimensional space. In fact it was Jean Cousin who painted the first known reclining nude in French painting: *Eva Prima Pandora*.

This period marked important changes in the portrayal of women who, no longer represented simply as Virgin Mary or model spouse, appear as, for instance, a Great Lady in François Clouet's *Anne d'Autriche* and in frescoes, idealized as a naked goddess. Look out for *Diane Chasseresse*, painted in about 1550; it has all the elements of the Fontainebleau School: lyricism, linear elegance and vast landscapes across which a tall woman proudly walks. This is yet another idealization of Diane de Poitiers, mistress of Henri II, who seems to have imposed a form of respect mixed with fear on all around her. She was one of the first patronesses of the arts to commission according to personal taste, inspiring several contemporary painters and sculptors to represent her as a mythological divinity.

Another famous painting of the same school is *Gabrielle d'Estrées et une de ses soeurs au bain*, in which one sister lightly pinches the right nipple of the other. The subject has naturally attracted some pretty diverse interpretations but is generally thought to be a satire on the flightiness of the aristocracy. Both paintings are good examples of the tendency of the Fountainebleau School to merge elegance and eroticism, beauty and sophistication, coquetry and grace.

Seventeenth century: This century was an extremely fertile period for French artists. Painting a woman, however, was no easy undertaking, since in the collective imagination she represented not only God and piousness (the Virgin Mary) but also witches, peasants and dangerous intellectuals! In fact, all the century's ambiguities are reflected in the portrayal of women, whether the art form be official, religious, mythological, allegorical or symbolic; and images of women range from royal and distant, bourgeois and natural, to lonely or surrounded by family, divine or low-born.

Poussin, king of Classicist painting, was probably France's greatest seventeenth-century painter. He spent most of his life in Italy – primarily for study, but also because he preferred it. The Louvre has one of the most important collections of Poussin, including his famous self-portrait (1650); *Echo et Narcisse*, much influenced by Titian (note how the nymph Echo merges into the rock); *Bergers d'Arcadie*, expressing more melancholic ideas, such as the fragility of human happiness; and *Apollo Lover of Daphne*, his last unfinished painting, seen as the artist's final statement on the wounds caused by love, juxtaposed with the theme of life flowing by and the beauty of nature.

Eighteenth and early nineteenth century (until 1848): Here at last we see women celebrated on a wide scale. The art of this period is said to be especially "feminine;" you can see why in the choice of form, the comfortable and gracious furniture, the abundance of mirrors and the brightness of the materials. But it was also the first time women had a strong, independent image: female writers, philosophers, poets, dancers, actresses and – last, but not least – painters, suddenly began to flourish, among them Elisabeth Vigée-Lebrun, Adélaide Labille-Guiard, Alexandre Roslin, Marie Loir, and Anna Vallayer-Coster. All were talented portrait painters except Vallayer-Coster, who preferred to paint still lifes. They were often barred from entering the Academy, which imposed a restriction on the number of women accepted, and could not attend workshops featuring male models as a matter of decency! A significant result was effectively to prevent them from becoming history painters, the top-ranking category of artist at the time.

Most famous among successful eighteenth-century female painters was undoubtedly Marie-Antoinette's private portraitist, Elisabeth Vigée-Lebrun. She is also one of only two women painters currently to be represented in the Louvre. Vigée-Lebrun painted her first portrait of Marie-Antoinette at the age of twenty-four. In her self-portrait (*Autoportrait avec sa fille*), mother and daughter have their arms round each other in a tender embrace. The monochrome background focuses attention on the two graceful figures, dressed in the style of the Ancients.

When the Revolution broke out, Vigée-Lebrun, closely associated with royalty, escaped just in time with her daughter Julie. For twelve years, they lived in exile in Italy, Austria and Russia. Everywhere she went, Vigée-Lebrun painted portraits of the nobility, opening up the doors of the Academies which enabled her to build a personal fortune. In 1802 she returned to Paris and stayed there for the last forty years of her life, holding a very fashionable salon.

Marie-Guillaumine Benoist is especially famous for her Portrait d'une Négresse, which she showed at her first exhibition in 1800 and was later bought by Louis XVIII. At twenty-three she worked under Vigée-Lebrun, then joined the workshop of Jacques-Louis David. In true Neoclassical style – perhaps in celebration of the 1794 bill abolishing slavery – her Portrait d'une Négresse made her reputation, winning her commissions from – among others – Napoleon, who ordered several portraits of himself and his family. Then suddenly, under the French Restoration, Marie-Guillaumine Benoist had to give up exhibiting her works in public, because her husband accepted an important government position. This was a bitter blow to her and her career. "Let's not talk about this any more, if not the wound will only open up again," she wrote in a subsequent letter to her husband.

Nineteenth century: By the early nineteenth century, the French Romantics were in full swing, most famously represented by Géricault and Delacroix. The upsurge of national and military glory, the lure of the East, the stirrings of a new revolution, became allied themes from classical mythology, with a distinct penchant for macabre realism.

The great French poet Baudelaire sums up this element in the work of Delacroix, whom he greatly admired:

> Everything in his world is desolation: everything bears witness to the eternal and incorrigible barbarity of mankind. Towns set afire and smoking, victims with their throats cut, raped women, children thrown between the hooves of horses or about to be stabbed by distracted mothers; the whole œuvre seems a terrible hymn composed in honor of fate and irremediable pain.

Some of Delacroix's most famous paintings are indeed full of sadistic details: the woman dragged along by a Turkish horseman in the *Massacres of Chios*, the stabbing to death of the female slave in the foreground of *The Death of Sardonapalus*, the violence of

The Abduction of Rebecca. Delacroix did much to introduce the French Romantics to the Orient, but his painting *Women of Algiers at Home* is one of the few to depict a peaceful, harmonious scene.

Italian Painting *(Denon, 8, 10).* Of all foreign schools, the Italians are by far the best represented because they were popular with the kings and queens of France.

Among the early masterpieces is Cimabue's *Virgin and Angels* where the freedom of outline and the delineation of space and volume mark the beginning of complete innovation. Have a look, too, at Botticelli's beautiful *Madonna* and *The Virgin and Child* and, of course, Leonardo da Vinci's *Mona Lisa.* This, the first masterpiece to enter the Louvre, is so famous and ubiquitous that it is almost difficult to appreciate. Supposedly a portrait of Mona Lisa Gherardini del Gioconda, wife of a Florentine doctor, the painting is so popular that it is protected by armored glass to prevent damage from over enthusiastic admirers or the constant flash of cameras. Hopefully there won't be too many people to block your view.

The Louvre houses several works by Leonardo da Vinci – thanks to King François I, who called the artist to France and gave him a dwelling at Cloux, where he died in 1519. Among his other masterpieces are *The Virgin of the Rocks*, in which, under the protection of an enigmatic angel, divine figures seem to emerge in a play of chiaroscuro from the shadows of a grotto surrounded by dark rocks; *The Virgin, the Infant Jesus and St. Anne*; and *La Belle Ferronière*.

Dutch, Flemish and German Schools *(Denon, 8, 10).* The Dutch School is fully represented in all its genres: landscapes, portraits, still lifes, and chronicles of everyday life. Rembrandt's self-portraits are not to be missed and don't miss the Medici Gallery either – it's a vast room devoted to Rubens's splendid sequence of large-scale compositions from the life of Marie de'Medici, commissioned in 1621 for the Luxembourg Palace.

Reached through a separate entrance from the Grand Louvre, on rue de Rivoli, are two thematically linked museums: the Musée des Arts Decoratifs and the Musée des Arts de la Mode. Each makes a separate admission charge.

Musée des Arts Decoratifs

107 rue de Rivoli, 75001. Metro Palais-Royal/Tuileries. Tel. 42 60 32 14. Open 12:30–6 p.m. Wednesday–Saturday; 12–6 p.m. Sunday; closed Monday, Tuesday. Guided tours September–July.

This entirely renovated part of the Louvre Palace houses on its six floors thousands of items, including furniture and applied arts, from the Middle Ages to the 1980s. The various collections are not organized in any clear order; this, together with bad directions, makes it hard to find your way around. Nevertheless, many items are worth seeing.

The most original part of the museum is undoubtedly that devoted to Art Nouveau and Art Deco on the first floor: there's an impressive range of furniture, ceramics and glassware, and even whole interiors, all dating from 1900 to 1925. The Art Deco room is especially famous for Jeanne Lanvin's private apartments. Lanvin rose from humble origins to become one of the top designers of Parisian fashion. Alongside her success in the world of *haute couture*, she had a strong interest in the arts; among her close friends were many famous names. In this apartment, originally located at 16 rue Barbet le Jouy, hang paintings – all of women – by Renoir, Bonnard, Vuillard and Boudin. Other treasures include the doll collection in the boudoir and, in the bedroom, the "Lanvin-Blue" bed-recess and a small black-and-white marble-topped dressing-table, supported by four bronze legs embellished with daisies – an allusion to Lanvin's daughter, Marguerite. The bathroom, decorated with stucco paneling by Paul Plumet, is famous for its bath and flower-shaped washbasin. If you're interested in toys, you should visit the important collection of ancient dolls, animals, mechanical cars, fortresses and other small-scale models on the third floor of the museum.

Musée des Arts de la Mode

109 rue de Rivoli, 75001. Metro Tuileries/Palais-Royal. Tel. 42 60 32 14. Open Wednesday–Saturday 12:30–6 p.m.; Sunday 11 a.m.–6 p.m; closed Monday, Tuesday.

Opened in 1986 with the support of many *grands couturiers*, this museum of fashion conveys a strong sense of industrial and artistic pride. The various collections are displayed over five floors, the first reserved for rotating exhibitions of the permanent collection. If you're lucky you might catch Anne d'Autriche's gloves or Brigitte Bardot's wedding dress.

The next three floors are dedicated to prestigious collections by the likes of Pierre Cardin and Jeanne Lanvin (see above). There's also a library, a workshop where ancient costumes are restored, and the Institut de la Mode, where trainee designers take intensive courses. Finally, don't leave without looking in the *boutique de la mode* where, if you can afford it, you can buy all manner of designer clothing, jewels, home furnishings, and some typically French objects.

While you're still close to the Louvre, take a moment to visit the former royal parish church whose bells are said to have rung out, on the orders of Catherine de' Medici, to signal the terrible Massacre of St. Bartholomew on August 24, 1572.

Saint-Germain l'Auxerrois
2 place du Louvre 75001. Metro Louvre. Tel. 42 69 13 96. Open daily 8 a.m.–12:30 p.m.; 3–7 p.m.

An architectural hodgepodge, featuring a Romanesque belfry, Gothic chancel, flamboyant porch and Renaissance doorway, Saint-Germain was begun in the twelfth century, but rebuilt many times. Haussmann – whose bulldozing zeal was restrained for once by the fear that the destruction of the church would be blamed on his Protestantism – nevertheless indulged his obsession for symmetry by flanking Saint-Germain with a mirror-image copy, now used as a town hall. The chapel dedicated to Sainte-Geneviève shows her carrying loaves in her apron, a reference to the fact that she fed the poor. Above the belfry door on the right is a fifteenth-century wooden statue of Jesus and the Virgin, who has a bird perching on her arm. She is in rich contemporary dress as a crowned queen. On the right of the door is a colorful Chapel of the Holy Sacrament, with murals depicting the coronation of the Virgin and a fifteenth-century statue of St. Mary the Egyptian dressed in nothing but her hair. According to legend, Mary was a prostitute who was divinely inspired to go into exile in the desert, and having paid for the boat trip out by sleeping with the sailors, she lived there for the rest of her life, eating berries and receiving instruction from God. Naturally enough, her clothes wore out, but her hair had grown so long that she was saved from embarrassment when a monk happened to pass by.

PALAIS-ROYAL, LES PASSAGES
AND L'OPÉRA

A short walk north from the Louvre takes you to the rectangular Palais-Royal which at various points in its four-hundred-year history has served as a refuge for royal widows, a gambling den and pleasure dome and home to writers such as Colette. It now combines the roles of shopping mall, park and government offices. Built in the seventeenth century by the Prime Minister Cardinal Richelieu, it was later bequeathed by the Cardinal to Louis XIII. The first royal residents were the king's widow, Anne d'Autriche and her young son Louis XIV, ousted in 1648 by the anti-royalist Fronde faction. Once his mother and her adviser, Cardinal Mazarin had quashed the Fronde, Louis XIV moved into the more secure Louvre, and gave the Palais-Royale to an equally hard-pressed Catholic monarch – Henrietta Maria, widow of assassinated Charles I of England. By day the gardens are the main attraction, drawing a mixed crowd – from office workers hurrying through to the financial district to the north, to Louvre-goers swigging bottled water and the odd reader taking a break from the nearby Bibliothèque Nationale. After dark, once the gates to the gardens are locked, the Palais-Royal turns outward to the cafés and bars which attract theater-goers from the adjoining Comédie Française.

"A Meeting of Extremes" was the epigraph to Restif de la Bretonne's 1790 book on the Palais-Royal. Little of this sense of the old Palais lingers today: neither the executives from the Japanese district to the west nor the occupants of the Ministry of Culture which takes up one wing bear much resemblance to the prostitutes and gamblers who haunted the Palais in the eighteenth century. The arcades, now divided between dusty shops and cafés advertising "garden view," were added on to the original seventeenth-century structure by Louis-Philippe of Orléans, a flamboyant aristocrat who condescended to dabble in real-estate speculation and later changed his name, in honor of the Revolution, to Philippe-Egalité. Orléans scandalized polite society by hiring his mistress, Madame de Genlis, to teach his children. (His eldest son was a possible successor to the throne.) At a time when a male chef earned twice the salary of a female cook, the idea of confiding a prince's education to a woman appeared not only crazy but bourgeois. Orléans offered her the equivalent of a male tutor's salary; out of modesty Madame de Genlis accepted only half the amount, but she was still lampooned as "master by day and mistress by night." Lower down the social scale, one house in the Palais trained each prostitute to impersonate a particular lady of the court, bribing dressmakers and maids to reveal the secrets of their mistress's toilette so that men too low-born to approach the objects of their desire could at least enjoy them "in effigy." Honest women were allowed to come before 5 in the evening without damaging their reputation, but the famous nineteenth-century Parisian chronicler Louis-Sebastien Mercier (who boasted that a person imprisoned in the Palais-Royal would never miss the outside world) complained that even a professional physiognomist could mistake a whore for a courtesan, a duchess, or an "honest woman." Even a provincial like Charlotte Corday had heard of the Palais-Royal: when she arrived in Paris, she came straight to number 177 to buy a knife to kill Marat.

After the Revolution billiard parlors, cafés, gambling dens and houses of ill-repute moved in, along with a scale model of Paris, presumably in the hope that the city's wasters would seize the opportunity to improve their geography before removing their clothes. For prostitutes continued to do good business! The galleries built of stone on one side of the garden belonged to upscale brothels that rented arcades as display space; the wooden galleries on the other side were open to all. Towards the end of the eighteenth cen-tury, at the Queen's request, such activities were outlawed. Inexplicably, the shops and restaurants aren't as fashionable as the elegant architecture and the central location would lead one to expect, but the music-box store and the ceiling of "Le Grand Véfour," one of Paris's most prestigious restaurants (Galerie de Beaujolais, on the northern end), are worth a look in the window. And even if the Palais is no longer the "capital of the capital," as it was called in its heyday, in winter, when the trees are bare it's still the city's most austere and classical garden.

The Comédie Française

Place Colette, 75001. Tel. 43 25 70 32. Metro Palais-Royal. Box office open daily 11 a.m.–6:30 p.m. Guided tours in French, third Sunday of every month. Phone the Caisse des Monuments Historiques for reservations: 48 87 24 12.

To the south of the Palais-Royal is France's national theater, the Comédie Française, where a classic repertoire with no surprises is dependably performed for low (subsidized) prices. Marriage to a *fille de théâtre* was, for a long time, a bourgeois mother's worst nightmare for her son, but the profession of actress has come a long way in terms of respectability since then. Today most performances feel like matinées, and once you leave the theater the area is not especially entertaining.

Northeast of the Palais-Royal complex, heading towards the financial district and the Passages, don't miss the place des Victoires, whose nearby church, Notre-Dame des Victoires, Colette would visit from her apartment in rue de Beaujolais (window marked "C"):

> This is a church where all come to slake their thirst, as if at the village fountain. The oyster-seller turns up the corner of her blue apron and pays a neighborly five-minute call to Notre-Dame. The greying delivery boy lays down his parcels, lights his candle, crosses himself and departs ... In the time it takes to walk two hundred steps, to take the shortcut past the "cravat clinic" and one end of Galerie Vivienne, I plant a small flame on a thorn of the burning bush like everyone else. The church is warm with petitions, candles and gratitude. Between the services there is complete silence, but every stone is engraved and speaks. How many candles, how many tears!

PLACE DES VICTOIRES

This elegant square was designed by the architect Jules Hardouin-Mansart in 1685 to house the statue of Louis XIV commissioned by the Maréchal de la Feuillade in 1679. Hardouin-Mansart intended it to be a tribute to his king, so the square was designed specifically to show off the statue to its best advantage. The roads leading into it

(text continued on page 62)

PALAIS-ROYAL, LES PASSAGES AND L'OPÉRA

COMÉDIE FRANÇAISE

Created in 1680 by the fusion of Molière's own theater group with actors of the Théâtre du Marais and of the Hôtel de Bourgogne, the Comédie Française was dissolved in 1792 to be reconstituted in 1804. Nowadays the name is synonymous with the theater in the Place Colette where an undiluted program of plays by such French notables as Corneille, Racine and Molière are performed.

It was in plays such as *Bérénice* and *Phèdre* by Racine and *La Mort de Pompée* by Corneille that the great women of the Comédie Française found the recognition and fortune they were seeking. The list of actresses – La Champmeslé, Adrienne Lecouvreur and Mlle. Mars from the seventeenth, eighteenth and nineteenth centuries respectively – show how through the centuries, actresses have cut their teeth on the same enduring roles.

Later stars in the firmament were Marie Ventura, who came to the Comédie in 1919 at the age of thirty-eight and Eugénie Segond-Weber who thrilled audiences at the turn of the century in her renderings of Cleopatra and Joan of Arc. Most recently, the Comédie Française has been a proving ground for well-known contemporary French actresses such as Madeleine Renaud, who went on to found her own theater with her husband, and Jeanne Moreau who learned her trade on the boards of the Comédie Française before launching herself on a film career.

Today's lines at the ticket office for last-minute returns are as long as ever, so if you want to see some of the greatest tragedies and comedies of French theater, arrive in plenty of time.

JEANNE MOREAU (BORN 1928)

Jeanne Moreau graduated from the Paris Conservatoire at the age of twenty and made her début at the Comédie Française before going into films. Of the same era as Brigitte Bardot, she was the modern intellectual woman, symbolic of the sexual liberation of the 1960s in contrast to Bardot's sexy, blonde pussycat image.

One of her more famous roles was in Louis Malle's *Les Amants*; she played a rich bourgeois wife who falls in love with an intellectual who drives a 2CV and for whom she is obliged to leave her smart, cushioned milieu, in a stark illustration of the social divide.

Jeanne Moreau's dedication to her work kept her at the forefront of her profession. She began to work with filmmakers of international renown such as Orson Welles and Buñuel, as well as making two autobiographical films.

Her life has not been without personal tragedies, experiences which she has channeled into her work. With the encouragement of the couturier Pierre Cardin she returned to the stage in 1976. In 1988 she was awarded a Molière (the equivalent of an Oscar) for her role in *Le Récit de la servante Zerline*. She is an actress with a zest for life that does not diminish with age.

CHARLOTTE CORDAY (1768–93)

At the age of twenty-five, Charlotte Corday became famous for her cold-blooded killing of Marat, one of the heroes of the Revolution.

A fervent reader of Plutarch, Tacitus and Rousseau, she was in her twenties when she joined the right-wing Girondin faction of the Revolution. Incensed by the ineffectiveness of her leaders, she was determined to obtain an audience with the leftist Montagnard Marat, whom she held responsible for the suppression of the Girondins and the instigation of a Reign of Terror. On July 13, 1793, he received her in his bath, whereupon, as every schoolchild knows, she stabbed him to death.

Corday's trial established that she had been working independently and entirely on her own initiative, and that her crime had been carefully premeditated. Throughout her trial and her subsequent imprisonment she remained calm and serene, as reflected in her portrait by Hauer, whom she summoned to her cell as one might call a priest. Her journey to the scaffold was conducted with equal composure, provoking some to see her as a heroine of the Revolution. Others, like this observer, merely used her as a target for their misogyny:

This woman who was said to be very pretty, was certainly not so. She was a virago more brawny than fresh, graceless and dirty in her person as are almost all female philosophers and intellectuals .... Decent men do not like such women, and they in turn affect to despise the sex that despises them.

MADELEINE RENAUD (BORN 1903)

Maudeleine Renard studied acting at the Conservatoire d'Art Dramatique and joined the Comédie Française in 1921. Her performance as Agnès in Molière's *L'Ecole des femmes* brought her immediate fame and the title of leading actress, a position she occupied for twenty-five years. In 1940, she married the actor Jean-Louis Barrault, director of the Comédie; in 1947 they left the company and founded the Compagnie Renaud–Barrault, which gradually included an extended range of classical, experimental and mime plays. Madeleine Renaud excelled in both modern and classical roles. She appeared in *Oh! Les beaux jours* (Beckett), *Des Journées entières dans les arbres* and *L'amante anglaise* (Duras), in *Harold et Maude* (Colin Higgins) as well as in plays by Claudel (*Le Soulier de Satin*) and Montherlant (*La Reine Morte*). She also acted in innumerable films, among them *Vent debout* (1922) and *La Maison du lac* (1988) and wrote the script of *La vie offerte* (1977).

COLETTE (1873–1954)

Colette is one of the most original figures in French literature. Born Sidonie Gabrielle Colette in rural Burgundy, she enjoyed an unusually free and happy-go-lucky childhood with an understanding and whimsical mother who taught her to respect nature, animals and human beings.

She began writing during her early marriage to writer-about-town Henri Gauthier-Villars, under whose instruction and pen name, "Willy," she wrote the scandalous *Claudine* novels. Despite almost immediate popular success, it took some time for the author's true identity to emerge. In 1904 Colette published *Dialogue de bêtes* under the name "Colette Willy," divorced her husband in 1906 and plunged headlong into the Bohemian life of *tout-Paris*. Notorious for a string of male and female lovers, she was by turns model, actress, music-hall performer, journalist but, above all, writer.

Colette's work always remained semi-autobiographical. *La Retraite sentimentale* (1907) is about her divorce; *La Vagabonde* (1910) was inspired by her wandering life as a music hall artiste. Both her mother and her daughter, Sido and Bel-Gazou, appear in her stories, and her own affairs are barely disguised in the protagonists and plots of books like *Chéri* and *Gigi*. But it would be a mistake to see these works as mere confessions. As well as having a keen eye for the complexities of human nature, Colette wrote in a unique and wonderfully sensuous style. She ended her life as the grand old lady of French letters and was, on her death, the first French woman to be granted the honor of a State funeral.

were conceived in such a way that no one road led directly out to another; this gave the impression of enclosing the statue and made it the pivotal focus of attention. At night four torches burned in the square to throw the statue into relief, and yet further emphasize its importance. Neither statue nor square has survived intact. The construction of the rue Etienne Marcel disrupted the form of the original square, while Louis XIV's statue fell victim to the Revolution. It was replaced by the present figure of the Sun King in 1822.

Despite these disruptions, the square retains much of its original beauty and charm, and it's hard to say which are more elegant – the clothes in the shop windows or the harmonious seventeenth-century façades. Louis-Sebastien Mercier called nearby rue Vivienne "the pocket of Paris," perhaps because people are irresistibly tempted to pour their money into it. Financial wealth is further symbolized by the presence, just to the north, of the Stock Exchange, the Palais de Bourse.

PLACE DU CAIRE AND SENTIER

Among the roads leading off the place des Victoires towards the north-east is rue Aboukir, named after Napoleon's victories in Egypt. So impressed was he by Egypt during these campaigns that he also named a square situated halfway up rue Aboukir, Place du Caire (Cairo). Appropriately enough, number 2 is covered with Egyptian motifs in the form of sphinxes, lotuses and hieroglyphics.

This is the heart of the city's rag trade district, known as Sentier. Sewing machines buzz away behind doors, while racks of identical garments are whisked past you on their way to the wholesalers. A lively area crammed with small streets where immigrants sweat away in dark workshops making fortunes for the fat cats of the fashion trade, it's enhanced by the smell of kofta kebabs mingling with the guttural sound of Arabic and other languages that waft from various bars. Take time to wander down these streets, and you'll discover another cosmopolitan face of Paris.

Not far away, the Passages and *galeries* represent yet another widely undiscovered aspect of the city.

THE PASSAGES

The Parisian Passages, delightful covered pedestrian arcades with elaborate glass roofs and smart tiled floors, are the precursor of our modern-day shopping mall. They were built in the nineteenth century as a place to walk, meet, eat and shop, sheltered from the elements and the hurly-burly of the streets outside, with the added benefit of providing a shortcut from one street through to another. The idea came from a cousin of Louis XVI who, finding himself short of cash, rented out the arcades of the Palais-Royal to shopkeepers. Other businessmen, seeing the effectiveness of this scheme, followed suit and started to build Passages and *galeries* of their own.

Of the 280-odd Passages that survive today, over 80 percent were constructed between 1822 and 1848. Under the Restoration the Passages enjoyed immediate success, for they afforded an unexpected comfort, luxury and protection hitherto unknown in street life. Here the nineteenth-century bourgeoise could find everything her heart desired: there were restaurants, cafés, reading rooms, bookshops and couture boutiques – not to mention the *cabinets d'aisance*, or upscale lavatories – all under one roof. After an exhausting day's shopping, eating, seeing and being seen, she might slip directly through a specially constructed entrance into either the theater or a museum. Alternatively, balls were held in the Passages – some of them more reputable than others – while in certain *galeries* men's evening entertainment was catered for by the prostitutes who would parade up and down in the seductive light of the gas lamps. Others, like Comte Muffat in Zola's great novel *Nana*, would hang around near the Théâtre des Variétés, waiting for their favorite actress to emerge:

> It was at the junction of the Galerie des Variétés and Galerie St-Marc, a shady-looking corner full of obscure shops, and a smoky, somnolent reading room whose shaded lamps cast a sleepy green light all evening. There was never anybody in this corner but well-dressed, patient gentlemen prowling around among the drunken scene-shifters and ragged chorus girls who always congregate about stage doors.

Gas lighting was greatly responsible for the fairy tale appeal of these Passages as the blue flames flickered and multiplied in a myriad of sparkling reflections all around. In the end a combination of the advent of electric lighting, which cast a harsher, less flattering light on the *habitués*, and the efforts of Haussmann, who created tarmacked streets with pavements, rendering the town a much more pleasant and safe place to stroll, put an end to the attraction of Passage life. By 1870 the former prides of Paris were no longer being mentioned in guidebooks, and the Passages fell into disrepair.

The process of renovating the Passages and *galeries*, and along with it the return of chic couturiers, restaurants and cafés, began some ten years ago. Now restored to their former glory, a few are positive jewels, hidden behind narrow arched entrances. Others remain in a state of more or less genteel disrepair; the following are among the more interesting and spectacular.

Galerie Véro–Dodat

Begins: 19 rue Jean-Jacques Rousseau, 75001
Ends: 2 rue du Bouloi, 75001
Metro: Palais-Royal.
Named after the two pork butchers Véro and Dodat, who founded the Galerie in 1824, this arcade has a wonderful black-and-white-checked tiled floor and classy mahogany shop fronts, but much of

PALAIS-ROYAL, LES PASSAGES AND L'OPÉRA

its charm lies in the preservation of its original character. It's easy to imagine a buxom courtesan leaning out of one of the shuttered windows, ready to ruffle her petticoats for a passing gentleman.

It was here, at number 38, that the famous actress Rachel lived when, at the age of seventeen, she made her début as Camille in *Horace* at the Théâtre Français. A consummate actress, fêted throughout France and at the courts of England, Germany and Austria, as well as by the Russian Emperor, she rose from humble beginnings as an orange-seller to be one of nineteenth-century France's most acclaimed actresses. Her rendition of the *Marseillaise* alone was enough not only to send the French into ecstasies but to actually dissuade a bunch of revolutionaries from burning down the Comédie-Française. Her private life was no less dramatic: among her lovers were Alfred de Musset, the son of Louis-Philippe, Count Walewski, the bastard son of Napoleon, and finally the President of the Republic, Prince Jérôme. She lived here until 1842 and died in Cannes fourteen years later after carefully ensuring that all her love letters were returned to their authors. Nowadays another well-known woman is associated with the Galerie: Yannick Bellon, film maker and director of *La Femme de Jean* (1974), *L'Amour violé* (1978) and *L'Amour nu* (1981), has her company office at number 18, and shot parts of three of her films in the Galerie. Her neighbors include R. Capia, a doll expert whose shop is a veritable Aladdin's cave of elaborate antique dolls crammed together with every possible curiosity: bowler hats, toy trains, gaudy china ornaments, old postcards, an antique matador outfit and a phonograph jostle for position in a chaos reminiscent of some long-abandoned attic. In comparison, the nearby Café de l'Epoque, established in 1826, is a haven of orderliness, with its clean salmon-pink decor and typical neat lace curtains – the ideal place to stop for a hot chocolate or a slice of quiche before continuing your explorations.

Galerie Vivienne
Begins: 4 rue des Petits-Champs, 75002
Ends: 6 rue Vivienne, 75002
Metro: Bourse.

Designed by Delannoy, this *galerie*, made up of three main sections and a side alley, was also opened to the public in 1826. Eighteen years later Hermance Marchoux, painter, sculptor and the future Comtesse de Caen, created the four caryatids which act as supports for the balcony above the Passage at rue Croix-des-Petits-Champs. It was this same woman who in 1870, as daughter of the founder of the *galerie*, bequeathed it to the current owners, the Institute of France. After a long period of decline, in 1974 it was declared a historic monument. However, its fortunes changed with the comparatively recent arrival of fashionable clothes shops and art galleries. Delicate wrought-iron gates lead into a Passage whose arched stone-carved ceiling, interspersed with glass panels, gives it a light, airy feel. Well-kept, classy shops represent a mixture of the old and the new – from the outrageous creations of Jean-Paul Gaultier to the venerable bookshop on the corner, where books are spread out on the pavement. If you're gasping for refreshment, try the Brasserie "La Bougainville," favored by journalists and brokers from the nearby Stock Exchange, where you can sit on green rattan chairs and contemplate a beautiful carved white stone clock flanked by two angels, and walls extravagantly carved with serpents and cornucopia. Finally, don't miss the lively toy shop, home to a lovely selection of teddies whose fluffiness is rivaled only by the *galerie*'s oddest resident: an Old English sheepdog lounging across the entrance.

Galerie Colbert

Begins: 6 rue des Petits-Champs, 75002
Ends: 6 rue Vivienne, 75002
Metro: Bourse.

Composed of two sections at right angles to each other, linked by a rotunda, this *galerie*, built at the same time as the Galerie Vivienne, was never as popular. Like Vivienne it fell into decline after the Second Empire until, in 1980, it was discovered that the rotunda was being used as a garage. It was another six years, however, before its owners, the Bibliothèque Nationale, stepped in and renovated it. The friezes were restored and the sumptuous fake marble columns were repainted, but the renovation has been somewhat overzealous, and though it is beautiful, it lacks the charm of its sister. Apart from the Grand Café Colbert – worth a visit for its turn-of-the-century decor – it's a usually lifeless place housing offices and the occasional Bibliothèque exhibition.

Passage des Panoramas

Begins: rue Saint-Marc, 75002
Ends: 11 boulevard Montmartre, 75002
Metro: rue Montmartre.

This Passage, also mentioned in Zola's *Nana*, opened to the public in 1800, and owes its name to the invention of "panoramas," vast panoramic vistas painted on a circular wall and viewed from a raised, enclosed platform which gave a bird's-eye view of the 360-degree scene below. Although people flocked to see the paintings here, the passage retained its popularity even when they had disappeared. It was one of the first places, besides the Palais-Royal, where fine products such as coffee, bonbons and patisseries could be bought.

PALAIS-ROYAL, LES PASSAGES AND L'OPÉRA

Today, if you can ignore the neon signs, you'll still find a few shops and eating places worth lingering over. The Arbre à Cannelle, a restaurant and *salon de thé*, has been restored with the original Empire decor, and has a gorgeous carved and painted diamond-patterned ceiling. Despite the tawdry lighting outside, the mood within is refreshingly authentic, making it a charming spot for a light lunch of delicious home-made quiche or a slice of pear tart. At number 13 is Ciboulette, a pretty shop selling stylish kitchen and bathroom accessories, and beyond you can linger over the window of Stern, one of the original shops; they've been engraving menus and invitations for the courts of Europe since 1834. Indeed, three years ago the current Monsieur Stern and his fellow occupants set about restoring the new Passage des Panoramas to its former glory.

Passage Jouffroy
Begins: 10 boulevard Montmartre, 75009
Ends: 9 rue de la Grange-Batelière, 75009
Metro: Richelieu–Drouot.

Officially inaugurated on February 7, 1847, this Passage enjoyed a less checkered history than most blessed with a public that has been less fickle over the years. This is probably because it was the first to have heating – hot air blown through iron grills in the floor – and because of the presence of the Musée Grevin, Paris's pale equivalent of London's Madame Tussaud's. Other notable features are the, then innovative, metal columns, the attractive lamps and the arched glass ceiling.

Three years ago the floor tiling was restored to its original state, and upscale shops started to drift back. Among them is M.C. Segas, a specialist in antique canes and walking-sticks displayed in a theatrical setting, complete with huge draped gold mirrors; and Thomas Boog, worth visiting for the original wood interior now teamed with an alarmingly bright red chandelier. Thomas Boog is a self-styled "color merchant" selling an intriguing selection of photo frames and candlesticks made of unusual materials in stunning primary colors. Pain d'Epices have two shops, the first full of indulgently scented bits and pieces for the bathroom and home, the second, more tempting for children, a far longer-established toy shop. Beneath a ceiling hung with puppets is a wonderlandish plethora of doll-sized toys: tiny tea sets; fingernail-sized plates, glasses, decanters and tumblers; miniature cereal packets, gilt mirrors and garden tools, and Lilliputian period furniture.

These, of course, represent only a fraction of the Passages and *galeries* in Paris, all of which are in various stages of reconstruction and decay. Others worth a visit include the tiny Passage des Princes for the renovated ironwork and tiled floor, the Passage de la Madeleine, home to one of the most prestigious restaurants in Paris, the Lucas-Carton, and the recently renovated three-storied Passage du Grand-Cert. This list is by no means exhaustive. If you take the trouble to discover the Passages for yourself, the reward will not only be finding a treasure trove of nineteenth-century decor off the beaten track, but the satisfaction of knowing that you are visiting something of which few Parisians – born or adopted – are even aware.

THE OPÉRA DISTRICT

The area around the Opéra is clogged with banks, travel agents and large hotels. By day the streets are lively and animated, bustling with office workers – not to mention tourists rushing from bank to travel agent before collapsing gratefully in one of the many well-known and expensive cafés. The district enjoys a lull at nightfall until late evening, when theater- and movie-goers disgorge on to the pavements and head off into the brightly lit restaurants and bars to discuss the evening's entertainment over dinner or a *café crème*.

Garnier's Opéra
Place de l'Opéra, 75009. Metro Opéra. Tel. 42 66 50 22.
Open 11 a.m.–4:30 p.m. daily except holidays and during matinee performances. Box office open 11 a.m.–7 p.m.

To the west of the Passages, this unmistakable green-domed building, probably the most important surviving example of Second Empire style, was completed in 1875 by the architect Charles Garnier. He was unknown, and lucky enough to win the competition to build a new opera house launched under the auspices of Napoleon III. Garnier, whose rather sheepish bust can be seen on the rue Auber side of the theatre, sought to impose his own style on the building. The result, an extravagant mishmash of Baroque, prompted Empress Eugénie to ask precisely what style he was aiming at, since in her opinion it was clearly neither Grecian nor Louis XVI. Garnier is said to have replied that the style was Napoleon III, which no doubt pleased the Emperor, if no one else.

The Opéra – known as the Opéra Garnier, to distinguish it from the new Opéra at Bastille – is now largely reserved for dance. When it was built it was as much a place to see and be seen as to watch opera. This accounts for the fact that in surface area it is one of the largest in the world, yet it seats little more than 2000 people – and not in great comfort. The imposing Rococo staircase leads up to the immense and highly decorated galleries and halls, where you can wander around during the intermission, admiring the ornate ceilings painted with allegories by Paul Baudry in the grand foyer, complete with a fireplace at either end. From here you can step through glass doors on to the balcony for a Haussmannian perspective straight down the avenue de l'Opéra as far as the Louvre. To get to the grand foyer you pass through a smaller foyer whose mosaics by Salviati make it one of the most beautiful parts of the opera house.

The main theater is typical of the period: plenty of red and gilt, and an enormous chandelier weighing six tons. It inevitably draws the eye up to the ceiling repainted in 1964 by Chagall whose gorgeous colors and weird naïvety refreshingly reinterpret scenes from well-known operas and ballets – Mozart's *Magic Flute*, Wagner's *Tristran and Isolde* and Berlioz's *Romeo and Juliet*.

The Opéra also houses a library and a museum; if you want to know more go to the Musée d'Orsay, where there's a brilliant cross-section model of the building that gives a clear idea of how the incredible amounts of scenery are stored and manipulated. Underground is a vast natural cavern with fountains and pools, supposedly the grotto that inspired Leroux to set his *Phantom of the Opera* here.

The exterior is liberally sprinkled with statues by no fewer than seventy-two sculptors. Among the most notable is Carpeaux's *La Danse* whose nudity caused outrage amongst the prudish nineteenth-century public, feeling it went well beyond the bounds of modesty; at least one of them was inspired to vandalism: On the night of August 27, 1869, the marble statue was subjected to an ink attack! Nearly a hundred years later it was moved to the safety of the Louvre, then to the Musée d'Orsay, eventually to be replaced by a copy.

AROUND THE OPÉRA

On the huge rectangular place de l'Opéra is the Café de la Paix, the most famous of many cafés on Boulevard des Capucines and understandably a favorite resting-place for sight-weary tourists. Part of the Grand Hôtel, it was built in 1867 to welcome the VIPs flocking to the Universal Exhibition. Despite considerable renovation, the main dining room has been preserved and the exuberant molding and gilt by Millet is worth a visit.

GRANDS MAGASINS

Heading down rue Auber, away from the Opéra, running parallel to boulevard Haussmann, is rue des Mathurins – famous for being home to two of Paris's greatest department stores, Galeries Lafayette and Printemps. Rue des Mathurins still retains a little of its nineteenth-century literary refinement from the time when Marie d'Agoult had a *salon* at number 10 – as did Sophie Gay at number 40, the house where Germaine de Staël died.

MARIE D'AGOULT (1805–97)

French writer and *salon* hostess Marie d'Agoult wrote under the pseudonym Daniel Stern. She welcomed to her *salons* some of the most outstanding figures of the nineteenth century, including Chopin, Rossini, Vigny, Heine and Sainte-Beuve, as well as providing a meetingplace for the political opposition during the Second Empire.

She left her husband, the Comte d'Agoult, in 1835, and for nine years she was mistress of the musician and composer Franz Liszt, by whom she had two daughters. Her works include political essays and an autobiographical novel, *Nelida*, which openly describes her passionate affair.

Off rue des Mathurins in rue Pasquier is the Chapelle Expiatoire, built by Louis XVIII to the memory of Louis XVI and Marie-Antoinette on the site where thousands of victims of the Revolution were buried.

LA MADELEINE

Open Tuesday–Friday 12:30–8 p.m.; Saturday 12:30 for matinees, 2–8 p.m. for evening performances; Sunday 12:30–4:30 p.m.

Further on down the boulevard des Capucines is the place de la Madeleine, dominated by a Greek-temple-style church which, when construction started in 1764, was originally dedicated to Mary Magdalene. But the Revolution intervened, and the building underwent an identity crisis until Napoleon decreed that it should be completed in its present form as a temple to glorify his army. One of the best things about it is probably the view away down rue Royale, where suffragettes once blocked the street by chaining themselves together, across the place de la Concorde to the Assemblée Nationale. The place de la Madeleine itself is a gourmet window-shoppers' paradise. The window displays of Fauchon are a Parisian institution, despite being the scene of periodic *foie gras* raids by latter-day revolutionaries during the 1960s – and Hédiard, an equally exclusive grocer, attract crowds of salivating tourists intent on capturing these gastronomic tableaux on film. Another of the square's attractions is the flower market on the east side of the church, which has been there since 1832. Every day except Monday it provides a dash of color against the looming grey mass of La Madeleine. Finally, it's worth knowing about the ticket kiosk opposite number 15, where – following in the footsteps of London and New York – a large number of Paris theaters have undertaken to offer at least four seats for that day's performance at half-price.

PLACE VENDÔME

Not far from place de la Madeleine is place Vendôme, an aristocratic seventeenth-century oval, and resort of those with serious money. It would be unthinkable for it to house anything but the most expensive jewelers (including Boucheron and Van Cleef and Arpels) – not to mention their customers, types who reside at the square's Ritz. The jewelers' windows display rocks the size of hard candy nestling on dark-blue velvet, beyond which impeccably turned out Parisian shop assistants wait to size up your net worth in the blink of one painstakingly curled eyelash. The square was originally graced by a statue of Louis XIV, a victim of the Revolution, but is now dominated by an enormous column erected by Napoleon wrapped with bronze reliefs of military scenes made of melted Austrian guns from the Battle of Austerlitz (1805). A predictable exercise in Napoleonic self-flattery, it's modeled on Trajan's warmongering column in Rome, and is now crowned with a statue of Bonaparte dressed up as Julius Caesar.

Church of Saint-Roch

Continuing southeast along snooty rue Saint-Honoré studded with designer boutiques, you cross rue Cambon, where the supremely elegant Coco Chanel held *salons* at number 31. The shrines to *haute couture* soon give way to the equally dazzling church of Saint-Roch, one of the largest churches in Paris, and the richest in religious art.

Saint-Roch, begun in 1653, was finished only in 1719, thanks to a donation from a Scots banker named Law (who subsequently went bankrupt). The façade on the rue Saint-Honoré side was

---

COCO CHANEL (1883–1971)

The American writer Djuna Barnes sums up Chanel perfectly: "She is famous for two things, perfume and severe-tailored suits – in other words, for the height to which she has brought olfactory sophistication, and for the depth out of which she evolved the almost lowly severity of chic, terribly chic, creations."

Born Gabrielle Bonheur into a family of farmers, she went to Paris to become a milliner at the stylish hat-maker's Lucienne Rabaté. By 1913 she had set up a shop of her own in the fashionable seaside resort of Deauville, where she sold the first sailor-style sweater and encouraged women to abandon corsets and long skirts. Three years later she had opened what was to become her famous Maison de Couture in rue Cambon.

Chanel was one of the first women to adopt the boyish haircut that became so popular in the 1920s, and revolutionized fashion by doing away with the abundant frills of the *belle époque* in favor of simple, skillfully-cut clothes in supple materials that cleaved to the body. As well as the celebrated little black dress, she launched knitted materials, the tweed suit, costume jewelry and, of course, Chanel No. 5, in its distinctive rectangular bottle.

Chanel was not only the embodiment of French *haute couture* but a lively figure in artistic life between the wars; one-time mistress of – among others – Grand Duke Dmitri, the Duke of Windsor and the poet Reversy, she was also friends with Cocteau, Picasso and Stravinsky. An affair with a German officer during the Occupation cast a shadow on her reputation. She died at the age of eighty-eight, just as she would have liked, hosting her own fashion show.

added in 1735, and a chapel was tacked on twenty-five years later. Today the church houses numerous works by well-known religious artists and sculptors, mostly from the eighteenth and nineteenth centuries, salvaged from convents that are no longer in existence. Among them is a bust by Coysevox (1707) on the right of the door leading to rue Saint-Roch – all that remains of the tomb of the landscape artist Le Nôtre, a Nativity group by Michel Anguier (1655) in front of the communion chapel, and the famous statue of *Christ in the Olive Groves* by Etienne Falconet (1757) at the entrance to the choir. The *salonière* Madame Geoffrin and playwright Corneille are also buried here.

The church is bordered on one side by the rue des Pyramides, named after Napoleon's victory in Egypt in 1798, which leads down to the small place des Pyramides, notable for its gilded statue of Joan of Arc by Frémiet.

Nowadays this statue is a place of political pilgrimage both for the extreme Right, led by Jean-Marie Le Pen, as a symbol of hardcore French nationalism, and for the Left, as a symbol of the triumph of the patriotic girl from the people. The Catholics revere the saint who received direct inspiration from God, but the truth is that Joan of Arc transcends all parties: her simplicity, her bravery, her purposefulness, made her one of the greatest feminine heroines of all time. Marina Warner sums up the uniqueness of her standing in her excellent *Joan of Arc*:

> She is a universal figure who is female, but is neither a queen, nor a courtesan, nor a beauty, nor a mother, nor an artist of one kind or another, nor – until the extremely recent date of 1920 when she was canonized – a saint. She eludes the categories in which women have normally a higher status that gives them immortality, and yet she gained it.

MADAME MARIE-THÉRÈSE GEOFFRIN (1699–1777)

Married at fifteen to an affluent mirror-manufacturer, despite little education, Madame Geoffrin succeeded in becoming the ultimate *salonière*. Some of the greatest minds of her time came to her *salon* at number 374 rue Saint-Honoré, popular with French and foreigners alike. Some, among them Gibbon, Hume and Walpole, said that if you had not been to rue Saint-Honoré then you hadn't been to France. King Poniatowski of Poland reputedly called her "Maman" and she was welcomed to the court of Austria by the Empress Marie-Thérèse and her son Joseph II on a visit to Vienna in 1776. A generous patron, she ensured that Diderot did not go without furnishings, and helped Julie de Lespinasse to set up her *salon* in the Hôtel de Hautefort. She also amassed an important collection of works by contemporary painters such as Vien and Vernet and commissioned works by Carle Van Loo and Hubert Robert, several of which she sold to Catherine II of Russia in 1772.

JOAN OF ARC (1412–31)

The young Joan of Arc was a shepherdess, tending her family's sheep in the Lorraine village of Domrémy, when she heard angelic voices commanding her to the rescue of her King, Charles VII, whose territory was being torn apart in a war with King Henry VI of England. Immediately Joan set off for Charles's residence at Chinon, in the Loire Valley, and introduced herself as a divine envoy sent to save his kingdom. She managed to convince the King, who commissioned her to lead an army and recapture the occupied city of Orléans; thanks to the combined action of soldiers and a local population galvanized by her leadership, she did so. Then she marched northwards to conquer Reims with the aim of having Charles anointed at the cathedral as the true king of France; this again she achieved with flying colors.

Her mission completed, Joan was nevertheless induced to try to liberate Paris. In this she failed, marching instead to Compiègne, where she was captured by the Burgundians, supporters of Henry VI, on May 23, 1430, and handed over to the English. In order to discredit her King, Henry's counselors advised him to charge Joan with heresy and witchcraft and have her tried by the court of Inquisition in Rouen; their motive was to reveal that Charles VII had in fact been anointed king through the offices of a witch.

On May 30, 1431, Joan was sentenced to be burnt at the stake. Her attitude during her trial, her simple confident answers and unshakable faith, made a lasting impression on public opinion, even in English- and Burgundian-held territory. So it was that she was hallowed as a martyr, becoming one of France's most moving historical figures. She was canonized in 1920.

TROCADÉRO AND THE EIFFEL TOWER

The place du Trocadéro is a busy semicircular "square" bordered on one side by the two monumental pavilions of the Palais de Chaillot.

Once simply a village on the outskirts of Paris, Chaillot first drew the attention of Catherine de' Medici, who built herself a palace here. Some years later it became the convent of the Visitation of Chaillot, founded by Henrietta of France, Queen of England, where one of Louis XIV's early mistresses, Louise de la Vallière, sought refuge on several occasions during her attempts to break off the relationship with the young king.

PALAIS DE CHAILLOT
1 place du Trocadéro, 75016. Metro Trocadéro.

The present Palais de Chaillot, built for the Paris Exhibition in 1937, is a typical example of thirties brutalism. The best thing about this great winged construction is undoubtedly the view from the wide flat terrace over the Trocadéro gardens, with their spectacular fountains and across the Seine to the Eiffel Tower, the Champ de Mars, the Ecole Militaire, the gilded dome of Les Invalides and the beautiful Alexandre III bridge, regilded in 1989 for the bicentennial of the Revolution.

Palais de Chaillot also houses four museums, including a film library, cinema, and two theaters, one of which is underground.

Musée des Monuments Français
Open 9 a.m. – 5:15 p.m. daily; closed Tuesday. Tel. 47 27 35 74.

This museum, situated in the palace's northeast wing, is more interesting than it looks, for it contains scale model copies of some of the greatest pieces of monumental sculpture throughout France.

Musée du Cinéma
Open 10 a.m., 11 a.m., 2 p.m., 3 p.m., 4 p.m.
Monday, Wednesday–Sunday. Guided tours (in French) only.
Tel. 45 53 74 39.

Located in the same wing, this is a temple of cinemabilia that traces the history of filmmaking from its very early beginnings up to the present day. Exhibits include film scripts, costumes, stills, posters and film sets, all lovingly assembled by the museum's creator, Henri Langlois. The next-door *cinémathèque* shows an impressive selection of films from various eras.

Musée de la Marine
Open 10 a.m.–6 p.m. daily; closed Tuesday. Tel. 45 53 31 70.

The marine museum, housed in the southwest wing, has a magnificent collection of model ships illustrating some of the great moments in French naval history since the end of the eighteenth century. You'll also find paintings, old maps, navigational instruments – in short, everything to satisfy an interest in boats and the sea.

Musée de l'Homme (The Museum of Mankind)
Open 9:45 a.m.–5:15 p.m. daily; closed Tuesday and public holidays. Tel. 45 53 70 60.

This somewhat dusty museum contains a wide range of extraordinary exhibits illustrating the history of humankind through the way of life, costumes, and characteristic occupations of numerous countries all over the world. It also provides a comprehensive overview of anthropological and ethnological sciences. The exhibition starts with a prehistory and a palaeontology section, followed by a room dedicated to African prehistory.

The African section contains beautiful objects from all over the continent illustrating the diversity of the regions and the various materials – iron, bone, ivory, wood, stone, gold – to be found there. Among the most beautiful pieces on display are jewels from the Ivory Coast, masks from Gabon, and some Maori earrings.

The museum also houses more than 3000 different costumes as well as thousands of samples of textiles from all over Europe. There's also a good musical instruments section, items from which are occasionally roused from sleep on Sundays for use in public performances. Children's activities are available on Wednesdays and Sundays from 2:30 p.m. (phone for details).

Underneath the palace's vast terrace, where skateboarders and itinerant sellers of African ivory and masks weave among tourists and flocks of schoolchildren, lies the Théâtre National de Chaillot (tel. 47 27 81 15), whose interior is a veritable monument to thirties design. From here, you descend the sloping gardens of the Trocadéro and cross the Pont d'Iéna to find yourself beneath the Eiffel Tower.

THE EIFFEL TOWER
Champ de Mars 75007. Metro Bir-Hakeim–RER Champ de Mars.
Tel. 45 50 34 56. Open 10 a.m.–11 p.m.
School holidays 9:30 a.m.–11 p.m.

The most easily recognized building in the world and quite possibly the most familiar symbol of any capital city, the Eiffel Tower celebrated its centennial as Paris was reveling in the excitement of the Revolution's bicentennial. This was no coincidence. Gustav Eiffel, an engineer who specialized in viaducts and pylons, originally built the Tower as a temporary structure for the Paris Exhibition of 1889 to commemorate the Revolution's centennial. It was only the inconvenience of dismantling it, and its use as France's tallest radio mast, that saved the structure from demolition. Indeed, it had some harsh critics. The poet Paul Verlaine made a specific detour every time he found himself in the vicinity to avoid having to look at it, and the novelist Joris Karl Huysmans likened it to a candlestick without its candle. But it seems to have found favor with Edward VII of England who, on June 10, 1889, made the first ascent of the Tower with his family.

At a height of 320 meters, it affords a bird's-eye view of Paris which, on a clear day, extends almost fifty miles, although visibility is often reduced by the haze. From the ground the most striking thing about the Tower is its size. Picture-postcard images totally belie its monumental proportions which, from beneath, create the impression of a great steel colossus, feet firmly planted in the four corners of the two-acre site while its head disappears into the clouds.

The urge to climb, whether on foot or by elevator, is irresistible, but be warned: from spring through summer the lines can be daunting. The crowds are smaller in winter, but you'll still probably have to wait outside. Provided you're feeling rich, one way to avoid hanging around is to have lunch in one of Paris's smartest and most expensive restaurants, the Jules Verne, spectacularly situated on the second floor. Booking is essential, preferably weeks in advance, but you will be rewarded by a trip up to the restaurant by private elevator, as well as the remarkable view.

FROM THE EIFFEL TOWER TO FAUBOURG ST-GERMAIN

CHAMP DE MARS AND ECOLE MILITAIRE

The former parade ground of the Ecole Militaire, stretching away from the Eiffel Tower, was transformed into a very pleasant park between 1908 and 1928. Landscaped with various shrubs, waterfalls and a pond, with plenty of benches beneath the trees, it's a good place to rest weary limbs and contemplate the Tower (incidentally given a feminine gender in French, regardless of any possible Freudian interpretations) and popular with tourists, joggers and children, who have fun in the playground. At the far end – and often neglected by tourists – the Ecole Militaire is a truly beautiful classical eighteenth-century building. Created at the instigation of Madame de Pompadour, the brilliant mistress of Louis XV, as a military school for penniless gentlemen, until 1966 this was the NATO officer training school for all countries belonging to the Treaty. It has since become the French Military Staff College.

LES INVALIDES TO
FAUBOURG ST-GERMAIN

Further into the seventh *arrondissement*, it's a short but lovely walk from Ecole Militaire to the Hôtel des Invalides and the unmissable Rodin Museum, also featuring the work of Camille Claudel, and then on to the Musée d'Orsay beside the river on the fringes of Faubourg St-Germain.

LES INVALIDES

Les Invalides was originally built by Louis XIV as a home for soldiers wounded while serving king and country.

This seventeenth-century building, with its glittering dome, houses the tomb of Napoleon and a war museum, and serves as a memorial to France's military victories over the centuries. One of the quotations decorating Napoleon's final resting-place – "By its simplicity my code of law has done more good in France than all the laws which have preceded me" – is a direct reference to the *Code Napoléon* or Napoleonic Code. This document, conceived by Napoleon and ratified in 1804, sets out all the laws relating to the civil rights of the French people. Some French laws are based on it even today, although it has undergone considerable modification over the years. As far as women are concerned, this modification started back in 1848 when Jeanne Deroin, a founding member of a club for emancipated women and a journalist on the first feminist newspaper, *La Voix des Femmes* (*The Voice of Women*) spoke out against the status of women in the Napoleonic Code. In the eyes of the state they were regarded as legal minors with no right to vote or, indeed, to act at all independently of men.

MADAME DE POMPADOUR (1721–64)

France's most famous royal mistress was born Jeanne Antoinette Poisson, the daughter of a financier. She married a tax inspector and was very soon introduced to the dazzling social life of the Parisian *salons*, hosted by the likes of Madame Geoffrin. Here she met scientists, wits and philosophers such as Voltaire and Fontenelle, but what made her fortune and fame was her long and influential involvement with the Court as Louis XV's mistress.

She received first the title of marchioness, then of duchess, and by 1756 she had been appointed lady-in-waiting to the Queen. Madame de Pompadour was known to influence the King's choice of ministers, and even his political decisions, but she is perhaps best remembered for her passionate support of the arts. A staunch friend of the Enlightenment intellectuals, she extended royal subsidies to many artists, and had castles built and remodeled – including the Elysée Palace, which she decorated with contemporary works – before dying, apparently in full glory, in Versailles.

Due east of Les Invalides is the Hôtel Biron, home of the Rodin Museum. Many of Rodin's works stand in the hotel's large, leafy garden, making it particularly tempting on a warm summer afternoon.

THE RODIN MUSEUM

Hôtel Biron, 77 rue de Varenne, 75007. Metro Varenne Tel. 47 05 01 34. Open 10 a.m.–6 p.m. (5 p.m. winter); closed Monday. Half price on Sunday.

Housed in the beautiful eighteenth-century Hôtel Biron, leased by sculptor Auguste Rodin from the state for what was surely one of the most lucrative landlord coups of all time – the ownership of virtually all his works after his death – the Musée Rodin is one of the most appealing of all Paris's art museums.

Rodin's extraordinarily lifelike sculptures were so shocking to the academic conventions of the time that no artist was more criticized or more insulted, despite numerous ardent admirers. In 1900 Anatole France wrote in the French national newspaper *Le Figaro:* "Insult and outrage are the wages of genius and Rodin, after all, only got his fair share." Yet Rodin did not have to face the prolonged hostility extended to his friends the Impressionist painters, and he eventually became a famous and respected figure. In the words of fellow sculptor Brancusi:

> Ever since Michelangelo, sculptors had been striving to be grandiose but succeeded only in being grandiloquent. In the nineteenth century, sculpture was in a desperate state. Rodin came along and changed everything.

No praise whatsoever greeted the work of Camille Claudel, Rodin's disciple, model, assistant, muse and lover for fifteen years. Only in recent years has her immense talent as a sculptor been recognized. Amid much controversy, she has been rehabilitated, and her work is well represented in this museum alongside Rodin's.

CAMILLE CLAUDEL (1864–1943)

Claudel, born into a provincial bourgeois family, passionately wanted to pursue an artistic vocation and persuaded her parents to move to Paris, where she could study sculpture. By 1883 she was sharing a studio with other artists when Rodin came in one day to give his opinion of their work. So began the long, painful, passionate affair that bound her to a man twenty-four years her senior, who never gave up his other lifelong woman companion and eventually broke off with Claudel in 1898, just as her talent as a sculptor was beginning to be recognized.

There is no doubt that Rodin made a forceful impact on Claudel's work, and he helped her to express herself with power and sensitivity, as in L'Abandon, La Valse, and L'Age mûr. But her own talent is already apparent in the visionary pathos that pervades these works.

Unfortunately, a combination of the break-up with Rodin and family pressures led to the gradual deterioration of Claudel's mental health. Having locked herself up and smashed her sculptures, she became increasingly erratic until, in 1913, her family had her committed to a mental asylum where she remained, virtually forgotten, until her death thirty years later. It was only after 1981, when a play by Anne Delbée brought her to public attention, that posthumous fame brought new interest to her work.

Judith Cladel and Gustave Coquiot, friends of Rodin, had already launched the idea of setting up a Rodin Museum in the Hôtel Biron. The artist was very enthusiastic, and offered to donate all his sculptures and his collection of ancient marbles and paintings, together with his copyrights to the state, on condition that he should be allowed to live in the Hôtel for the rest of his days. The offer was considered, and much debated. Rodin's enemies used every possible device to prevent the museum's creation, including petitions and a vicious press campaign. Proceedings dragged on until 1916, when the Senate passed the Bill. The museum opened in 1919, two years after Rodin's death.

The Sculptures There are sixteen rooms altogether. *The Broken Nose*, an early bronze sculpture displayed in Room 1, was refused entry to the *Salons des Artistes* in 1864. It was said to lack "moral elevation," and that the artist had used a "strange technique," in fact, what shocked the judges was Rodin's use of rippling flesh, indicating the sensuality that was to characterize so much of his work. In contrast, *Girl in a Flowered Hat* seems naïve and unsophisticated with the lovely hair, bold delineation of the eyes and velvety softness of the skin. This and the bust *Mignon* were both inspired by one of Rodin's early models, the long-suffering Rose Beuret, with whom he lived for fifty-two years.

Room 3 with its beautiful examples of eighteenth-century paneling holds the famous *Age of Bronze*; Room 4 contains *The Hand of God* or *The Creation*: "When God created the world, it is of modeling he must have thought first of all," wrote Rodin. The large hand holds a rugged mass of matter from which the smooth forms of a man and a woman emerge. Room 5 is dominated by the famous *Kiss*, an illustration of passion so successful that when it was exhibited in Chicago in 1893, some considered it indecent.

Next we move on to the work of Camille Claudel. Most of Room 6 is dedicated to her, and to two sculptures by Rodin inspired by her. Her pieces share the lyrical fervor of Rodin's art, but at the same time fiercely assert their independence. *The Waltz*, modeled in 1891 during a period of reconciliation with Rodin, is often considered her *chef d'œuvre*. In the same year, she wrote to the Ministry of Fine Arts requesting a commission to produce a marble version, but she was told that "the closeness of the sexes is rendered with surprising sensuality," and ordered to dress the figures. For months Claudel labored with the sculpture, and finally half-enveloped the couple in flowing drapery. But she never received the commission. *Chattering Women* is in onyx, a particularly difficult stone to sculpt. The complex lines of these four tiny figures, with their crossed arms and curved backs, were inspired by the sight of young women talking in a railway compartment.

Room 8 contains portraits of women from Rodin's life, both friends and lovers, among them Vita Sackville-West, while on the staircase stands a large bust of Rose Beure. Works in the upper rooms beyond include *The Thinker*, probably the most famous of all Rodin's works.

Outside the museum's gardens, containing yet more monumental sculptures, are lovely and well worth lingering in before you head back on to the streets.

FAUBOURG ST-GERMAIN

Art, fashion and politics – three things dear to a French person's heart – are closely associated with the area known as Faubourg St-Germain. Covering much of the desirable part of the Left Bank, the Faubourg St-Germain can be roughly divided into three sections. To the west towards rue de Sèvres and rue des Saint-Pères (where American poets, Edna St. Vincent Millay lived at number 65, and Ezra Pound and Dorothy Shakespeare at number 59) temples of *haute couture* display neat little suits and shoes with amusing heels at exorbitant prices while classy interior designers advertise their skills with swathes of fabric draped artfully over Louis XV furniture. This is the liveliest part of the Faubourg. Between the boulevard St-Germain and the Seine you'll find street upon street of art galleries and antique shops, a fitting prelude to the Musée d'Orsay, holding Paris's best selection of nineteenth- and twentieth-century art. But the heart of the Faubourg lies further west, between rue de Babylone and the Seine as far as boulevard des Invalides. This is the

JEANNE DEROIN (1805–94)

Jeanne Deroin, one of the earliest socialist feminists, spent her life struggling for better working conditions and the emancipation of women. From working on *La Voix des Femmes* she went on to found her own paper, as well as a club for emancipated women. In 1849, she put herself forward for election to the National Assembly. Since this was illegal, she could succeed only in highlighting the question of women's eligibility to be elected.

Oblivious to the scorn poured on her by the bourgeoisie, Deroin founded an association of socialist teachers with Pauline Roland and tried to unite all workers' organizations under one banner against capitalism. She was imprisoned for six months for subversion before eventually fleeing to London, where she continued her fight in exile with the help of like-minded British women.

land of politics and foreign affairs, where embassies and ministries occupy the former homes of the aristocracy. These beautiful old houses surround the Palais Bourbon, seat of the National Assembly.

PALAIS BOURBON (ASSEMBLÉE NATIONALE)

126 rue de l'Université, 75007.
Metro. Chambre des Députés/Invalides.
Visits on application to the Office of Administrative Affairs.

Built between 1722 and 1728 for the Duchess of Bourbon, daughter of Louis XIV and Madame de Montespan, with its familiar classical façade overlooking the place de la Concorde, the palace is now the seat of the lower house of French Parliament, known as the National Assembly or Chambre des Députés, whose members meet in an ornate white-and-gold room. Access to debates for visitors is rare, and the building may be visited only as part of a guided tour.

The eastern half of the seventh arrondissement remains one of the most exclusive residential areas in Paris. Unlike the Marais, whose nineteenth-century decline allowed the government to buy up mansions and open them to the public, here many hôtels *particuliers* (the name given to a substantial townhouse, generally owned and occupied by characters of wealth and high social standing) are still owned by the original families. Others have passed on to millionaires, who keep the heavy courtyard doors locked, or ministries which keep them patrolled. Among the few exceptions are the Musée Rodin and the Palais Bourbon (see above) and the Musée de la Légion d'Honneur. Or – at a price – you can dine in the park of the Maison de l'Amérique Latine at 217 boulevard St-Germain. This Latin American cultural center, very much linked to the embassies, offers classes in the language and culture of Latin America, as well as providing a meetingplace for Latin American students. Also worth a visit is the garden at 33 rue de Babylone, which is open to the public. It was once the orchard of a convent; the vines and apple trees provide a welcome respite from the sight of so many walls.

SIMONE VEIL (BORN 1927)

Simone Veil, née Jacob, was born in 1927 in Nice. At the age of seventeen she was deported by the Nazis to Auschwitz, together with her whole family – only she and her sisters survived. Her training as a magistrate aroused her interest in prison administration, and later in the legislation of child adoption. As the Secretary-General of the Conseil Supérieur de la Magistrature, she caught the attention of Jacques Chirac and of President Valéry Giscard d'Estaing, who appointed her Health Minister in his 1974 Cabinet.

Simone Veil's constant concern for the dignity of the individual inspired her to instigate two bold reforms, on which her fame rests. The first one introduced the legalization of abortion; the other initiated a government campaign against excessive smoking. To those measures should be added decrees that prolonged maternity leave and extended social security payments to all French citizens. Thanks to the energy of women like Simone Veil and Françoise Giroud – then director of the weekly magazine *L'Express* and Simone Veil's colleague as junior minister in charge of women's issues – France became the first country in Catholic Europe to soften its legislation on abortion, which until then had been illegal.

Simone Veil has since pursued her political career in the moderate Republican Party, and was President of the European Parliament between 1979 and 1982. She remains active as a committed European and is resolutely hostile to the racist ideology of the National Front, and to all extremist positions.

Musée de la Légion d'Honneur
2 rue de Bellechasse, 75007. Tel. 45 55 95 15. Metro Solferino/ Chambre des Députés. Open 2–5 p.m. daily; closed Monday.

The Légion d'Honneur is France's highest and most prestigious award. Before the time of Napoleon it was reserved for an elite made up of the aristocracy and officers of the King. Abolished in 1791, it was re-established under Napoleon as a reward for those who had contributed to the prosperity and defense of the country. At the end of the Empire there were 30,000 members; now there are 250,000. The museum, worth visiting for its location, also covers similar orders existing throughout the world.

The French do not appear to be as proud of their women *Légionnaires* as might be hoped. When we tried to obtain information about the number of women who have received this honor, or even learn of a few names, we were put off on the telephone and told to make the request in person, by appointment only, on a Wednesday. We agreed to arrange a meeting with the archivist, only to be told that he was reluctant to comply owing to the Metro strike which already threatened to delay his journey home. We again asked the woman receptionist if the archivist couldn't be persuaded to supply the information (which he presumably had in his head) over the phone. No, came back the answer. Had we hit a raw nerve, a male chauvinist, or simply a Frenchman at his most unhelpful? We'll never know.

As you go east, the neighborhood becomes livelier, and from the clothes shops at the end of rue de Grenelle you catch a glimpse of the church of St-Germain-des-Prés. The streets parallel to the Seine were built for purely residential purposes, confining shops to the cross streets – an innovation in urban planning that persists today. Although antique dealers have moved into the northern streets like Lille and Université, in rue de Varenne or Grenelle the only sign of life tends to be armed and uniformed embassy guards or ministerial protection squads.

At the same time, the occasional glimpse of trees above a wall still hints at garden parties and a *douceur de vivre* not so different from the area's heyday, when everyone who was anyone lived within a few blocks of each other; even Marie-Antoinette's dog is buried in the garden of 80 rue de Lille – the plaque marked "Coco" still stands. The writer Germaine de Staël called exile from the rue de Bellechasse a fate worse than death; in fact, it was in the elegant building at 50 rue de Varenne (now the Italian Embassy) that her first meeting with Napoleon Bonaparte launched the mutual disapproval that eventually led to her banishment from 102 rue de Grenelle (later inhabited by Elizabeth Barrett and Robert Browning) and the one neighborhood where life was worth living

The Faubourg St-Germain hosted an array of *salons*, the most influential run by bossy Madame du Deffand, Julie de Lespinasse and Madame de Geoffrin.

On rue de Bellechasse, a Protestant church and part of the Defense Ministry occupy the site of the unconventional convent of the Dames de Bellechasse, which moved here in 1671. The convent's pupils, recruited from the finest families, spent far less time praying

MADAME DE STAËL (1766–1817)

Germaine de Staël-Necker grew up in the enlightened atmosphere of her mother, Suzanne Necker's *salon*, an institution so influential that Necker managed to secure her husband the role of finance minister to Louis XVI.

Despite her father's position, Germaine became a wholehearted supporter of the Revolution, hailed the advent of Napoleon Bonaparte but soon turned against him for betraying the revolutionary ideal of liberty, and her *salon* became a center of opposition. She also accused him of misogyny, though in this aspect he was no different from any other man of the time. Staël herself was lampooned for her "mannish" participation in politics; "Miserable hermaphrodite that you are," one disparager ranted, "your sole ambition in uniting the two sexes in your person is to dishonor them both at once." Women were simply not *meant* to have opinions, let alone express them! In 1803 Napoleon sent Madame de Staël into exile, which she spent traveling around the continent and staying at her house in Switzerland with her lover, the writer Benjamin Constant. Her belief in women's rights pervades her two best-known works, *Delphine* and *Corinne*, featuring heroines determined to live out their own desires against the demands of social convention.

than cultivating the connections which were to last them through a lifetime of Court politics. Another well-known figure, Madame Récamier, retired to a different convent, since destroyed by the construction of the street named after her; she planned to flee the world once her looks and money were gone, but ended up entertaining the artists, writers and politicians who had surrounded her throughout her youth. Once cloyingly described by Chateaubriand as being as seductive as Venus and as inspirational as a Muse, she's now best known in France for having a type of chaise lounge named after her. She would doubtless find this as insulting as Chateaubriand would the fact that he's now most famous as a slab of steak.

Once you reach the Sèvres–Babylone Metro, houses give way to shops, and the atmosphere becomes less rarefied. The intersection of rue de Sèvres and rue de Babylone is dominated by Le Bon Marché, the world's first department store (1876), where ladies would spend their husbands' wealth as conspicuously as possible. The size and innovations of the store (self-service, sales, mail order) opened a new career to young women, but it wasn't the dream job they'd imagined. Although the need for armies of salesgirls allowed them a greater freedom than service in paternalistic traditional shops, the workers were wretchedly housed, treated like children, and paid too little to keep up the smartness that their employers demanded. Zola's novel *Au Bonheur des Dames* gives one account of their experience.

Meanwhile, in the Square Boucicaut outside is a statue of the founder's wife, Madame Boucicaut, who commissioned a pseudo-Chinese pagoda at 57*bis* rue de Babylone which has been turned into a tearoom and movie theater. To the south, rue Placide is a great street for secondhand clothes, while on rue de Sèvres mid-market clothing stores alternate with a succession of hospitals. All the land round here was once owned by the Church. Among the surviving religious monuments is the Chapel of the Miraculous Medal (at number 140), the burial place of a nun to whom the Virgin appeared in 1830. In the courtyard a coin-operated dispenser sells "miraculous medals" – to bring good luck! Turning back towards the river, between rue du Bac and rue de Bellechasse, you come to the impressive Musée d'Orsay.

MUSÉE D'ORSAY
62 rue de Lille, 75007. Tel. 40 49 48 14. Metro Solferino, RER Musée d'Orsay. Bus 24, 68, 84, 73. Open Tuesday, Wednesday, Friday, Saturday 10 a.m.–6 p.m.; Sunday 9 a.m.–6 p.m. (half-price Sunday); Thursday 10 a.m.–9:45 p.m. Opens 9 a.m. during the summer. Closed Monday. Free guided tours in English 11 a.m.–2 p.m.

The Musée d'Orsay, inaugurated in 1986, is France's most "female" museum. Housed in the fin de siècle Gare d'Orsay, it was rebuilt by a woman architect, Gae Aulenti; Madeleine Rebérioux, a historian specializing in workers' movements, was vice-president of the public establishment responsible for preparing the first exhibitions. She introduced music, film and photography; and for the first time in a large national French museum, the head curator is a woman, Françoise Cachin, a specialist in Gauguin and Manet. Two-thirds of the other curators are women, including the general secretary.

Women painters are still a rarity here – there are only a few paintings by Rosa Bonheur, Suzanne Valadon, Berthe Morisot and Mary Cassat, and some sculptures by Camille Claudel, but naturally there are a host of women created by men: allegorical and sensual nudes, housekeepers and dancers, mothers and prostitutes.

This museum holds some of the capital's most prestigious art collections, yet not so long ago it was a railway station. Amid much controversy, the Gare d'Orsay was constructed by the architect Victor Lanoux in 1898. The building, with its heavy metallic structure, was considered daring, especially given the proximity of the Palais du Louvre immediately opposite on the Right Bank. From 1900 to 1939 the station was an important part of the French railway network, but by the end of the Second World War, the Gare d'Orsay was no longer used for public transportation and became a rest center for prisoners coming back to France after the Liberation. Some three decades later, in 1978, it was decided to transform it

MADAME DU DEFFAND (1697–1780)
AND JULIE DE LESPINASSE (1733–76)

At the age of sixteen Julie de Lespinasse was informed by her aristocratic mother that she was illegitimate. The consequences were harsh – instead of sharing the financial and social fruits of her family's position with her half-sister, Julie was forced to become governess to her children. She was rescued in 1752 when Madame du Deffand, a leading *salonière* and one-time mistress of the Regent of France, came to visit the family. By this time du Deffand – whose *salons* had attracted the likes of David Hume and Voltaire, along with a glittering array of economists and politicians – was going blind, and she decided to take Julie back to Paris as her eyes and companion. For the first ten years things went brilliantly, and the two women presided over one of the most dazzling *salons* of Enlightenment Europe; they were an exhilarating couple – du Deffand spiking the proceedings with her dry cynicism and Julie with her youthful optimism. Eventually, however, the women's relationship soured, and Julie secured herself a new patroness, Madame Marie-Louise Geoffrin, du Deffand's rival *salonière*, who sold three paintings to Catherine the Great of Russia in order to provide her new protégée with a pension and apartment. Her investment paid off. Julie's *caché* attracted the likes of Boucher, Diderot and Horace Walpole to Geoffrin's Wednesday dinners, where they would eat well and tolerate the rather tame topics of conversation before moving on to Julie's for more stimulating mental exercise. "Nowhere," said the writer Marmontel, after Julie died aged forty-three, "was there a livelier, a more brilliant, or a better-regulated conversation, than at her house."

into a museum. Thanks to Gae Aulenti the result is stunning – and the dramatic glass and steel vaults only enhance the brilliant collections of paintings, sculptures, photographs and objets d'art. They are displayed on three levels; works are generally arranged chronologically, and according to style. There is a lot to see in the Musée d'Orsay, so allow at least three hours.

Ground floor *Section A*: Ingres and his disciples, Delacroix, Chassériau, historical painting, and portraits 1850–80. To the right of the central gallery are Classical and Romantic nineteenth-century works. Among the former, have a look at Ingres's *Virgin with a Host* intended as a statement on the Western ideals of religion and art, but striking, too, in its contrasting piety and sensuality, and at Chassériau's *Tepidarium*. Artists of his ilk loved the excuse to show off women's bodies in various languid positions, usually in harems or baths disingenuously elevating their theme by historical accuracy: the *Tepidarium*, for example, is an exact depiction of the baths of Venus Genitrix, in Pompeii.

Section B: Daumier, Chauchard Collection, Millet, Rousseau, Corot, Realism, Courbet. Honoré Daumier was a lithographer and painter but he was also the most famous French caricaturist of his time, especially popular for his social and political satires. In his painting La République, two sturdy children suck milk from the breasts of a monumental, but tellingly almost featureless woman.

The Chauchard Collection is one of the museum's most important, comprising the work of L'Ecole de Barbizon, the school that preceded the Impressionists. Before the Impressionist movement, a significant group of painters, working at the end of the last century, decided to abandon their studios to paint in the countryside, usually close to Paris. Barbizon, a small village in the heart of the forest of Fontainebleau, fitted in well with their dream of rural harmony. While impoverished peasants were flocking to the cities in search of work, Parisians tended to see the forests, farms, cows and cultivated fields as a paradise lost. Ten such painters became famous, among them Théodore Rousseau, whose *Une Avenue, Forêt de l'Isle-Adam* depicts a typical rural scene in which time seems suspended and all work has ceased, while in the far distant background a small peasant girl stands surrounded by her cows amid a sea of exuberant nature, rendered in detail to the last thorn bush. Upstairs in Section B animal painting, also in vogue at the time, is represented by artists such as Troyon, Rosa Bonheur, Daubigny and Jules Breton. Rosa Bonheur's *Labourage nivernais* was much admired, after an early exhibition of her work.

At the very end of the gallery containing the Chauchard Collection, a large area is devoted to Gustave Courbet's work. *Un enterrement à Ornan* is considered to be his masterpiece. The funeral is attended by the rural community of Ornan, roughly

ROSA BONHEUR (1822–99)

Rosa Bonheur turned away from the male preserve of "noble" themes in favor of painting domestic animals and the daily lives of country people. The daughter of a landscape artist from Bordeaux, she was something of a child prodigy whose first exhibited work, *Goats and Sheep*, attracted immediate interest for its bold simplicity. As early as 1849, she was widely acclaimed for the almost photographic *Labourage nivernais* based, it is thought, on a passage in George Sand's pastoral novel, *La Mare au Diable*. In order to research her gigantic and vigorous *Foire aux Chevaux (The Horse Fair)* she went to the horse market in Paris, disguised as a man – having first got a "permission de travestissement" from the police! She became massively popular among the animal-loving middle classes of Britain not only because of her themes, but also because this was a time when animal rights issues were being hotly debated. Queen Victoria was a fan, and arranged to meet Bonheur and have a private showing of the *Foire aux Chevaux* at Buckingham Palace.

divided into three groups: on the left the Church, with its clergymen; in the middle the local dignitaries, with a Justice of the Peace, a fat mayor and two honored ancients dressed up in 1793 costumes for the occasion; and on the right the villagers, huddled together. Like the chorus in some Greek tragedy, the women form a separate group. Courbet was a scrupulous realist: the figures represented were all inhabitants of Ornan; more than half of them were identified, including the gravediggers. His realism is also displayed in *Naked Woman with a Dog* in which he broke with tradition and painted the real face and body of his model, Léontine Renaud, instead of adapting her features to correspond with those of a Classical Venus.

Section C: Contains paintings by Puvis de Chavannes, a Neoclassical painter whose monumental works are more often found in national libraries and universities than in museums. His vast allegorical fresco *The Summer*, on show here, influenced many painters of the next generation, including Seurat, Gauguin and Picasso.

There are also several paintings by Gustave Moreau, an early Symbolist. Note especially the bizarre *Orpheus*, whose head lies on a lyre held by a dreamy young woman, and the way in which the symbolism of color takes over from realism in his portrait of his two sisters: the younger one, Marguerite, half-natural, half-self-conscious is painted in pale tones; the elder, Thérèse, strong and haughty, is rendered in sharp colors dominated by her black dress.

Section D: Concentrates on early Impressionist paintings (before 1870); mainly Claude Monet, Auguste Renoir, Alfred Sisley, Camille Pissarro and Berthe Morisot.

Morisot, one of the few women artists in "the group," contributed to the first Impressionist exhibition of 1874 and to subsequent shows, except that of 1878, the year in which her daughter was born. Her painting is characterized by light shades and a refreshingly lively spontaneity; her subjects are mostly the private concerns of leisured middle-class women and children and the everyday rituals of domestic life – notable for the absence of men. Although Morisot's pictures are regarded nowadays as invaluable, they were somewhat looked down on at the time. Sewing, boating, drinking tea, looking after the children and reading are all observed with acute, though empathetic insight. Among the paintings displayed are *Dans les blés, La Jeune Femme se poudrant,* and *Le Berceau,* with the serene and pensive mother looking at her sleeping baby (the models were Edmé the artist's sister, and Edmé's baby daughter Blanche).

Mary Cassatt also played an important part in the French Impressionist movement. Born in the United States, she spent four years at the Philadelphia Academy of Art before coming to Paris. She contributed to the spread of Impressionist painting across the Atlantic, but remained in Paris until her death. Like Morisot, her paintings reveal an interior domestic life; but again, like Morisot, scenes of the everyday are infused with sometimes startling insights.

The rest of the Impressionist exhibition is located on the top floor, easily reached via the back escalators.

Top floor   *Section K*: Impressionism, Monet, Renoir, Pissarro, Sisley, Degas, Manet after 1870. Personal Collection, Gachet Collection, Guillaumin, Van Gogh, Cézanne.

With the Impressionists, the public discovered another way of painting feminine beauty, illustrated by Manet's *Déjeuner sur l'herbe,* which drove the critics wild when it appeared in 1863. The image of a naked woman in a forest, unabashedly sharing a picnic with two fully dressed men, was deemed totally indecent and unacceptable. What particularly outraged many of Manet's contemporaries was the woman's total lack of self-consciousness. Bathed in bright light, she sits by her companions with an air of serene confidence, very much on equal terms. Manet's *Olympia* caused another shock to the well-meaning bourgeoisie of the time. Although the work follows a tradition of "female nude with attendant" (as in the work of Titian, Ingres or Goya), this Olympia is defiant and again, totally self-possessed. She looks out of the painting in a way that makes it plain that (despite working as a prostitute) she submits to no man. The fact that Manet was unusual in having many platonic friendships with women may be significant.

You'll also find many works by Claude Monet – mostly landscapes, but there's one poignant portrait of his wife painted while she lay dying from a long illness. Camille Monet is shown under her bedclothes, her face faded like the bunch of flowers she is clutching in her hands, and her body already almost turned to dust.

This section also has some of the best-known Renoirs, including *Les Baigneuses*. Renoir had a definite preference for group studies and portraits – above all portraits of women from all walks of life, from the elegant high-society girl in *Danse à la ville* to the manifestly low-born *Gabrielle à la rose*. In his later period, nudes fill his landscapes, seeming to get larger and larger to the point of filling the whole canvas.

Degas, of course, is famous for his paintings of women, whose unflattering realism early led him to be charged with misogyny. No one but he would have chosen to paint, in *Les Repasseuses*, the very moment when an anonymous ironing woman stops to yawn. Yet as Degas himself said, this apparent spontaneity was in fact minutely calculated; indeed, the figures are caught in a grid of perpendiculars and diagonals which seems to fix them on the spot. He was also fascinated by the way women move their bodies – hence his numerous paintings of dancers: *La Classe de danse, Le Foyer de la danse à l'Opéra de la rue Peletier, Danseuses bleues*. The dancers' positions echo each other like some clockwork mechanism: contraction and rest, tensing of the muscles by leaning forward, stretching back to relax them.

Cézanne was taught the Impressionist style by his friend Pissarro, whose influence is evident in *La Maison du Docteur Gachet* and the *Carrefour de la rue Rémy à Auvers*. *La Nature morte aux oignons* and the important still-life painting *Pommes et oranges* were to have a significant influence on twentieth-century artists. Cézanne gave substance to all objects, even to air, mist or vapor. The skies and seas in his landscapes have as much solidity as the trees, rocks and houses.

With a steady hand, he ordered and combined in the space of the picture the cubes of his houses, the architectures of his trees, the concrete blocks that are his people, the spheres that are his fruits. His still lifes heralded the most radical creations of the artists to come.

Van Gogh has a whole room dedicated to him – albeit rather small, given the number of visitors who crowd in, all too often video camera in hand. Note his portraits of very different women: the orange and yellow *Italian Woman* (modeled by Agostina Segatori, who owned a café in Paris, and with whom he had a brief affair), *l'Arlésienne* and *La Paysanne près de l'âtre*.

Section L: One painting by Seurat – his last unfinished piece, *The Circus,* the central figure of which is a girl performing on a very wild-looking horse – is joined by a number of works by Toulouse-Lautrec. Known for his representation of prostitutes, Toulouse-Lautrec was something of a voyeur and spent many months of his life in brothels, where he was fascinated by what went on behind the scenes. There's a warped nastiness to many of his paintings, which definitely reveals more about the artist than his subjects.

Tending to choose moments of rest, he was adept at capturing the personal, often lesbian, relationships between the women in the *maisons closes*. *Seule* (*Alone*) is a particularly striking painting of a prostitute lying across her bed in a state of complete exhaustion.

Section M: Dedicated to the Symbolists, among them Gauguin, Henri le Douanier Rousseau, Odilon Redon and Serusier. Gauguin, of course, is famous for his portrayal of Tahitian women, of which there are many examples in the Orsay collection. *Vairumati*, all red and gold, mingles myth and reality through the features of a young Polynesian representing the goddess Vairumati, the "original woman" in Polynesian cosmology. In Gauguin's words: "the sun's fire shone through her golden skin while all the mysteries of love slumbered in the night of her hair."

Rousseau's allegorical *La Guerre* (*War*) was first exhibited at the 1894 *Salon*, to great derision and condescending amusement. Considered a simpleton, Henri le Douanier Rousseau turned out to be the precursor of twentieth-century so-called primitive or naïve painting. This particular canvas shows the Goddess of War, her white dress torn to shreds, sitting in front of her horse, brandishing a sword; under her lies a battlefield full of corpses being fed on by crows. The immediate impact is one of violence, even though the whole scene has the appearance of a dream – or rather, a nightmare.

The *Charmeuse de serpent* conveys a quite different mood: in a primitive Garden of Eden, a strange woman plays on her flute to charm the snakes around her – an image of woman's sexual power subduing a host of phallic serpents.

Mezzanine Level Half of the gallery is dedicated to Naturalism, historical painting and Symbolism, as well as works from the 1880–1900 *Salons*.

SÉVÉRINE (1857–1929)

Sévérine, a confirmed radical, supported workers' and women's rights and equality for all before the law; she participated in all the conflicts that tore at the fabric of French society during her time.

Her career in journalism began as assistant editor of the revolutionary paper *Le Réveil*, moving on to become editor of *Le Cri du Peuple* (*Cry of the People*), for which she wrote under a masculine pen name. However, she gradually became disillusioned by the dogmatism of the radical press and briefly swung the other way: towards the right-wing movement of Général Boulanger. At the same time, Sévérine never hesitated to enter mine shafts in support of striking miners, rose to the defense of persecuted anarchists, and vigorously campaigned for women's rights, contributing to Marguerite Durand's feminist paper *La Fronde*. Inspired by the Russian Revolution, she later joined the Communist Party and wrote for *L'Humanité*, before again renouncing the authoritarianism of rigid political doctrine and, in particular, the puritanism that was victimizing her as a woman militant. She died, more or less an anarchist, inveighing against the horrors of Fascism.

The Meeting by Maria Bashkirtseva was extremely well received by the critics. The realism of the facial expressions, the precise style, the accuracy of observation and the natural postures accrued great success and universal acclaim. But the dream did not last. One critic was very upset by the fact that despite her elegant aristocratic upbringing, Bashkirtseva, a Russian who came to study in 1880s Paris, showed a great passion for the ugliness, the commonness and the roughness of the deprived areas of the city. She was denied the medal of the *salon* she was attending on account of her sex—she died nine months later aged only twenty-five.

The *Portrait de Sévérine* by Hawkins is notable, too. Sévérine was one of the first female journalists in France. The portrait's layout is unusual, very much like a still life, with Sévérine in the center, hands clasped, staring at something we cannot see.

This middle level also houses late-nineteenth-century sculptures, including those of Camille Claudel and Rodin and decorative arts.

While you're here, take a look at the former station's *Salle des Fêtes* and the Belle Epoque restaurant. There's also a handy café upstairs, just behind the face of the massive station clock, worth fighting the crowd to get a table. Finally, don't forget to step out on to the roof terrace for a sensational view across the Seine and a bird's-eye view of the Louvre and surrounding area.

THE HISTORIC CENTER

Here, all within walkable distances are some of the oldest – and most jewel-like – parts of Paris. In the middle of the Seine, tethered by bridges to the mainland are the Île de la Cité, where the city began, the home of Notre-Dame and the Conciergerie, where Marie-Antoinette spent her final hours; and the tiny lozenge-shaped Île St-Louis, as well as a mass of appealing narrow streets bordered by *les quais*, where rows of exquisite, balconied *hôtels* are a reminder of seventeenth-century elegance.

From the tip of Île de la Cité a short walk across Pont Neuf to the Right Bank plunges you full tilt into the hub of contemporary French life around Beaubourg–Les Halles. This unabashedly commercial area, dominated by the echoing curves of the great tubular Pompidou Center and the nearby Forum des Halles, contrasts strongly with the sedate gentility of the islands or the Marais beyond. On summer lunchtimes the grass of Les Halles is thick with deshabille office workers eating *carottes rapées* out of plastic boxes. Street performers try to interest the clientele of Café Costes, where people go to be seen rather than to see, while scruffy young things sit on the cobblestones in the shadow of the Pompidou Center, strumming guitars and drinking cheap wine in an echo of the 1960s.

ÎLE DE LA CITÉ

All road distances in France are measured from Notre-Dame from a point known as *kilomètre zéro* by the west door. Whatever you think of centralism, this standard seems somehow right, for this is where France began. The Île de la Cité was a town when there was nothing but trees on the mainland. People have lived here since at least the third century BC, and the combination of its position as the center of trade and the protection afforded by the river attracted Gauls and Romans alike. Not until a fourteenth-century revolt turned the royal family against a site on which they felt trapped did the center of Paris begin to shift towards the Right Bank, and even today the concentration of newer administrative buildings on the Île de la Cité echoes its original importance.

Until the nineteenth century the island still looked like a medieval city, and novelists like Eugène Süe and Victor Hugo seized upon it whenever a sinister setting was called for. Haussmann put a

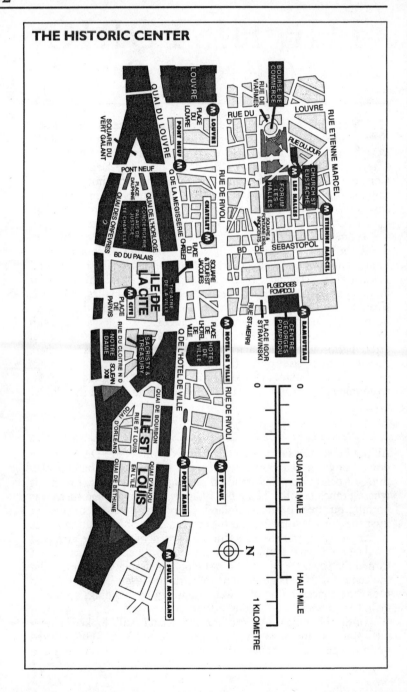

PONT NEUF
(75001 AND 75006 METRO PONT NEUF)

If Paris is one of the most romantic cities in the world, then the Pont Neuf is one of the most romantic spots in the city.

Presided over by Henry IV on a magnificent charger, this bridge, despite its name, is the oldest bridge in Paris. It is also the most famous and the most popular. Built to allow the King to move easily between his palace at the Louvre on the Right Bank and the Abbey of St-Germain-des-Prés on the Left Bank, the bridge effectively slices through the most western tip of the Île de la Cité, to which it gives access via the pretty place Dauphine.

The first stone was laid by Henri III in 1578 but the bridge was not actually finished until 1607, when it was officially opened by Henri IV. It was an instant success. The first bridge to be built of stone, and wider and larger than any previous one, it was especially popular for promenades because its width allowed for pavements which afforded protection from the mud and horses crossing the bridge, and because of the little semicircular indentations along its length, where there was just enough space for four or five people to rest for a few moments and pass the time of day.

Today the bridge is just as well loved. With its grey arches spanning the river majestically, the authentic old square Parisian-style gas lamps casting their gentle glow at night, and the breathtaking view of a pinky red sun coming up over the river as the mist rises in the early morning in front of the Conciergerie, it is quite simply one of the most beautiful spots in Paris.

One of the added benefits of the Pont Neuf is the perfect uninterrupted view it affords of the Pont des Arts, located a little further downstream towards the west.

---

stop to this by leveling the insalubrious alleys to make way for naked thoroughfares lined with his favorite kind of building: police stations and law courts. Two-thirds of the island's population were driven out between 1856 and 1900. There were objections – "Notre-Dame is not a pyramid, a desert is not its proper setting" – but this sort of criticism never stopped Haussmann. Now all that survives of the medieval city are a few residential streets on the northeast tip of the island, and to the south the unmistakable silhouette of Notre-Dame Cathedral.

NOTRE-DAME

Place du Parvus Notre-Dame, 75004. Metro Cité. Tel. 43 26 07 39.
Visits daily 8 a.m.–7 p.m.; chancel 10:30 a.m.–12 p.m., 2–5:30 p.m.

It is no accident that a church begun in 1160 was dedicated to the Virgin, for the poetry of courtly love had helped to shift attention from the feminine evil represented by Eve to the feminine purity symbolized by Mary. Since Louis IX's barefoot entry bearing the Crown of Thorns in 1239, almost every important event in French history has been marked by a ceremony in the cathedral: here Joan of Arc was rehabilitated, Marie-Antoinette was churched (presumably after being soiled by giving birth) and thanks were given for the Liberation of Paris in 1944. The construction of the original cathedral stretched over nearly two centuries. During the seventeenth and eighteenth centuries it suffered from some dubious interior decoration, not to mention misplaced revolutionary zeal. During a takeover by the Jacobins an actress representing the goddess Reason managed to upstage the Virgin by posing on a papiermâché mountain to the sound of "La Marseillaise."

The 1841 publication of Victor Hugo's *The Hunchback of Notre-Dame* came just in time to alert public opinion to the state of the dilapidated church and save it from demolition. The controversy surrounding Viollet-le-Duc's ambitious reconstruction project (1857–79), which added a spire, gargoyles and other Gothic frills, had the merit of bringing Notre-Dame into a spotlight which it has never lost since.

Before you go into the cathedral, take a moment to glance up at the figures adorning the arches of the three doorways known as the King's Gallery. These twenty-eight kings are the Kings of Judah and Israel, restored by Viollet-le-Duc after being destroyed by the revolutionary mob who mistook them for the kings of France. Viollet-le-Duc has made his bid for immortality by casting himself as one of the kings. Some of the original heads, which date from the twelfth and thirteenth centuries, were found on a construction site, and are now on display in the Cluny Museum. The other entrances have equally richly carved doorways.

Once you're inside, don't let the rumbling of buses revving up outside or the multilingual buzz detract from the play of dark and light that streams through the magnificent stained-glass windows on a sunny day. The immense rose window on the north side, depicting the Kings of the Old Testament and the prophets surrounding the Virgin, was the largest made in the thirteenth century, and is mostly original. Adorning the small side chapels are a wealth of tombs, paintings, bas-reliefs and other art works dating as far back as the fourteenth century. The eighteenth-century organ, which you can hear in action at a free concert every day at 5:45 p.m., is the largest in France. The decoration of the choir, covered in beautiful carvings and bas-reliefs, was carried out at the instigation of Louis XIV according to a vow his father had made to build a new altar at Notre-Dame. Included in the altar was to be a sculpture of the Virgin and Christ after the Crucifixion, made for the choir, as a way of giving thanks for the birth of a male heir. Louis XIV carried out the vow sixty years after his father's death.

The Sacristy and Treasury displays a selection of manuscripts and religious objects (open Monday–Saturday 10 a.m.–6 p.m.; Sunday 2–6 p.m.). In the south tower, up in the belfry, you can watch tourists doing hunchback impressions and declaiming "de bells, de bells" while visiting the thirteen-ton bell, or alternatively climb the 387 steps up the north tower (open 10 a.m.–5 p.m.) to enjoy a magnificent view over Paris. Out in front of the cathedral is the Crypte Archéologique, an underground museum with an excellent exhibition showing the remains of the original cathedral of Notre-Dame, together with houses and streets of the Cité going right back to Roman times. If you want to bone up on more history, head for the Musée de Notre-Dame at Rue du Cloître 10.

If you can stand the bus fumes, there are rows of benches with a view of the buttresses on Square Jean XXIII, at the eastern edge of the cathedral; a quieter place to sit is the Square de l'Île de France across the quai de l'Archevêché, which is rather plain but overlooks the river and the Île Saint-Louis. Below it is the moving Memorial to the 200,000 French deported by the Nazis. A claustrophobic staircase leads down to a bunker with barred cells and windows through which 200,000 points of light commemorate the deportees.

PLACE DAUPHINE

A walk down the island, in the direction of the Louvre, brings you to sights of a different kind. On the very tip is the sunken Square du Vert-Galant, a haven for sunbathers and lovers jutting into the Seine like the prow of a ship. Running above it is the Pont Neuf which, despite its name, is the oldest bridge in Paris and the first to be constructed without having houses built on top – perhaps that's why it has survived its predecessors. Built to allow the King to move easily between the Right Bank Palais du Louvre and the Abbey of St-Germain-des-Prés on the Left Bank, the bridge effectively slices through the western tip of the Île de la Cité.

But don't cross from one bank to the other without visiting the pretty Dauphine, tucked into a triangle of the Île. The red-brick façades of this elegant seventeenth-century triangular "square" provide a welcome relief from the ubiquitous beige stone and white plaster that predominate elsewhere in Paris. One of France's best-known actresses, Simone Signoret, lived here. In another era number 37 was the childhood home of the revolutionary Madame Roland, whom opponents on the left accused of corrupting her husband and "wearing the pants in the house." Her father taught her to paint miniatures, but she fled to a convent when her father's apprentice began to caress her after lifting her on to a window sill for a better view of a procession passing on the Pont Neuf.

Palais de Justice

Boulevard du Palais (entrance by the cour de Mai), 75001. Tel. 43 29 12 55. Metro Cité. Open 8:30 a.m.–6 p.m. Monday–Friday.

As you go east you will come upon what seems like an endless stretch of administrative buildings, each housing a different aspect of law and order. The first is the Palais de Justice, a hulking mass of law courts built piecemeal since Roman times. Once you're past the obligatory security check you can rub shoulders with the barristers

SIMONE SIGNORET (1921–85)

Simone Signoret was not only a celebrated actress, but an active campaigner against social and political injustice. Attracted in the 1940s by the people who made up the eclectic radical world of the Café Flore, she ended up supporting a range of other international causes.

Her first big role was in a film called *Les Démons de l'aube*, made by Yves Allégret, by whom she had a child, Catherine, and whom she married soon after, in 1947. Three years later she met and fell in love with a young unknown singer called Yves Montand. They eventually married and stayed together for the rest of her life, nurturing their love and their careers side by side.

The 1950s saw her undertaking weightier roles, as in Jack Clayton's *Chemins de la Haute Ville*. Her interpretation of a young Frenchwoman trapped in a sad and tragic marriage won her an Oscar in 1960. This period was also marked by a brief flirtation with Communism. Many roles followed, both in films and on stage. In later years she took to writing – first her memoirs, then a novel.

milling around the Salle des Pas Perdus. But the main attractions of the Palais de Justice are the two buildings that it has gradually swallowed up: the Sainte-Chapelle, located to the left of the main entrance and occupying part of an interior courtyard; and the Conciergerie, which is incorporated into the right wing of the Palais, overlooking the Seine towards the Right Bank.

SAINTE-CHAPELLE

4 boulevard du Palais. Tel. 43 54 30 09. Open 9:30 a.m.–6 p.m. summer; 10 a.m.–4:30 p.m. winter

The Sainte-Chapelle is a narrow church originally built as the showcase for a Crown of Thorns which Louis IX brought back from one of his Eastern crusades. Its vast unbroken wall of stained glass is no longer the technical novelty it was when the chapel was built – at the time Parisians could *not* understand what was holding the glass up! Executed by the same master-craftsmen who made the stained glass at Chartres Cathedral, the windows depict 1134 scenes based on the theme of Christ's Passion; 720 of the original windows survive. On a sunny day the effect from inside is breathtaking. At night the chapel is equally impressive: its Gothic vaults are studded by a thousand painted gold stars on a Prussian-blue background as though imitating the night sky beyond the impenetrable black of the windows. It is well worth checking the listing for one of the numerous concerts given in the Sainte-Chapelle.

The Conciergerie

1 quai de l'Horlogerie.
Open 9:30 a.m.–6 p.m. summer; 10 a.m.–5 p.m. winter.
Combined ticket available with Sainte-Chapelle

The second attraction crushed under the weight of the law courts is the Conciergerie, a fairy-tale castle that combines nineteenth-century fake with genuine fourteenth-century Gothic, especially in the Salle des Gardes, the Salle des Gens d'Armes, and the vast adjoining kitchen. In fact, the era that lingers in the public memory is neither of these centuries but the Revolution, which is also the overwhelming focus of the current museum. The list of people imprisoned here while awaiting the guillotine reads like a biographical index of the period. The vaguely anti-Jacobin exhibition includes reconstructions of different types of cells ranked according to the class of prisoner. Even revolutionaries thought it perfectly natural to put rich prisoners in private beds and the rest on piles of straw. There is also a *salle de toilette*, where prisoners' hair was trimmed so that it did not obstruct the guillotine.

Women, for whom a reactionary Church was often the only possible ally, were especially active in fostering the nineteenth-century cult of martyrs of the Revolution. It was Empress Eugénie who reconstructed the chapel where the Girondin(e)s spent their last night, and commissioned the nineteenth-century paintings of their last hours. Marie-Antoinette is remembered in two places: in the expiatory chapel decorated with paintings of her last communion and Bible reading, painted just after the fall of Napoleon; and in a reconstruction of her cell containing objects said to have belonged to her.

MARIE-ANTOINETTE (1755–93)

Queen Marie-Antoinette, "l'Autrichienne" (the Austrian woman), remains one of the most celebrated figures in France's history. Attached to her fame are the climactic years of the *ancien régime*, with their mindless extravagance and luxury, her stubborn resistance to change and, finally, the brutal fall of that regime with the French Revolution.

Marie-Antoinette spent her childhood at the Court of her father, the Emperor of Austria, who used her to serve the political ends of his dynasty by marrying her off to the French Dauphin, the future Louis XVI, in 1774. The initial welcome which her grace and beauty attracted at the French Court was short-lived. The young Queen's thriftless and frivolous behavior in times of national economic hardship soon antagonized a significant portion of the Court and also discredited her with the people at large, who accused her of serving the interests of Austria – hence her nickname.

On the eve of the Revolution she staunchly rejected the progressive ideas of the Enlightenment, schemed against all reforms initiated by the King's own ministers, opposed any notion of a constitutional monarchy, and put all her hopes in the intervention of foreign armies. On hearing from an attendant that the people had no bread, she is said to have uttered the famous retort: "*Qu'ils mangent de la brioche!*" (Let them eat cake!), thus effectively signing her own death warrant.

When the Reign of Terror came, she was locked up in a dungeon with her children, then transferred to the Conciergerie before being condemned to death by Revolutionary Tribunal and finally beheaded on October 16, 1793.

Before leaving the island, take time to visit the Flower Market at the entrance to the Metro – a delightful leafy oasis in the middle of all the rather severe imposing buildings.

ÎLE ST-LOUIS

The hospital, law courts, headquarters of the Paris Police, and above all the mass-market tourism surrounding Notre-Dame, have conspired to make the Île de la Cité a place where everyone passes through and nobody lingers. The neighboring Île St-Louis is just the opposite. Narrow streets keep coaches out, and high prices limit the number of tourists (and Parisians) who feel comfortable here. But it's easy to see why millionaires are willing to pay exorbitant prices for a property on the island. Quite apart from the thrill of having the Seine as your private moat, this is one of the few examples in Paris of a homogeneous period style. The harmony of the façades and the regular grid system on which the streets were planned bear witness to the rapid construction of most of the island, which was undeveloped until a bridge was built to the mainland in 1614, and has had only one new street added since the eighteenth century. The island's population has undergone a lot of changes: *nouveaux riches* soon succeeded the original artisans, but in the nineteenth century poets like Baudelaire and Théophile Gautier turned it into a center for hashish consumption and literary production – hard to imagine once you've seen the current rash of irreproachably respectable tea-rooms. Some of their names are cringingly fastidious, and the atmosphere tends to be a bit stuffy (or "cozy," an English word the French are fond of), but they all sell the delicious local *glaces de la Maison Berthillon* of well-deserved fame.

Rue St-Louis-en-Île, which runs down the middle of the island, is the liveliest and most commercial street, and everything you will find in the shops, from rare varieties of tea to marbled-paper address books, is sure to be painstakingly packaged and displayed.

THE QUAIS

In contrast the *quais* bordering the Island house the grandest *hôtels particuliers*, large town houses designed for a single family (often parvenus who could not break into the exclusive Marais) and at dusk, when the light reflects off the water through the trees, they're surprisingly romantic. All the façades are interesting, and most bear a plaque. Worth singling out is the Hôtel de Lauzun (17 quai d'Anjou; tel. 48 87 24 14. Open April–October Saturday and Sunday 10 a.m.–5:40 p.m.) built by the King's architect, Le Vau, who was responsible for the transformation of Versailles. The house was bought in 1682 by the Duc de Lauzun, a favorite of Louis XIV until he secretly married Mademoiselle de Montpensier. This is one of the few seventeenth-century residences in Paris to have preserved its original interior: the exuberantly carved wood and painted ceilings contrast sharply with the simplicity of the exterior. Most of the ceilings are attributed to Michel Dorigny, with paintings by Le Brun and Le Seur. The staircase, reconstructed in 1949, is decorated with a tapestry depicting the Labors of Hercules. The main room on the first floor is filled with Louis XIV and Napoleon III furniture, and retains the original chimneypiece. On the second floor is a portrait of Mademoiselle de Montpensier, previous mistress of the house, and a music room in the first room installed in the nineteenth century, when the gallery was added.

Other former residents have been equally interesting. From 1899 to 1913 Camille Claudel had her studio in an elegant seventeenth-century building at 19 quai de Bourbon. A century or so earlier, the Marquise de Lambert, a champion of girls' education and the hostess of an influential *salon*, lived at 27 quai d'Anjou. Lower down the social scale, washerwomen rented space on barges anchored at the quai Bourbon, using the river water to rinse the clothes; the last barge was destroyed in 1942. Take a look at the eighteenth-century sign on Le Franc-Pinot, at number 1: it was already a restaurant during the Revolution, but the plaque declaring it to be the home of Cécile Renault, guillotined for her unsuccessful attempt on Robespierre's life, is wrong. (Her real house, on the Île de la Cité, was one of the many torn down by Haussmann.)

MADEMOISELLE DE MONTPENSIER (1627–93)

One of the richest women in Europe, Mademoiselle de Montpensier, daughter of the royal Gaston of Orléans, made a name for herself as *La Grande Mademoiselle* during the Fronde, the conflict that pitched the Paris Parliament and the higher aristocracy into battle against the monarchy under the government of Cardinal Mazarin (1648–52).

She was Louis XIII's niece, and her status and ambition drove her to seek marriage into royalty. Having set her sights on virtually every available European monarch, she refused the hand of the Prince of Wales in 1646 and threw herself into the Fronde, on the side of the rebels. On horseback, she led the rebel Prince's army as it conquered Orléans before marching towards Paris, where she was popular and admired.

But the rebellion failed, and Cardinal Mazarin's victory drove Mademoiselle de Montpensier into exile until 1657. The passions of love succeeded political passions and twelve years later, at the age of forty-two, she fell in love with and secretly married the Duc de Lauzun. This liaison, however, was swiftly opposed by Louis XIV, who threw Lauzun into prison. He was freed in 1682, but the marriage did not last and Montpensier became absorbed in religious devotion. Her memoirs cover more than fifty years of her life and their witty style, together with their clearsightedness, testify to the intelligence and originality of the woman who richly deserved her title, *La Grande Demoiselle*.

On the quai d'Orléans, at numbers 18 and 20, is the beautiful Hôtel Rolland, built in 1639; and at number 6 vestiges of a once thriving Polish community linger; the library founded in 1838 by the exiled Polish Prince Adam Czartoryski is now the new Musée Adam Mickiewicz (6 quai d'Anjou; tel. 43 54 35 61; open Thursday only: 3–6 p.m.). The museum focuses on this Romantic poet who corresponded with George Sand (who had an affair – and a miserable sojourn on Majorca – with Polish expatriate Chopin), among others. Several of her letters are here, as well as assorted mementoes connected with Polish Romantics in Paris. In the Hôtel Lambert the same prince also created a Polish literary circle and center for refugee Polish intellectuals. Princess Anna Czartoryska founded the Polish Women's Relief Committee, which raised money through charity events. In 1845 an Institute for young Polish girls to teach them the language and literature of their motherland was established. There is also a Polish bookshop at number 10.

A clock jutting out from the wall points the way to the church of St-Louis-en-l'Île, whose interior is one of the best surviving examples of Baroque religious architecture in Paris. The rich collection of sixteenth- and seventeenth-century European art and twelfth-century tapestries fittingly reflects the affluence of the *quartier*.

While you're on the island wander down the quai de Béthune, where virtually every house is the work of Le Vau, seventeenth-century France's leading Baroque architect, or members of his family. Cardinal Richelieu lived at numbers 16 and 18 from 1729 to 1791, Baudelaire lived at number 22 in 1842 while attending soirées in the Hôtel Lauzun. More recently, in 1935, Helena Rubinstein had a house built at number 24 on the site of the former Hôtel Hesselin; the only remaining vestige of Le Vau's original building is the doorway. President George Pompidou died here in 1974.

AROUND CHÂTELET

Once you've left the Île St-Louis and crossed the *Pont Marie* over on to the Right Bank, you can wander down the *quai* towards Hôtel de Ville and Châtelet, pausing to squint in at the steamed-up windows of small crowded cafés and looking back across the river to the two islands you have left behind.

HÔTEL DE VILLE
Place de l'Hôtel de Ville, 75004. Metro Hôtel de Ville.
Tel. 42 76 59 37. Visits in French every Monday 10:30 a.m.

Rebuilt in 1874 after the supporters of Paris's short-lived Commune burnt it down in 1871, this Neo-Renaissance building is highly decorated and festooned with female statues of French towns and male statues of French citizens. A town hall has stood at this site since the thirteenth century, and it's always been a despised symbol of the power of Paris against the rest of the country: it was here, for instance, that Etienne Marcel urged peasants to rise up against the Crown in 1357.

Théâtre de la Ville and Tour Saint-Jacques

Continue your wander down the *quai,* and you will come to busy place du Châtelet, home to the Théâtre de la Ville, originally owned and run by the actress Sarah Bernhardt, whose dressing room you can visit by phoning in advance (tel. 42 74 22 77).

To the east of place du Châtelet, a grimy tower pokes into the air – Tour Saint-Jacques, a disembodied belfry, is all that remains of the sixteenth-century church, Saint-Jacques-de-la-Boucherie, that stood on this spot. The Revolutionaries manufactured bullets inside the belfry after the Revolution had destroyed the church itself.

A few steps across busy rue de Rivoli take you to the heavily commercialized area known as Beaubourg–Les Halles, home of the city's largest modern shopping complex – on four levels underground – and the famous tubular Pompidou Center, often referred to simply as Beaubourg.

SARAH BERNHARDT (1844–1923)

Sarah Bernhardt, born Rosine Bernard, Germanized her surname and adopted a new first name before setting foot on the stage and becoming one of France's legendary theatrical stars.

A tall, slim woman with long dark hair and brilliant blue eyes, she first caught the attention of the public in 1869 playing a man's role in François Coppée's *Le Passant.* Bernhardt was one of the first actresses to move away from the wooden performances characteristic of the time. She clearly succeeded, for it is said that no one died on stage more convincingly – so much so that more sensitive members of the audience would sometimes faint at such a realistic portrayal of death. Through her professionalism she managed to separate the profession of actress from its dubious reputation but, like all stars, she was not without her caprices: she had public affairs, and liked to sleep in a satin-lined coffin.

By 1880 she was touring worldwide and was regarded as one of the most famous Frenchwomen of her time. Her dazzling career continued unabated to the end – all the more surprising given that in 1915 she had a leg amputated owing to a wound that had been troubling her for many years. Refusing to let this impede her work, she continued to act, either seated or reclining; indeed, she performed in Turin only four months before her death in 1923 at the age of seventy-nine.

A statue of Sarah Bernhardt in Racine's play Phèdre was erected in place Malesherbes, in the seventeenth *arrondissement,* in 1926; in 1945 she became the second woman after Marie Curie to be featured on a postage stamp.

THE HISTORIC CENTER

BEAUBOURG–LES HALLES

Approached on foot, this area can be quite confusing to navigate. Despite the fact that the Forum and the Pompidou Center are virtually cheek by jowl, it is relatively easy to lose one or the other, and the abundance of single men eager for an instant "English lesson" means standing on a corner with map unfurled is best avoided.

Arriving by Metro does not help matters. Although entrances lead out of the station (Metro Châtelet–Les Halles) on every side of the Forum except rue de Viarmes, finding them is not easy. To make matters worse, there's a separate RER (suburban train) station called Les Halles. Your best plan from here is to keep an eye out for the bright orange maps posted at various points, and take any escalator leading down below ground level. Although most of the basement is taken up by shops, the inside is better labeled than the streets.

THE FORUM DES HALLES

The Forum des Halles occupies the site of what was once the capital's central fruit and vegetable market, on the lines of London's old Covent Garden. Les Halles had operated throughout eight centuries before being exiled to the suburbs in the 1960s. Under the *ancien régime* market women had special rights; in times of famine their protests were tolerated, even expected. It was a procession of market women from Les Halles who began the Revolution by marching to Versailles to force the royal family back to virtual imprisonment in Paris. Nineteenth-century historians claimed that they must have been men in drag. More recently, Les Halles became synonymous with decadence; after a night on the town it was *de rigueur* to stop for coffee near the market at the crack of dawn before going to sleep, just as the workers were beginning their day. This is still the place for all-night restaurants where you can grab a bowl of onion soup before staggering to bed after a long night's clubbing.

For years the gaping hole left by the market's demolition provoked furious arguments among different lobbies, each with its own ideas of what central Paris needed most. The fact that a shopping complex won the day would have been absurd had it not been linked to the creation of a suburban train system, the lines of which cross in Les Halles. The RER filled a desperate need; a million people pass through this station every day and comments such as one architect's complaint that Les Halles "isn't Paris, it's the suburbs" are merely insensitive to the experience of exhausted commuters for whom convenience counts more than charm.

For visitors, the Forum offers some of the best people-watching in Paris, especially if you want a window on ordinary French life and consumer habits. On the other hand, those who condemn it as one big cash register have a definite point. All the main Paris chain stores are represented, as well as countless shops of varying quality that stock everything from refrigerators, to earrings, Opéra tickets or the complete works of Molière.

The gardens, like the building itself, look flimsy and cheap, and some of the cultural attractions meant to gloss over the commercialism – a "House of Poetry", *vidéotheque, discothèque* library, holography museum, swimming pool, exhibition spaces and workshops for "cultural expression" – are, to say the least, gimmicky. As a result, they are usually less crowded than the rougher-edged, more spontaneous street performances outside. The animated clock that is the pride of the newly built complex of low-income housing between rues Rambuteau, Saint-Martin, Beaubourg, and Grenier Saint-Lazare is worth a visit, especially if you have children in tow.

Saint-Eustache
2 rue du Jour, 75001. Metro Les Halles.
Tel. 42 36 31 05.
Open daily 8:30 a.m.– 7 p.m.

Somewhat incongruously juxtaposed to the brash concrete, glass and steel of the Forum is the Church of Saint-Eustache, rising majestically ahead as you emerge by escalator from the Forum's Porte Saint-Eustache. This massive construction, complete with flying buttresses and Gothic doorways, was built between 1532 and 1637. Inside, the chancel has an impressive multicolored nineteenth-century marble floor, and eleven stunning stained-glass windows executed in 1631 by Antoine Soulignac. As you wander around you'll discover a wealth of seventeenth-century paintings, sculptures and frescoes, but perhaps one of the most fascinating features of this church is its historical associations. It was here that Molière was baptized in 1622, as was the future Madame de Pompadour in 1721, and Louis XIV took his first communion. This was also the scene of many celebrated funerals: an illustrious list of poets, painters and composers as well as Diderot's mistress, Sophie Volland, and Mozart's mother. Saint-Eustache has always had a musical connection. Berlioz's *Te Deum* was performed here for the first time, and the choir of Saint-Eustache give an excellent sung mass every Sunday at 11 a.m.

Fontaine des Innocents
Diagonally opposite the church, on the other side of the Forum in the southeastern corner, the Renaissance Fontaine des Innocents is now the center of a lively café-lined square where young people hang out day and night. The pretty Renaissance fountain is the

only one left in Paris. The work of the architect and sculptor Jean Goujon, it originally stood on the corner of rue Saint-Denis and rue Berger; then it had only three sides. The fourth, indistinguishable from the rest, was added in 1788 when it was transported to its present location.

The big round domed building at the west end of the park of Les Halles – formerly the Halle au Blé, or Corn Exchange – now houses the Bourse au Commerce, or Commodities Exchange – not to be confused with the Stock Exchange near Palais-Royal, where there is plenty of *blé* – French slang for money– around.

To the north of Saint-Eustache, rue du Faubourg Montmartre is packed with bustling food shops, and rue du Faubourg Montorgeuil hosts one of the city's most colorful produce markets, a welcome contrast to the rather soulless Forum. Nearby, music blasts from the clothes stores lining rue Saint-Denis, running all the way up from place du Châtelet to boulevard Saint-Denis. Rue Saint-Denis – one of the oldest in Paris – is best known as a street of ill repute, where 80 percent of Paris prostitutes ply their trade: as you head north the jeans shops trail away, to be replaced by X-rated cinemas which, in turn, give way to women standing in doorways. The Halles end, usually thronging with tourists, feels perfectly safe, but wandering alone farther up, especially at night, is not recommended.

AROUND THE POMPIDOU CENTER

On the other side of boulevard Sebastopol, halfway between the modern, middlebrow Forum and historic yuppified Marais, the streets surrounding the Center Pompidou are pleasantly schizophrenic. Rue Saint-Merri is full of crêpe and frites (french-fries) stands, and attracts the spillover of street entertainers from place Georges Pompidou, the cobblestoned square that slopes gently down towards the great museum. Towards Hôtel de Ville, place Igor Stravinsky, bordered on one side by the church of Saint-Merri, is dominated by a riot of brightly colored sculptures in the midst of which stands a fantastic Tinguely fountain. You'll also find a few tearooms and stores full of vaguely arty, impeccably tasteful but totally useless objects. Café Costes, with its designer chairs, is trying – fairly successfully – to attract movers and shakers in the art world, and good bookstores like the Bibliothèque du 20ᵉ Siècle and Banque de l'Image are scattered among the shops offering fanny packs and American brownies. Ultimately, though, you are bound to be drawn down the slope into the transparent entrails of the Richard Rogers creation.

THE POMPIDOU CENTER

Plateau Beaubourg, 75004. Metro Hôtel de Ville/Rambuteau/Les Halles. Tel. 44 78 12 33. Open 12–10 p.m. Monday, Wednesday, Thursday, Friday: 10 a.m.–10 p.m. Saturday, Sunday and holidays; closed Tuesday.

Admission tickets for all paying exhibitions, on any floor, are on sale at the central cash desk only, situated on the ground floor.

This temple to contemporary art is made entirely of glass, metal and multicolored pipes, specially color-coded so that they are easily distinguished from each other; blue for air conditioning, green for water circulation, red for transport, and yellow for electrical circuits.

Since opening in 1977, the Center has housed more than 700 exhibitions, 1000 debates and 650 concerts. It welcomes an average of 24,000 people a day, making roughly 90 million visitors in the first fifteen years. According to pre-1988 statistics, two-thirds of visitors to the museum are male, one-sixth come for the building, more than 60 percent are from in and around Paris, and a quarter come once a week – all of which goes to show that, despite the controversy that surrounded it when it was built, the museum is a huge success, nowadays attracting more than double the number of visitors who go to the Louvre.

The National Museum of Modern Art

The fourth floor of the Pompidou Center houses one of the most important permanent collections of modern and contemporary art

---

SUZANNE VALADON (1865–1938)

Suzanne Valadon, illegitimate child of a seamstress, received little academic education, working instead as an apprentice dressmaker, vegetable seller, waitress and groom. At the age of sixteen she was hired as a circus acrobat, but that career soon ended – she fell from a trapeze.

Like so many women painters, Valadon first moved into the artists' world as a model. She sat for Puvis de Chavannes, by whom she had a son, Maurice, unrecognized by his true father but later acknowledged by Miguel Utrillo, who gave him his name. (Maurice Utrillo later became famous as a painter in his own right.) She also modeled for Toulouse-Lautrec, Renoir and Degas, all of whom recognized her talent and encouraged her work. Her first exhibitions in the early 1890s consisted mainly of portraits – for example, of her lover, the composer Erik Satie.

A brief marriage to a banker ended in divorce; she returned to Montmartre to live with André Utter, one of Maurice's friends, whom she married in 1914. In later years Valadon's work became increasingly violent and personal, always with the bold colors and vivid outlines typical of the Fauvist style. With the utmost freedom of expression she painted nudes, landscapes, still lifes, flowers and portraits, and produced an abundance of work among which *Lancement de filet* and *Mère Utrillo, sa grand-mere et son chien* can be seen in the Pompidou Center.

---

in the world. Most of the 25,000 works were formerly displayed in the Palais de Tokyo; others came directly from artists' private collections. The schools represented are as follows.

Fauvism This word, derived from the French *fauve*, meaning wild animal, was coined by the art critic Vauxelles in 1905; he used it to express his disapproval at the new bold approach, especially in the use of color, which was to revolutionize the history of painting. One of the most prominent Fauvists was Suzanne Valadon. Although she painted landscapes, still lifes and portraits, she is recognized above all for her female nudes. One of the most forceful and colorful works shown here is *Adam and Eve*: the model for Adam was her second husband André Utter, twenty-one years her junior.

There are many works by Bonnard, more of which are on show in the Musée d'Orsay. Note especially *L'Atelier aux mimosas* and *Le Nu à la baignoire*. There are also some good Matisses: his expressive use of color is shown to perfection in *Le Rêve*. Speaking of his models – in this case Lydia Delectorskaya – he once said:

> My models, which I see as *human* figures, are never extras in an interior decor. They are the principal subject of my work. I absolutely depend on my model. I spend time freely observing her, and it is only after a while that I decide to fix her pose, the one which most naturally corresponds to her.

Cubist and Abstract Painting The Cubist collection starts with the *Cheval majeur*, a bronze sculpture by Duchamp-Villon which is seen as a key work for its fusion of vital and mechanical force. In the next room, Braque's *Le Géridon* and *L'Homme à la guitare,* and Picasso's *Portrait de jeune-fille*, illustrate the two different periods in Cubist painting. "When we began Cubism," writes Picasso, "we had no intention of it being Cubism. We only wanted to express ourselves." *Les Demoiselles d'Avignon* is one of the most famous Cubist paintings: it represents the first and decisive step towards the new movement.

Orphism, a style derived from Cubism, was developed in 1911 by Robert and Sonia Delaunay. Sonia played an important part in the evolution of painting, and was also instrumental in bringing about dramatic changes in the decorative arts. *Prismes électriques* is a complex series of bright colored circles reminiscent of electric light. A contemporary of the Delaunays was Natalia Goncharova who used not only painting – see, for instance, *Porteuses* – but also fashion and industrial design to express her ideas. The abstract painters Kandinsky, Klee, Brancusi and Malevich are also on show in this section. Thanks to Kandinsky's donations through his wife Nina, the Pompidou Center houses one of the most important existing collections of art that has influenced abstract painting.

SONIA DELAUNAY (1885–1979)

Born into a family of Jewish factory workers near Odessa in the Ukraine, the young Sonia Terk was educated by an uncle in Saint Petersburg. She had intended to be a mathematician, but she went to Karlsruhe in Germany in 1903 to study drawing. Two years later, at the age of twenty, she moved to Paris, where the strength and originality of her work drew the attention of Picasso, Braque and Derain. After a very brief marriage to the art critic Wilhelm Uhde, she met and married the British painter Robert Delaunay; the couple had a son in 1911.

Together the Delaunays invented the aesthetics of Orphism and Simultanism, a pictorial theory based on chromatic and formal harmonies. In addition to painting, Sonia illustrated a book, decorated pottery and designed book bindings, textiles and dresses, some of which were shown at a great Exhibition of Decorative Arts in 1925. Like her compatriot, Natalia Goncharova, she also collaborated with Diaghilev on the *Ballets Russes*.

She left Paris in 1940 for the Auvergne. A year later, after Robert's death, she moved to Grasse, and then to Toulouse. As a measure of her success, in 1964 she became the first women to have a painting exhibited in the Louvre in her lifetime. More recently, her textile work has aroused great interest and enthusiasm among both designers and the public, and in the 1980s a large exhibition was arranged at the Musée d'Art Moderne de la Ville de Paris.

Surrealism According to the Surrealists, artists must seek inspiration inside their own subconscious. As a result, objects from very different origins, sometimes unidentifiable, come together in paintings and sculptures, producing strange, often violent or erotic images, as in Dali's *Hallucination partielle*, Magritte's *Le Modèle rouge* and works by Tanguy, Ernst, Miró, Breton and Calder. Several women, such as Kay Sage, Dorothea Tanning and Leonora Carrington, took part in this movement, but none of them is exhibited here.

As in the Musée D'Orsay – though not as attractive – the museum's café is situated on this top floor, with marvelous views of Paris in every direction. Before rounding off with a browse in the Center's wonderful bookshop downstairs, French-speakers at least might be interested in two other features, the second of which should appeal to musicians.

Public Information Library This enormous library – free and open to all – contains an encyclopedic quantity of contemporary information in the form of books, images and the most advanced information technology. The only negative point is its popularity. Allow at least fifteen minutes to get in, and once you're through the doors, be patient while you're looking for somewhere to sit. Also, keep a close eye on your bags and personal belongings.

Institut de Recherche et de Coordination Acoustique/Musique Founded by composer/conductor Pierre Boulez in the mid-seventies, IRCAM is considered by its deriders to be no more than a production line for music. Its supporters would point out that the idea is to use electronic technology to explore and create new sounds, to analyze music and instruments from all over the world, creating new materials for contemporary composers to work with. In recent years the most successful young IRCAM composer has been the British George Benjamin. Concerts, workshops and seminars are open to the public, as is the musical information and documentation center on the first floor.

THE MARAIS

Though only a stone's throw away, the area known as the Marais meaning "marsh" or "swamp" has none of the brashness of Beaubourg–Les Halles. Intimate museums, important galleries, tasteful shops, cafés, restaurants, tearooms, and well-restored *hôtels particuliers* occupy most of the available space, and pleasant parks take up the rest. The architecture is usually homogeneous: little was built in this swampy area before Henri IV made it fashionable at the turn of the seventeenth century, and by a miracle Haussmann refrained from flattening it all. The area fell out of favor in the nineteenth century and artisans moved in, converting the vast spaces to workshops and the private houses to apartment buildings (as you can still see in the northern Marais, where gentrification hasn't yet taken over). When heritage-conscious Parisians undertook the res-

---

NADIA (1887–1979) AND LILI (1893–1918) BOULANGER

The Boulanger sisters have left their mark on the history of French music — not only because of their exceptional talent, but because of their creative originality and energy. Brought up in a musical family, their grandmother, a Russian princess, was a concert singer; their father was a renowned composer and violinist. The greatest musicians of their time, including Gabriel Fauré, had a share in their training; both sisters made flamboyant débuts and reaped more than their fair share of prizes. The Boulanger sisters became the talk of the town; a musical publisher offered the younger sister, Lili, a contract for her compositions, and Nadia's début as an orchestral conductor was an immediate success. But Lili's untimely death at the age of twenty-five completely upset her sister's life. She resolved to devote her life henceforth to publicizing her sister's works, gave up composition altogether, and took up conducting and teaching full time. She was the first woman ever to conduct symphony orchestras in London, New York and Boston; she also became one of the most influential teachers of her time. She was faithful not only to her sister's works but also to those of her master, Gabriel Fauré, whose *Requiem* she made known to the musical public. In addition, she also introduced her fellow musicians to a whole group of Renaissance composers, chief among whom was Monteverdi. In 1950 she became director of the American Conservatory at Fontainebleau, where her courses were attended by devoted students from all over the world, including Elliott Carter, Aaron Copland, Roy Harris, Leonard Bernstein and Igor Markevich.

cue of the Marais the old tenants were moved out and the buildings turned into museums, often, one suspects, simply as an excuse to open them to the public, as is clear from museums on subjects like hunting or locks and keys.

The Marais is bounded by rues Beaubourg and Turbigo to the west, boulevard Beaumarchais to the east, rue du Temple in the north and the Seine to the south. This area, roughly corresponding to the third and fourth *arrondissements*, is ideal for exploring on foot: you can push doors open (a silver button will normally give access to a coded door during the daytime) and admire quiet seventeenth- or eighteenth-century courtyards with fountains, statues and beautiful staircases. No one will object if you step inside what are mostly private buildings as long as you're discreet, lost in admiration, and remember to close doors behind you.

Architectural treasures apart, the Marais is also one of the liveliest and most popular parts of Paris. Day and night, it's frequented by artists, writers, the chic and the would-be chic, for whose benefit the neighborhood is crammed with shops, designer boutiques (not all of them unaffordable) and any number of places to eat and drink.

THE WORLD OF SALONS

The Marais's seventeenth-century heyday coincided with a moment when upper-class women's status was higher than ever before. The elegant *salons* (drawing rooms) you can still visit were presided over by women who made an art out of conversation; both sexes considered publication beneath them, although Madame de Sévigné agreed to circulate her letters in manuscript form. Men vied for admission to these houses, where they knew they could meet other important men, although the stream of gallant compliments which men were expected to keep up sometimes turned sour. "In Paris one can get nothing done without women," Rousseau complained. "Ladies are like curves and philosophers their straight lines: we approach them endlessly without ever touching." Molière ridiculed bluestockings and their "preciosity," which tried to rid language of vulgarity and love of sex, while debates on the finer points of vocabulary and ethics provided drawing-room conversation. Some decades later, the *salonières* who inspired his *Précieuses ridicules* were being berated by women experiencing the first glimmers of a burgeoning feminist rebellion that was to develop until the Revolution, only to be quashed in the 1800s before reviving with even greater force this century.

QUARTIER DU TEMPLE ET DES ARCHIVES

The rue du Temple is an old road that once belonged to the Knights Templars, a religious order of monks who were also knights and fought in the Crusades in the fourteenth century. Most of the many beautiful old *hôtels particuliers* here are still unrestored.

THE MARAIS & THE BASTILLE

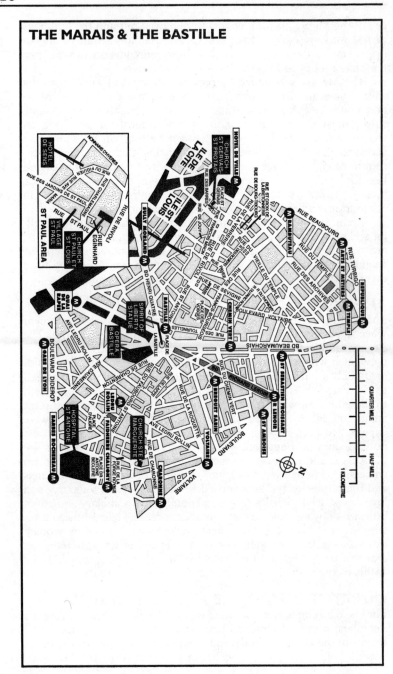

Hôtel Saint-Aignan

At number 71 is the Hôtel Saint-Aignan, one of the most singular houses of the Marais with a mask-studded gateway and *trompe l'œil* windows in the false (left) side of the courtyard. Built in 1640 by the architect Pierre Le Muet, it is now half restored though its romantic decadence almost increases its appeal.

Hôtel de Montmor

At number 79 is the Hôtel de Montmor, built in the seventeenth century by Jean Herbert de Montmor. His son, Henri-Louis de Montmor, was a friend of Madame de Sévigné and had created a sort of academy, sometimes called the Montmor academy, attended by the great doctors of the day along with Descartes, Molière, Madame de Sévigné and Gassendi. The first experiment in blood transfusion also took place in this mansion in 1666.

Hôtel de Hallwyl

At number 28 rue Michel-le-Comte, to the east of rue du Temple, this mansion was constructed in 1765 by Nicolas Ledoux, one of France's most brilliant architects, much influenced by Palladio as well as by Rousseau's philosophical ideas. Germaine Necker, the future Madame de Staël was born here in 1766.

Hôtel de Guénégaud

The Hôtel de Guénégaud – situated in rue des Archives, which runs parallel with rue du Temple, and originally built by François Mansart around 1648 – was bought by the City of Paris in a state

MADEMOISELLE DE SCUDERY (1607–1701)

Plain, poor and from the provinces, Mademoiselle de Scudéry would probably never have found the time or means to write her lengthy, popular and idealistically romantic novels, had she not been sponsored by the great seventeenth-century *salonière*, the Marquise de Rambouillet.

Having made her début as a guest at the Marquise's prestigious literary *salon* in the rue Saint-Thomas-du-Louvre, she opened her own *salon* at her home in the Marais. She gathered around her those of her bourgeois friends who shared her interest in romances and styling herself on the "illustrious Sappho," began to pen her own long, drawn-out works, less significant today for their literary content than for their sociological interest. Their characters are based on people living at the time; their dialogues and plots reflect the debates, ideals and incidents of the enclosed world of the *salons* – the *précieuses*' society. Ideal love, Scudéry believed, was sexless love – which not only freed women from the burden of pregnancy but, by making them unavailable, increased their power and moral value. "We marry," she declared, "to hate," and indeed, she never did, believing that it did nothing but provide a mutual dislike in both parties. A number of other early seventeenth-century *salonières* put the ideal into practice, dubbing themselves the "précieuses" (precious women) which not surprisingly made them the buff of many a male satirist, most significantly Molière, who lampooned them in his "précieuses ridicules."

MADAME DE SÉVIGNÉ (1626–96)

Nearly three hundred years after her death, Madame de Sévigné remains a household name in France, chiefly for the letters she wrote to her daughter, whose marriage had exiled her to a distant province.

De Sévigné's outstanding quality was an astonishing freedom of spirit. Widowed at twenty-five, she made full use of her independence through travel and a never-ending ability to observe and comment on everything around her. She showed great leniency towards her son's amorous adventures, dared to advise her granddaughter to read Corneille's plays against her confessor's counsel, and approached life in general with humorous, ironic detachment. Nothing escaped her notice; her writing describes with equally vivacious wit the pleasures of haymaking, the scandals of the Court, or her own distaste for Racine's tragedies. Still a great read, her letters are also an incomparable document – not only of aristocratic life in the seventeenth century but also of one woman's passage through it.

of near ruin. Its beautiful simplicity and harmonious proportions have been revealed by cleaning and restoration; the French garden, visible from rue des Quatre-Fils, has been similarly restored. Today it houses a museum dedicated to hunting and nature. The most schizophrenic museum in Paris, its displays celebrate hunting through the ages; yet it is always holding temporary exhibitions on the protection of nature and the environment.

Hôtel Soubise

Back down the rue Vieille-du-Temple you come to the intersection with the rue des Francs-Bourgeois. Here, at number 60, you'll find the Hôtel Soubise, today part of the city's National Archives. The doorway is all that remains of the original fourteenth-century château that stood here. Within its walls the Saint Bartholomew Massacre was planned.

Hôtel de Rohan-Strasbourg

Further to the east, back in the rue Vieille-du-Temple at number 87, stands the main home of the National Archives. This seventeenth-century hotel was built at the same time as the Hôtel de Soubise, with which it shares a garden. In the second courtyard, added later, is a famous relief by Robert le Lorrain, the *Horses of Apollo*, one of the most magnificent pieces of eighteenth-century French sculpture. Inside are painted wooden panels, a music room, and a series of tapestries by Boucher known as the Chinese suite.

Hôtel des Ambassadeurs de Hollande

Beaumarchais lived in this seventeenth-century palace at number 47 in the same street while he was writing *The Marriage of Figaro*. He also used it as an arms store, having created a company to front his undercover activities. It's not as sinister as it sounds – he was raising money and buying arms to send to Americans rebelling against their English rulers. Once òne of the most beautiful mansions in the Marais (and home, incidentally to the Dutch ambassadors' chaplain – hence the name), it has unfortunately suffered extensive damage over the last two hundred years.

AROUND SAINT-PAUL
This area, located at the southern end of rue Vieille-du-Temple, encompasses the parish of Saint-Gervais–Saint Protais, one of the oldest in Paris. Today most of what survives from the Middle Ages are the street names, though there are a couple of fourteenth-century houses in rue de la Cloche Percée, rue des Barres and rue François Miron.

Hôtel de Beauvais
Bordering the church to the north is rue François Miron; at number 68 stands the Hôtel de Beauvais, whose Gothic cellars can be visited by appointment. It was built in 1657 by Catherine Belier – lady-in-waiting to Anne of Austria (nicknamed Cathan the one-eyed) – who was reputedly the sexual initiator and first mistress of the future King Louis XIV. She managed to make a small fortune in the Queen's service, became a baroness and succeeded in marrying her daughters off to nobles. Much later, Mozart stayed here and played the harpsichord while he waited to be received at the Court of Versailles.

VILLAGE SAINT-PAUL
At the end of rue François Miron, continue eastwards down the rue de Jouy, and you'll come to the Village Saint-Paul: four roads surrounding a delightful pedestrian precinct crammed with antique and bric-a-brac shops. Four times a year the whole place transforms itself into a huge antiques market. Many of the neighboring houses have been saved from demolition and lovingly restored; you can also see some original seventeenth-century staircases and medieval cellars – notably at number 14 rue des Jardins-Saint-Paul, leading into rue Charlemagne.

ANNE OF AUSTRIA (1601–66)
The daughter of Philip III of Spain and Margaret of Austria, Anne married Louis XIII in 1615. She was a great beauty who loved to be loved. In 1643, during the social and political uprising of the Fronde, she became Regent, and wished to keep abreast of both the situation and the government. Her political inexperience led her to share her power with the Prime Minister, Cardinal Mazarin, her great favorite and perhaps secret lover. After his death she withdrew from society to dedicate herself to a life of piety. Both her heart and that of Louis XIII were placed on public display in the church of Val-de-Grâce, which had been especially built for her.

Hôtel de Sens

If you retrace your steps up the rue Charlemagne, you'll find rue du Figuier on your left and, at number 1, the Hôtel de Sens, a rare example in Paris of a nonreligious medieval building. More a castle than a mansion, it was first built in the fifteenth century and occupied by the turbulent Queen Margot (Marguerite de Valois) after her husband Henri IV had divorced her for failing to produce a male heir. Bought in a state of near-collapse by the City of Paris in 1916, it took thirty years to restore. Today it houses the Forney Library (open 1:30–8:30 p.m. Tuesday–Friday; 10 a.m.–8:30 p.m. Saturday), founded in 1886 with a legacy from a wealthy Parisian industrialist and containing over 150,000 books on arts, crafts and architecture. The Library also has an extensive collection of periodicals, museum catalogues, slides, prints, drawings, fabric samples and wallpapers.

Church of Saint-Paul and Saint-Louis

Further up, back in the rue Saint-Antoine, is the church of Saint-Paul and Saint-Louis. A Jesuit church since the sixteenth century, it was rebuilt in the seventeenth in a mixture of Italian and Flemish Baroque. The sculpted doors were a gift of Cardinal Richelieu; inside is a Delacroix painting, and a pietà sculpted by Jean Guyon. In 1792 the church was stripped of its religious art works, and the Cult of Reason was celebrated there for several years.

Hôtel de Sully

Free entry into the courtyard daily 9 a.m.–7:30 p.m.
Special permission needed to visit the inside from the Caisse Nationale des Monuments Historiques, based here.

The rue Saint-Antoine, one of the oldest streets in Paris, dates back to Roman times. This hotel, located at number 62, is one of the most beautiful mansions of the Marais. Built in the seventeenth century, it was sumptuously decorated by its owner, the Duc de Sully. Then followed a period of total neglect until after the Second World War, when it was meticulously renovated according to original plans. It's rich in ornamental and sculptural decorations in the Flemish Baroque style; the eight bas-reliefs in niches in the courtyard and garden represent the seasons and the four elements – Earth, Wind, Air and Fire – depicted as graceful young women. The interior has a beautiful staircase, decorated ceilings, painted rooms and gilded pilasters, as well as some fine paneling in the duke's bedroom, the decoration of which is attributed to his wife, Charlotte Séguier.

PLACE DES VOSGES

Just behind the Hôtel de Sully is the magnificent place des Vosges, Paris's first square – and still, to many eyes, the most beautiful. Originally named the place Royale, it was completed in 1612 on the site of the Palais de Tournelle, which was destroyed on the orders of Catherine de' Medici, who could not bear to look at it after her husband Henri II had died there.

The square, meant originally for workers, enjoyed tremendous aristocratic popularity under Henri IV and until the reign of Louis XIV, who preferred Versailles. Quite forgotten by the rich during the nineteenth century, it has once again become a chic and desirable place to live, and is the home of many famous actors and writers: the late Delphine Seyrig lived here. In the middle of the main reddish-pink brick and stone quadrilateral, encircled by 36 houses, is a smaller square, rebuilt in the last century and surrounded by arcades of upscale shops, art galleries, cafés and restaurants where Parisians sit out on warm summer evenings, often besieged by street musicians.

Illustrious women residents have included Madame de Sévigné, born at number 1, the actress Rachel and the famous seventeenth-century courtesan Marion Delorme, who lived at number 11 in the Hôtel de Loménie de Brienne. number 6 – now the Victor Hugo Museum – was home to the poet and writer between 1832 and 1848.

Perhaps restored by a cup of coffee on the place des Vosges, it's time to visit one of the Marais's greatest jewels, the Musée Carnavalet, all too often skipped by tourists exhausted by the Louvre.

MUSÉE CARNAVALET

23 rue de Sévigné, 75004. Metro Saint-Paul. Tel. 42 72 21 13.
Open 10 a.m.–5:40 p.m. daily; closed Monday and public holidays.
Some rooms are closed 12:30–2 p.m. Notices are in French only,
but English guidebooks are on sale.

Housed in the hotel of the same name, this is the most Parisian of all the city's museums. Its rich collections on the history of the capital are interesting in themselves, and the rooms devoted to urban planning add to the interest of walking around present-day Paris.

The building, worth a visit in itself, was begun in 1548 and enlarged a century later. It has passed through the hands of several women, among them Françoise de Kernevenoch, a widow whose

DELPHINE SEYRIG (1932–90)

Much loved film star Delphine Seyrig was equally at home playing ordinary women or stunning *femmes fatales*, working with such famous directors as François Truffaut, Joseph Losey and Luis Buñuel. She was also a committed feminist and in 1973 was among the 343 women who signed a petition admitting publicly to having had an abortion, a criminal offense at the time. Eleven years later, with two others, she founded the Simone de Beauvoir audiovisual center, a library of audiovisual works by and about women, originally housed in the Palais de Tokyo.

refusal to remarry provoked much comment; Mademoiselle de Lillebonne, a princess whose husband's debts forced her to rent the house and live with her daughter in relative poverty; and, from 1677 to 1696, her tenant, Madame de Sévigné. Sévigné's famous correspondence with her married daughter includes detailed deliberations about how to arrange the rooms, and how much money to spend on their decoration. She was one of the first women to be considered a major writer, mostly because her gossipy and spontaneous epistolary form appeared to her male contemporaries appropriately feminine, and didn't threaten their monopoly on "real" literature. The success of her letter collection was unusual in a time when correspondence was often published, but women's letters were considered good reading only when they were addressed to male lovers; Sévigné, by contrast, invented a language for maternal affection. In Room 10 you can see both correspondents' portraits, the mother's writing desk, and the marriage contract that took the daughter away from Paris and forced the women to communicate by letter.

The Exhibits   There are more than 500,000 exhibits, arranged on two floors. The rooms devoted to prehistoric, Roman, and medieval Paris have more scale models and line drawings than actual artifacts; a few of the maps can help you to understand the layout of Paris today, but after the Renaissance the collections become more interesting. Rooms 16–23 and 30–60 are re-creations of period rooms, often reassembled from buildings whose woodwork was saved when they were demolished to make way for Haussmann's new constructions. Images of or by women are rare: exceptions include portraits of Mary Stuart and Catherine de' Medici (Rooms 7 and 8), a statue of Adelaide of Savoy as Diana (Room 11), and Catherine Lusurier's portrait of the philosopher d'Alembert (Room 48), but the porcelain figurines representing the cries of Paris (Room 39) remind one of the omnipresence of women on the streets.

In the rich and well-documented section devoted to the Revolution, a fan showing the meeting of the Estates-General, and a dressing table inlaid with Phrygian caps (Room 108), bring home how deeply politics permeated the daily life of all social classes. Room 102 contains souvenirs supposedly carved out of the stones of the Bastille; Rooms 105–106 are devoted to religiously preserved royalist relics, such as a ring intertwining the hair of Marie-Antoinette and her supposed lover, the Princesse de Lamballe, her son's handwriting exercises, and the miniature spinning wheel that she kept with her in prison as a sign of housewifely virtue. This appeal to bourgeois values was worse than useless: when she tried to be modest she was accused of being secretive; when she fled the company of men she was accused of lesbianism, and her declarations of mother love were misinterpreted as evidence of incest. One engraving shows her in court denying the charge ("Nature forbids a mother even to answer such an accusation"), while the painting next to it depicts her crying as her son is taken away to save him from "moral and physical degeneration."

A poster of the Rights of Man is displayed in Room 104; the *Declaration of the Rights of Woman* by the playwright Olympe de Gouges is not. The portrait in Room 108 of Mademoiselle Maillard, who played the goddess Reason in one of the elaborate festivals that the Revolution invented, is a reminder that artists used feminine figures more often to personify concepts than to portray individual women. When they do appear, it is usually to provide a contrast to their husband's virility: an engraving in Room 110 shows a wife protesting a volunteer's departure to war, and in Room 112 a wife is depicted laughing at her husband for wearing revolutionary costume. There are also naïve cutouts in this room showing men jeering at a woman wearing fine clothes, but this is counterbalanced by another image of the girl marrying her wounded fiancé, and suppliant girls preventing counter-revolutionaries from chopping down a liberty tree by prayers and tears.

The depiction of a Patriotic Women's Club shows women discussing the decisions of the National Convention – a reminder that they were capable of more than tears!

In the First Empire (Room 115) portraits of women become more common, but their subjects are as decorative as the paintings: witness the hostess Madame Récamier in an often-reproduced portrait by Gérard; Madame Hamelin, mistress of Napoleon and later Chateaubriand; the actress Mademoiselle Duchenois; and Boilly's engraving of prostitutes at work in the Palais-Royal. In Room 120 the Duchesse of Orléans, is immortalized in a charitable visit to an infant school; she was setting an example for the thousands of upper-class women who turned to philanthropy to fill their empty hours.

AROUND THE RUE DES FRANCS BOURGEOIS

Before you turn towards the Picasso Museum, there's at least one more hotel worth visiting, at 24 rue Pavée.

Hôtel de Lamoignan

This large, beautiful sixteenth-century building is one of the oldest remaining palaces of the Marais. Built in 1584 by Diane de France, it was embellished by her nephew Charles de Valois, illegitimate son of Charles IX and Marie Tronchet, who spent most of her life in the Marais. The hotel now houses the Bibliothèque Historique de la Ville de Paris (open daily 9:30 a.m.–6 p.m.; closed public holidays), with more than a million books and manuscripts on the history of Paris. The great hall on the ground floor is a reading room with a beautiful sixteenth-century painted ceiling.

The Marais is particularly rich in places to eat and drink in at any time of the day. There's a good selection of tea-shops where you can sink into a big comfortable armchair while your teeth sink into a succulent piece of tart. Le Loir dans la Théière in rue des Rosiers is particularly recommended, or you could try Paris's finest tea merchants, Mariage Frères, where you can sample different blends on the premises. For something more substantial Le Gamin de Paris, on rue Vieille-du-Temple, serves traditional French cuisine, and L'Auberge de Jarente in rue de Jarente specializes in regional cooking from southwest France. Rue des Rosiers in the heart of the Jewish Quarter is also famous for its Jewish cooking – or you could buy some of the best falafel and chopped liver in Paris from one of the many local delicatessens.

OLYMPE DE GOUGES (1748–93)

"O man, are you capable of justice? By what sovereign right do you oppress my sex? ... The sex superior in beauty as in its courage in the course of maternal suffering recognizes and declares in the presence of the Supreme Being the Following Rights of Women and the female citizen." So began the *Declaration of the Rights of Woman*, which established Olympe de Gouges as a passionate feminist, well ahead of her time.

She was born in Montauban; at the age of fifteen she married an army officer whose early death gave her the chance to head for Paris where, driven by ambition, she began to write – mainly plays. Despite all her efforts, only one work, a play about slavery entitled *L'Esclavage des Noirs*, ever reached the stage of the Comédie Française. In 1791, in response to the *Declaration of the Rights of Man*, she drafted her own *Declaration* in favor of equality between the sexes, causing a public scandal. Politically, Olympe de Gouges was a staunch Republican until the horrors of revolutionary Terror persuaded her to switch allegiances and defend the King. Having devoted the last shreds of her wealth to the printing of placards against Robespierre and Marat, she was duly imprisoned and guillotined in 1793.

Like so many of her contemporaries, this courageous and original woman fell victim to the very Revolution that ought to have implemented the rights for which she fought until her death. While the Revolution had tended to reduce the independence of upper-class ladies – they were told to stay home and nurse their children instead of using their charms to machinate behind the scenes – it had offered ordinary Parisian women a tantalizing glimpse of political participation. Women's activism posed such a threat that in 1795 the revolutionary government forbade any assembly of more than five women. Child rearing often disqualified women from political ambitions even when the government did not step in: the majority of militants were either under thirty or over fifty. In an image entitled *Divorce*, a judge holds up a child to persuade its parents to repent of their desire for a divorce: the Revolution had legalized separation and remarriage in an initial fit of enthusiasm for individual freedom, but by the time of the Terror the idea that a woman's place was in the home had returned more strongly than ever, and Jacobins distrusted women who aspired to being anything more than "good mothers and good daughters, sisters taking good care of their younger brothers."

Having taken your pick, you can wander past yet more undiscovered hotels on rue Payenne and rue du Parc before arriving at your last important landmark.

THE PICASSO MUSEUM

Hôtel Salé, 5 rue de Thorigny, 75003. Metro Saint-Sébastien.
Froissart/Saint-Paul. Tel. 42 71 25 21.
Open 10 a.m.–5:45 p.m.; closed Tuesday.

When Picasso died in 1973, the government was given an enormous collection of his works by his family, and the immediate question was where to display them. Eventually the Hôtel Salé was proposed, a beautiful empty mansion named after the collector of salt taxes who had built it in 1656. As usual in Paris, there were strong reactions: for some, the project was too audacious, while others didn't like the idea of a Louis XIV-style house to exhibit paintings by Picasso. However, the architect Roland Simounet took up the challenge and succeeded in transforming the Hôtel Salé into a very attractive museum.

Since 1978, 203 paintings, 158 sculptures, 83 ceramics, 16 collages and more than 3000 drawings and etchings have been on display in this sumptuous building. When you go inside, you will find yourself automatically drawn up the massive staircase to the first floor. From this starting point the collections are displayed in chronological order over 20 rooms, taking you down a gently sloping corridor to the sculpture garden and basement before returning to the ground floor, where the artist's last works are displayed.

MARIE TRONCHET (1549–1638)

Charles IX and Marie Tronchet met and fell in love in 1566, when he was sixteen and she seventeen. Despite the fact that Marie was not of noble birth, Charles's mother, the formidable Catherine de' Medici, encouraged the liaison to distract her son so that she could cling to power longer.

Charles brought Marie to Paris and installed her near the Louvre. She bore him two sons, one of whom died. The other became the Duc d'Angoulême; he inherited a Marais hotel in the rue Pavée from his aunt, Diane de France. In 1573 Marie gave the King a daughter.

Marie was resigned to the inevitability of Charles's formal marriage to the German Elizabeth, daughter of Emperor Maximilian. He also had several other mistresses, but it seems that he kept a special place in his heart for his first great love who, despite her unenviable position, was described as lively and gentle, with a delightful round smiling face. Driven mad by his hatred for his mother and her oppressive hold over him, the King eventually withdrew to Vincennes. Marie stayed by his bedside until he died in 1574. Encouraged by Catherine de' Medici, she went on to marry François d'Entragues, Governor of Orléans, by whom she had two daughters.

There is no recommended order in which to visit the Picasso Museum; everyone should feel free to discover its riches in their own way – perhaps by theme, for example.

Picasso and Women Women were very important to Picasso. He had many affairs and was married seven times. He invented a different "language" for every woman he loved, so that he could reflect her personality. Thus, the pale blues and blacks of his *Portrait de Marie-Thérèse* (Room 13) are in total contrast to the warm colors of his *Portrait de Dora Maar*. It was Dora Maar (Picasso's companion from 1936 to 1945) who pointed out to the artist's biographer, John Richardson, how much the artist's life changed with the influence of his women, even to the extent of transforming his circle of friends.

Picasso expressed his love through his painting – and sometimes even through the writing on his paintings, as in *J'aime Eva*. But as Richardson writes, this kind of tenderness was often replaced by hostility:

> Picasso's typically Andalusian upbringing at the hands of a doting mother and grandmother abetted by two doting maternal aunts, a succession of doting maids ... is in keeping with his subsequent alternations between misogyny and tenderness on the one hand, his affectionate though sometimes heartless manipulation on the other. Machismo, we would do well to remember, is a concept specifically associated with Andalusia; it is not surprising to find women bringing it out in the adult Picasso. It was the only possible attitude for an artist, he once said, when challenged. As an artist and an Andalusian, he felt entitled to have women cater to his deepest psychic needs as well as his childish caprices.

In *Le Grand Nu au fauteuil rouge* (Room 7) Picasso displays emotions he experienced during the deterioration of his relationship with Olga Koklova. He uses very bright colors to emphasize the feeling of chaos – it's as if he wanted to destroy the image of woman by refusing to represent the natural harmony of her body. This picture, far removed from our traditional concept of nude painting, was probably influenced by Surrealism, even though Picasso never liked to be identified with any particular movement. *Le Baiser* (Room 7) is from the same tumultuous period.

Les Femmes à la toilette (Room 12) is a gigantic collage where Picasso has summed up his art, covering all his different periods, especially Cubism. Look out, too, for the three versions of Manet's controversial *Déjeuner sur l'herbe* which Picasso did while living in Vallauris, as part of an exercise in studying masterpieces in order to reproduce them in his own individual style.

Picasso and Children Picasso had a lot of respect for children and their drawings, all too often dismissed by adults as "scribblings:" "When I was their age, I drew like Raphael. It took me a whole life to learn how to draw like them."

Just as children express themselves spontaneously, he wanted to paint what he felt, even if it wasn't exactly what other people saw. As a child himself, Picasso was far too talented to compete with others his own age. In *La Fillette aux pieds nus* (Room 1), painted when he was fourteen, he managed to represent the little girl's sadness not only in her face, but in her clothes and in the painting's dull-colored background. Not surprisingly, it was considered ineligible for any children's competitions.

Picasso painted children throughout his life. The "Blue Period" of his early twenties inspired some particularly sad and moving portraits, among them *L'Autoportrait* in Room 1. In 1906, aged twenty-five, he moved from Paris to Gosol in Spain. Strongly influenced by the sun and the arid ground, he changed his style and his way of painting children. Gone were the cold, ice-blue tones and sad faces in favor of red, ochre and orange, as in *Les Deux Frères* (Room 2).

Fascinated by the circus and bullfighting, Picasso often dressed his own children in clown or harlequin outfits – see, for instance, *Paulo en Arlequin* and *Paulo en Pierrot* (Room 6). Later, deeply affected by the outbreak of the Spanish Civil War in 1936, the artist's style of painting children changed yet again, as in the popular work, *l'Enfant aux colombes* (Room 15), where the child symbolizes hope and courage – the white dove represents peace. *Le Jeune Garçon à la Langouste* and *Le Chat* were also influenced by the war.

The Artist and his Friends Part of Picasso's own private collection is also on show at L'Hôtel Salé, including the work of great painters like Chardin, Cézanne, Braque, Renoir, Matisse and Derain (see *Donation Picasso* in Room 5 and on the second Floor).

LA BASTILLE

The eastern Marais is bordered by boulevard Bourdon, which runs up to the Bastille. On the other side of the boulevard lies a stretch of water known as the Port de l'Arsenal. This is the beginning of the canal, which – after disappearing underground at the place de la Bastille – re-emerges as the Canal Saint-Martin to run all the way to the Bassin de la Villette in the nineteenth *arrondissement*.

The approach from the Marais, down boulevard Bourdon, rue Saint-Antoine or boulevard Henri IV, brings you straight into the big oval square known as place de la Bastille. Whether it's the gilding on the famous central "Spirit of Liberty" column or the sight of the impressive new opera house, the whole area has an overwhelming feeling of affluence, but with none of the stuffiness of the sixteenth. The streets around the square are packed with bars, movie theaters and restaurants, making this one of the liveliest parts of Paris for a night on the town.

PLACE DE LA BASTILLE

The place de La Bastille was, of course, the scene of one of the most significant events of the French Revolution, for it was here, on July 14, 1789, that the French people stormed the Bastille, that fortress-like prison that symbolized the unquestionable power of the monarchy, and used to stand on this site.

One of the leaders of the uprising was Théroigne de Méricourt, whose dramatic impact is described by the poet Lamartine in his *Histoire des Girondins*:

> From the first moment of the uprising, she descended into the streets. Her beauty was like a banner to the multitude. Dressed in a blood-red riding habit, her saber by her side, two pistols at her waist, she flew to the forefront of the fray. She was in the vanguard of those who forced the gates of the Tuileries and carried off the cannon, first too in the assault which scaled the towers of the Bastille. The visitors ordered her a sword of honor in the breach.

The storming of the prison was largely a symbolic gesture, since it had barely been used in recent years and there were only seven prisoners to liberate at the fall of the Bastille. Nevertheless, the event was seen as a key triumph of the people over regal oppression and, as such, the day is celebrated each year with nationalistic pride. The central column, topped by the much-loved "Spirit of Liberty" – regilded in bicentennial fervor – was erected in 1833 to commemorate the victims of the July 1830 Revolution.

Opéra Bastille
Place de la Bastille, 75012. Metro Bastille. Tel. 44 73 13 00.

Yet another of Mitterrand's bicentennial extravagances, the new opera house on the place de la Bastille was built with a view to bringing opera to the masses, and opened in 1989. It is hard to see how its purpose has been achieved – seats are hard to obtain and by no means cheap. But politics aside, this is a very impressive building. The acoustics are state-of-the-art – even the absorption of sound by the audience's clothing has been taken into account – and every seat gives an uninterrupted view of the stage. The main auditorium seats 2700; a second auditorium, studio and amphitheater can accommodate as many again not to mention the workshops, rehearsal rooms, library, video and record library. The stage is surrounded by five other areas of exactly the same dimensions to allow fast scene changes, while the scenery is stored six floors down. At

THÉROIGNE DE MÉRICOURT (1762–1817)

Théroigne de Méricourt is one of the most interesting figures of the French Revolution, not least for her promotion of women's rights.

She was born in Luxembourg into a family of well-to-do farmers, whom she left at the age of seventeen to settle in Paris. Here she kept a *salon* in the rue Tournon that was frequented by a number of famous intellectuals, including Mirabeau, Danton and Camille Desmoulins, who evidently enjoyed discussing revolutionary ideas in her company. Through her energy and commitment – demonstrated at the fall of the Bastille – she became a symbol of the Revolution. Dressed in her legendary red riding habit, she became known as the Amazon of Freedom.

Following a period in exile in the aftermath of 1793, Théroigne de Méricourt returned to Paris to continue in the revolutionary struggle and, having reached the peak of her fame, took a resolutely feminist stand, demanding that women should be allowed to bear arms in the defense of their beleaguered country. At the same time, when the Terror-mongering Jacobin Party was holding sway over the revolutionary assembly, she dared to preach tolerance and moderation, thus losing her support overnight. Cornered and whipped by Jacobin women in the Tuileries Gardens – an incident which, legend has it, drove her to madness – she spent the rest of her years, from 1794 onwards, in the insane asylum of Salpêtrière Hospital.

night the building, designed by the hitherto unknown Venezuelan-Canadian architect Carlos Ott, resembles nothing so much as a ship in full sail, with its small square lights blinking in the curved white façade. By day the effect is more monochrome; the walls resemble a huge mosaic of tiny black-and-white tiles reminiscent of a public lavatory. If your French is up to it, a guided tour of the inside is highly recommended. Otherwise, splurge and buy a ticket for a performance: you won't be disappointed.

FAUBOURG ST-ANTOINE

Running from place de la Bastille to place de la Nation, the elegant rue du Faubourg St-Antoine, with its wrought-iron balconies and little hidden passages, forms one of the main arteries of what is one of the last authentic *quartiers* of Paris, the Faubourg St-Antoine. During the reign of Louis XI the presence of such famous cabinet makers as Boulle, Cressent and Jacob gave the area international renown as a center of seventeenth- and eighteenth-century cabinet making. This was the home of the classic styles of French furniture as we still know them: Louis Quatorze, Louis Quinze and the Second Empire. Today the tiny streets and courtyards still harbor craftsmen, inlayers, stainers, and polishers imitating these classic styles for the modern market. The place d'Aligré off the rue du Faubourg Saint-Antoine is worth a morning visit for its lively flea market, selling silver, jewelry, books, glass, some clothes and other bric-a-brac (open daily except Monday, till 1 p.m.).

In the nineteenth century this area was known for more than just cabinet making; it was a hotbed of revolutionary activity. This was due mainly to the low wages and poor working conditions suffered by the furniture-makers' employees; these, along with other social problems, provoked them to lead the insurrection that led to the revolutionary uprisings of 1830 and 1848. Some years earlier, on March 25, 1792, it was here too that Théroigne de Méricourt had addressed the "fraternal club" of Faubourg St-Antoine with the words:

> Let us arm ourselves ... Let us show men that we are not their inferiors in courage or in virtue ... Let us rise to the level of our destinies and break our chains; it is high time that women emerged from the shameful state of nullity and ignorance to which the arrogance and injustice of men have so long condemned them.

Leading off the Bastille end of the Faubourg St-Antoine is rue de la Lappe, which became celebrated early this century for its *bals musettes*, a sort of music hall, popular until the 1930s and a platform for such stars as Edith Piaf, Jean Gabin and Rita Hayworth. Only the vestiges remain today although the Balajo, the most famous, is still there. The seamier side of the street has been replaced by boutiques and art galleries, and for the most part Chinese restaurants have ousted the traditional Auvergne shops where clogs and sausages used to be sold.

Musée Edith Piaf

5 rue Crespin du Gast, 75011. Metro Saint-Maur/Ménilmontant. Tel. 43 55 52 72. Open every day except Saturday and Sunday; closed July. Admission by appointment only.

Edith Piaf, brought up in a brothel, became one of France's greatest legends. She went blind at the age of eight, but miraculously recovered her eyesight three years later, at the shrine of Saint Thérèse of Lisieux, and ever afterwards retained a naïve and superstitious faith. After a desperate life of poverty, singing on the street corners of Paris, her career finally took off in 1937 with an engagement at the city's major music hall theater, the ABC. She was twenty-three. From then on almost all her songs – mostly conveying the trauma of poverty and the torment of broken love – were hits, among them the famous *Je ne regrette rien* (*I regret nothing*), which never fails to tug at the heartstrings. When she died in 1963, her body racked by drug abuse, two million people attended the funeral.

This small private museum, situated in an apartment near Ménilmontant, contains every kind of memento from Edith Piaf's life: clothes, shoes, sculptures, letters, postcards, photos and paintings, all displayed in a quasi-religious atmosphere. Every existing recording is here too, and it will give the caretaker – a devoted fan – great pleasure if you ask him to play one.

Sainte-Marguerite

If you head back south, close to the Faubourg and up rue de la Forge Royale, you will come to the church of Sainte-Marguerite. The cemetery of this church, where the dead of the Bastille prison were buried, was also the scene of a mystery. There is a child's tomb here, said to be that of Louis XVII, who was imprisoned in the Temple Tower and subsequently killed. However, exhumation of the remains cast doubt on the identity of the corpse, leading to speculation that two boys were somehow switched. All the same, the young King was never seen again.

Further north, at number 94 rue de Charonne, is the Salvation Army. This typical 1920s building is sometimes referred to as the *Palais de la Femme* (Woman's Palace), presumably because it has provided a refuge for women. At number 98 is the site of the former Filles-de-la-Croix convent where Cyrano de Bergerac, the lovesick, big-nosed, tragic hero of Edmond Rostand's play is supposed to have hidden and died.

Returning to the Faubourg at place du Docteur-Bèclere, you'll discover the Hôpital Saint-Antoine built on the site of the old royal abbey of Saint-Antoine-des-Champs, founded in 1198 for women of noble birth. The abbesses tended to be princesses, and Madame Geoffrin's stay in 1772 was recorded for posterity by Hubert Robert, who made it the subject of some charming paintings. The façade of the current building dates from 1767, but between 1945 and 1965 a substantial extension was built by André Wogensky to house the first university college hospital in Paris, for 850 students. Wogensky, who once worked with Le Corbusier, has succeeded in softening the rigidity of the cement, steel and glass structure by skillfully employing the use of light and shadows as well as color. Also worth noting are a mobile by Marta Pan, a wall-painting by James Guitet, and John Koenig's glass windows.

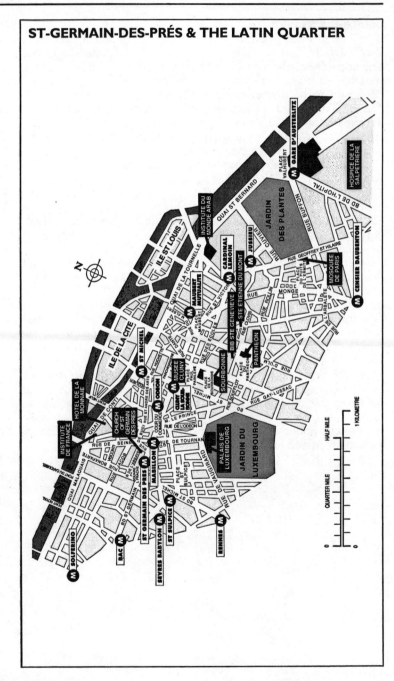

ST-GERMAIN-DES-PRÉS & THE LATIN QUARTER

THE PARIS OF ARTISTS AND INTELLECTUALS

When people first visit Paris they tend to concentrate on the grandeur of its monuments and museums – the Eiffel Tower, the Arc de Triomphe, the Louvre and the Arche de la Défense. It's perhaps only on a second visit that you get a sense of the extraordinary richness of its cultural life down through the centuries and of the men and women who continue to influence modern-day French thought and perceptions. In recording their reflections and describing their lives through words and paintings we, too, can see the city through their eyes.

Wandering the streets they lived in, drinking in the cafés where they used to gather, and visiting the places they immortalized in their art is one of the city's most stimulating pleasures. Inevitably, this focus on the city of artists and intellectuals concentrates on the Left Bank, the part of Paris that has always been connected with learning, creativity and dissent – from the origins of the Sorbonne in 1253 through to the bohemian days of the early twentieth century and the radical protest of 1968. St-Germain, the Latin Quarter, Montparnasse, all conjure up reminders of a fascinating past. But included for its associations is also Montmartre, that "mountain" on the other side of Paris, in the eighteenth *arrondissement*, where showgirls and painters, too, once lived at full tilt.

For generations of students from all over the world, the words "Left Bank" were synonymous with the Promised Land. Today, you'll still see backpacks on the streets, but many Parisian intellectuals have moved out: rents are steep, and those who can afford it often prefer the more recently trendy area around the Bastille. The aftermath of *les événements* of May 1968 split the University of Paris into thirteen campuses of which only a few are still located in the fifth *arrondissement*. But there are good reasons to make your own pilgrimage to the parts of the fifth and sixth that stretch in all directions from the intersection of boulevard St-Michel and boulevard St-Germain. To the west, the pleasant streets of St-Germain-des-Prés are lined with famous cafés and endless opportunities for window-shopping; once you cross boulevard St-Michel, the clothes stores are more affordable and the cafés give way to fast-food restaurants which, in a losing battle against Anglicization, official publications insist on calling *restaurations rapides*, while scruffier students replace the leggy young women who populate the sixth *arrondissement*.

ST-GERMAIN-DES-PRÉS

A good place to begin is one of the oldest churches in Paris, St-Germain-des-Prés, which gives its name to an avenue, a *place*, a Metro station and, above all, a neighborhood. Begun in the eleventh century and partially destroyed in an explosion set off by the saltpeter that was warehoused in the church by the revolutionaries, it is now bordered by a peaceful string of gardens. On boulevard St-Germain, in front of the church, mime artists and organ grinders compete for attention with a man who hawks Shakespeare's sonnets by the page. The railing as you come out of the Metro is the best place to look for posters advertising local church concerts.

The city's first coffee house was opened in St-Germain in 1672, and all along the avenue are the cafés whose names evoke the birth of Existentialism in the heady years following the Liberation of Paris: Les Deux Magots, Brasserie Lipp, Café le Flore, La Rhumerie. The American, Janet Flanner, writing in her *Paris Journal 1944–1965*, commented on the Left Bank's appeal to young Americans at the time:

> The St-Germain-des-Prés quarter has become a campus for the American collegiate set. The Café de Flore serves as a drugstore for pretty upstate girls in unbecoming blue denim pants and their Middle Western dates, most of whom are growing hasty Beaux-Arts beards. Members of the tourist intelligentsia patronize the rue du Bac's Pont-Royal B, which used to be full of French Existentialists and is now full only of themselves, often arguing about Existentialism.

Simone de Beauvoir used the Flore as a refuge from her unheated hotel room – an unofficial office where a receiving line of friends and colleagues would file by.

JANET FLANNER (1892–1978)

The American journalist Janet Flanner was born in Indiana into a family of Quakers. As Parisian correspondent for the *New Yorker*, she participated in the Franco-American literary movement that centered on the Left Bank of Paris between the wars. In 1939 she moved to London to write a column entitled *News Letters from Abroad* under the pen name "Genêt." Many of her articles, including profiles of many distinguished characters of the time, were later published in two volumes.

Around the corner at 2 rue de l'Abbaye is the Abbot's Palace, constructed in the late sixteenth century from a striking combination of brick and stone. By some miracle the narrow streets between the church and the river have kept their village atmosphere – it's especially strong in the lively food market on the corner of rue de Seine and rue de Buci. This is the place to come if you're planning a picnic or simply want to see how Paris's stall-holders have raised fish, fruit and vegetable arrangement to a fine art: plump red tomatoes stand out against heaps of creamy mushrooms and shiny avocados, and the loaded cheese stall competes for your attention with the smell of freshly roasted chicken wafting across from the butcher next door.

The courtyards of rue Jacob are almost provincial, despite its string of art galleries, antique shops, bookstores, clothes boutiques, publishers, hotels and restaurants. Every now and then, you'll come unexpectedly upon an oasis of trees and birds – Square L. Prache, behind St-Germain, or place Furstenburg, with its tempting fabric shops. Glancing at the chintz-draped teashop "Au Cour de Rohan," it's hard to imagine that it was here that the revolutionary Marat printed his sensationalist – often misogynistic – newspaper, and the inventor of the guillotine tested his new device on sheep.

All of present-day St-Germain-des-Prés once belonged to Marguerite de Valois, married to Henri IV but abandoned in favor of a more fertile Marie de' Medici, leaving Marguerite free to write poetry and scandalize Paris with a string of love affairs. The whole of quai Malaquais was built in one go when she sold the parcel of land; its harmonious seventeenth-century façade remains. Number 9, at the

SIMONE DE BEAUVOIR (1908–86)

For generations of women, Simone de Beauvoir's *The Second Sex*, first published in 1949, opened up a new world. In the words of one of her biographers, Deirdre Bair: "She was largely responsible for creating the current feminist revolution that changed the lives of half the human race in most parts of the world."

Born in Paris into an upper-middle-class family, the young Simone soon showed the spirit of independence and nonconformity that remained a hallmark throughout her life. After graduating from the Sorbonne, she took a job as a philosophy teacher in 1929 – around the time when her relationship with Jean-Paul Sartre was developing. It was another fourteen years before she began to write full-time.

Although her stature undoubtedly derives from the publication of *The Second Sex*, de Beauvoir also published several novels, including *The Mandarins*, which won the famous Prix Goncourt, as well as essays and memoirs. Everything she wrote explored the issue of human relations, the meaning of life and liberation in the inescapable face of death. To exemplify her own freedom of choice, she renounced marriage, motherhood and domesticity: "She lived life on her own terms, prepared to defend her stances and decisions and willing to take whatever circumstances came her way."

corner of rue Bonaparte, housed the famous gambling den which Prévost immortalized in his novel *Manon Lescaut*, a warning to young men who sank into debt in order to buy their mistresses jewels.

George Sand scandalized the residents of rue de Seine, where she lived at number 31 by cross-dressing, as did Natalie Barney, who entertained a succession of intelligent and cultivated women, friends and lovers in her Love Temple built in the garden of 20 rue Jacob – one of the many streets Colette also lived in. Among Barney's set were her lover Renée Vivien, the poet and novelist Lucie Delarue-Mardrus and the painter Romaine Brooks. They would get together, with others, scantily clad, to dance and celebrate the feminine form in a world devoid of men.

The residents of rue Dauphine threw pails of water out of the window on to the clients of Le Tabou, a smoky club where Juliette Greco sang after the war to her Existentialist friends. Nearly two centuries earlier, the less iconoclastic Adrienne Lecouvreur held her *salon* at 16 rue Visconti, where she lived until her death in 1730. This was known during the Reformation as "Petite Genève," owing to the number of Protestants who lived there – and died there on the night of Saint Bartholomew, when 20,000 Huguenots were massacred by their Catholic enemies. After the Revolution, the seventeenth-century building at 2 rue Séguier housed several generations of the publishing dynasty Didot which, like many presses, allowed widows to take over the family business at a time when most companies automatically passed into the hands of another man. Farther along rue Saint-André des Arts, a winding, animated street that ends where it meets boulevard St-Michel and the river, is Lycée Fenelon, the first girls' secondary school in Paris. Its opening in the 1880s had at least as much to do with anticlericalism as with pro-feminism. Throughout the Third Republic, women's education was used as a pawn between Church and state, and republicans might have been

MARGUERITE DE VALOIS (1553–1615)

Known as "La Reine Margot," she was the daughter of Henri II and Catherine de' Medici, and sister of Charles IX who married her off to the Protestant Henry of Navarre, the future Henri IV, in the hopes of reconciling Protestants and Catholics. The marriage was a disaster and Marguerite sought consolation in countless lovers. Her amorous adventures scandalized the court and caused her brother Henri III to make a public scene where he is supposed to have confronted her with the list of all her lovers past and present. Banished from Paris, she was later imprisoned in the chateau of Usson in the Auvergne where she succeeded in seducing her jailer, the Marquis of Canillac, with whom she lived from 1587 to 1605.

In 1605, she returned to Paris with her reputation rehabilitated and ended her days in religious devotion, writing poetry and her memoirs, and pursuing her lovers!

less enthusiastic about women's education if the Church had been more so. In 1870 the Minister of Education, Jules Ferry, declared: "Either woman belongs to science, or woman belongs to the Church." The possibility that women might belong to themselves does not seem to have crossed his mind.

LES *QUAIS*

On the edges of these narrow streets, St-Germain does contain a few monumental buildings, among them the eighteenth-century Hôtel de la Monnaie at 11 quai de Conti, and the domed Institut de France at number 23 which houses the venerable, if misogynist, Académie française.

After considering the matter for four centuries, the Académie française has condescended to elect three female members: Marguerite Yourcenar, Jacqueline de Romilly and Hélène Carrère d'Encausse.

The best things about the *quais*, though, are the tree-lined pavements and booksellers' stalls that stretch from around quai de Conti to quai de la Tournelle; you can also stroll or sunbathe below street level, along the river itself, although at night the area is too deserted for safety.

Saint-Sulpice
Place Saint-Sulpice, 75006. Metro Saint-Sulpice.
Open 7:30 a.m.– 7:30 p.m. Monday–Saturday.

To the south of boulevard St-Germain, a different atmosphere takes over. The streets are wider and more modern, the window displays less consistently precious and the cars more noticeable. Couture boutiques alternate with stores selling tinny earrings, antiquarian bookshops, and a cluster of Catholic shops between rue de Rennes and the great bright white church of Saint-Sulpice. The main attrac-

---

ADRIENNE LECOUVREUR (1692–1730)

Adrienne Lecouvreur, daughter of a poor hatter, made her name at the Comédie Française, where she excelled in both tragic and comic parts with a natural and simple diction that stands out in the history of drama. Among her most famous roles were Monime in Racine's *Mithridate*, Bérénice in his play of the same name, and Cornélie in Corneille's *La Mort de Pompée*. Intelligent and witty, she was also admired for her elegant letter-writing and respected by the brightest minds of her time.

Lecouvreur died at the early age of thirty-eight; it is believed that she was poisoned by one of her rivals, the Duchesse de Bouillon. As an actress and philosophers' friend, she was denied a Christian burial. Instead she was secretly buried at night in the rue Bourgogne, whereupon Voltaire, who shut Lecouvreur's eyes when she died, wrote a famous letter vigorously criticizing the Church's attitude and lamenting the tragic destiny of one of France's greatest performers. Her letters were published in 1894 and her life inspired several plays, including *Adrienne Lecouvreur*, with Sarah Bernhardt in the lead role, and an opéra by Francesco Cilea, first performed in Milan in 1902.

ARTISTS & INTELLECTUALS

tions of this church, built around 1700, are a Delacroix fresco and the imposing fountain set in the charming leafy square in front. Both the fountain (by Visconti) and the church are beautifully lit at night, giving an atmosphere of a Verdi opera setting. The Hôtel Récamier, which overlooks the square at 3*bis*, once sheltered the writer Djuna Barnes, a "refugee from Greenwich Village." Her most celebrated novel, *Nightwood*, includes a description of the "huge towers of the church which rose into the sky, unlovely and reassuring . . . the basins of the fountain loosing their skirts of water in a ragged and flowing hem."

A statue at 145 boulevard St-Germain marks the site of the house where the debt-ridden Encyclopedist Diderot wrote against the clock, studiously ignoring his wife's protests. She was his landlady's daughter, whom he married against his father's wishes and soon abandoned for the company of better-educated and better-

NATALIE BARNEY (1876–1972)

An American *salon* hostess, Natalie Barney was born in Dayton, Ohio and spent much of her childhood in Paris where her mother was studying painting. She was educated first by a French governess, then at boarding school in Fontainbleau.

Considered a great beauty and engaged to many eligible men, Natalie Barney openly declared her lesbianism. She established her *salon* on the rue Jacob. This became a center of both literary exchange and lesbian friendship and remained so for more than half a century. This famous *salon* is evoked by Barney in her own memoirs and in her *Pensées d'une Amazone*.

Among the usual guests at Barney's all-lesbian gatherings at the Temple à l'Amitié, an early nineteenth-century "Doric" shrine buried in her overgrown rue Jacob garden, one might find famous courtesans of the day who preferred women on their off hours; married ladies with the same off-hours preferences, poets, French aristocrats and American heiresses-turned-French-aristocrats. For entertainment, Mata Hari once rode into one of Barney's parties nude on a white horse, and Colette once reportedly danced naked.

Barney's life-companion was the painter and sculptor Romaine Brooks whom she seduced at the Pavillion Chinois (the preferred resting-place for lesbians after cruising the Bois de Boulogne). Between 1899 and 1901, she had a tempestuous affair with the woman poet Renée Vivien. Once, attempting to lure her back, it is rumored that Barney had herself delivered to morbidly romantic Vivien in a coffin lined with white satin. After Vivien's death in 1909 Barney awarded an annual prize to women writers in her memory. In 1920 she founded an "Académie des Femmes," also intended to support new writers.

Natalie Barney's legendary love affairs inspired many novels by her lovers: Liane de Pougy's *Idylle Sapphique*, (1901) and Djuna Barnes *Ladies' Almanack*, (1928). Her own literary work includes essays and collections of poems: *Eparpillements, Actes et Entractes, L'Amour défendu, Les Aventures de l'esprit* and *Quelques Portraits-Sonnets des Femmes* (1900), illustrated by her mother.

In 1969, after fifty years together, Romaine Brooks finally left Barney. Brooks's death, a year later, left Natalie desperate and ill; she died within two years at the age of ninety-five.

heeled women, advising friends to "choose mistresses who knew how to make novels and wives who knew how to make shirts."

Rue Princesse, where you can stop to browse in the Village Voice bookstore, was named after Mademoiselle de Montpensier, who fought in the Wars of Religion before repenting of her scandalous behavior and ending her life in seemly obscurity. At rue de Tournon the feminist revolutionary, Théroigne de Méricourt entertained Fabre d'Eglantine, Camille Desmoulins, and Danton. Her neighbor was the pamphleteer Hébert, who called her a whore. From here she moved to the less pleasant atmosphere of an insane asylum.

Between the wars Sylvia Beach and Adrienne Monnier ran facing bookstores on nearby rue de l'Odéon – one for English books, the other for French – both of which became important meeting places for writers. (Les Amis des Livre has recently been resurrected.) At number 1 the Centre Franco-Americain occupies the site of the venerable Café Voltaire, another meeting-point between the wars for such famous American writers as Scott Fitzgerald, who lived with Zelda at number 58 rue de Vaugirard, T.S. Eliot, Ezra Pound, Hart Crane, Ernest Hemingway, Kay Boyle, Sinclair Lewis, Gertrude Stein and all the others who divided their time between the café and Sylvia Beach and Adrienne Monnier's bookshops.

At the end of the rue de l'Odéon is the Carrefour de l'Odéon, a crossroads formed by the intersection of various roads with boulevard St-Germain.

ODÉON

This area, with its four movie houses and many well-known and well-loved cafés, bars and restaurants, is one of the most lively and popular night spots in Paris. During the Revolution the ten-year-old

PONT DES ARTS
(75001 AND 75006 METRO LOUVRE–RIVOLI)

Built between 1802 and 1804 on Napoleon's orders, this pedestrian bridge, built of iron, was only the third of its kind to be constructed: the other two are in England. One theory is that it was built to permit the students studying at the Ecole des Beaux-Arts on the Left Bank to go and visit the art works in the Louvre on the Right Bank, and the bridge is certainly strategically placed for the purpose. Another is that its name derives from the fact that under Napoleon the Louvre was known as the Palais des Arts. At the time of its construction it was made into a veritable hanging garden with small trees, flowers, and benches for people to rest on. It was closed in 1970 for safety reasons because the flimsy bridge had been damaged by passing barges bumping into it. Reconstruction work started in 1982, and it has now been reopened to the public, with only five arches in place of the original nine, made this time of steel. Nevertheless, it is a very pretty, delicate bridge, and a stroll along it will afford a good view of the Louvre on the Right Bank and the domed Institut de France on the Left Bank.

Théâtre de l'Odéon was "democratized" – as were the plays performed at the time; boxes were removed altogether and the square in front was covered with a red, white and blue awning so that everyone could see the performance. These days it's a double theater – the Odéon Théâtre de l'Europe and the Petit Odéon. The former specializes in foreign-language plays. The discreet little shops around it are rather exclusive, as are all the shops in the neighboring streets. The bookstore *des femmes* at 74 rue de Seine displays its books like jewels and you'll feel more relaxed if you're both well-heeled and well-versed in the press's own brand of feminist theory, which has given a new lease of life to the seventeenth-century *précieux* tradition of linguistic hair-splitting.

Further south is the Palais du Luxembourg, seat of the Senate or French Upper House.

Palais and Jardin du Luxembourg

Rue de Vaugirard, 75006. Metro Odéon. Tel. 42 34 20 00.
Palace open to the public only on Sunday or by prior arrangement,
two months in advance, when the house is not in session.

The Renaissance palace was commissioned and largely designed by Marie de' Medici, who wanted to be reminded of the Florentine

---

DJUNA BARNES (1892–1982)

Djuna Barnes left Greenwich Village, New York, in the 1920s for Paris where she settled upon first arriving at the Hôtel d'Angleterre (44 rue Jacob). The flamboyantly caped Barnes was one of the few of the Paris expatriates without an independent income who had to work to support herself as well as for personal fulfillment. She did this sitting on her bed at the Angleterre, most mornings, after spending most nights chasing around the bars after her alcoholic but good-looking sculptor girlfriend Thelma Wood. In Paris she met Natalie Barney, Gertrude Stein and Anaïs Nin. She soon gained a reputation for original, dazzling and sometimes formidable styles both literary and personal (as William Burroughs put it, "one sentence, and you know it is Djuna"). Her anonymous novel *Ladies' Almanac* (1929), apparently conceived to amuse her lover Thelma Wood, Is now recognized as one of the boldest pieces of writing produced by and about lesbian society in Paris of the time. But her ambivalences about *Ladies' Almanac* and the lesbian culture it parodies and celebrates led her many years later to exclaim, "I'm not a lesbian; I just loved Thelma." Her astonishing and brilliant novel *Nightwood* (1936), prefaced by T.S. Eliot, is now considered a classic of modern literature.

Djuna Barnes returned to the United States around 1940 at the height of her reputation, but shattered by the end of her relationship with Thelma Wood. She lived the rest of her life in poverty and seclusion under the protection of Peggy Guggenheim. She published little with the exception of a verse play, *Antiphon* (1958) and *Vagaries Malicieux* (1974). Djuna Barnes was virtually the last of the Paris expatriate modernists when she died just after her ninetieth birthday in 1982.

palaces of her youth. In 1625, she had the gallery decorated with twenty-four Rubens paintings which she had specially commissioned from him three years earlier. These were intended to glorify her as a person, as well as to celebrate her reign as regent, but the glorification was short-lived – following a dispute with Richelieu, she was exiled to Cologne.

Mrs. Frances Trollope complained in 1835 that women were not allowed into the Palace (then used as a law court), but she recounts an amusing anecdote about one woman who slipped the net:

> It is said, indeed, that in one of the tribunes set apart for the public, a small white hand has been seen to caress some jet-black curls upon the head of a boy; and it was said, too, that the boy called himself George S—d; but I have heard of no other instance of any one not furnished with that important symbol of prerogative, *une barbe au menton*, who has ventured within the prescribed limits.

The main attraction, however, is the gardens. These were opened to the public during the Second Empire when, for a fee, people were allowed to pick fruit from the trees. Today they draw a mixed crowd, ranging from rollerskaters and students cutting through on their way to the Latin Quarter to nuns from the many convents located on the southwestern edge. There are also plenty of activities to keep children occupied, including donkey rides, sandpits, merry-go-rounds and slides, as well as a big pond where they can sail boats. The Musée du Luxembourg sponsors temporary exhibitions (tel. 42 34 25 95. Open 11 a.m.–6 p.m. daily, except Monday). It's also a pleasure just to sit by the shady Fontaine de Médicis in the northeastern corner, or perhaps tour the statues of queens and famous citizens commissioned for the main terrace by Louis-Philippe, though be warned: this is a popular hunting ground for *dragueurs*.

MARGUERITE YOURCENAR (1903–87)

The novelist Marguerite Yourcenar was born into an aristocratic family in Brussels, where her erudite father saw to it that she received an austere but well-rounded education, including a thorough background in the classics. She went on to devote much of her literary energy to reviving great figures of the past, such as the Roman Emperor Hadrian, on whom she based the novel *Memoirs of Hadrian*, which brought her much critical acclaim in 1951. She also became an accomplished translator of Greek poets, both ancient and modern, such as Pindar and Cavafy, and also of Black spirituals.

Her life's work was completed by her memoirs, which also retrace her family's past. Yourcenar's interests excluded no area of intellectual activity. In the final stage of her life, spent with her woman companion in Maine, she became a devoted champion of conservation.

ARTISTS & INTELLECTUALS

Once you've crossed the boulevard St-Michel, you've arrived in the Latin Quarter, one of the oldest areas of Paris: the ruins of the Roman baths near the corner of the boulevards St-Germain and St-Michel and the arena (now a pleasant park) hiding in the court-yard of a nineteenth-century house at 49 rue Monge both testify to this. In the twelfth century a dissenting group of students, headed by the famous Abelard – lover of Héloïse – crossed the river from the Île de la Cité and set up courses which evolved into the official university. By the end of the Middle Ages these courses were attract-ing students from all over Europe – a foretaste of today's inter-national jumble of backpackers.

Despite the occasional demonstration on the tree-shaded place de la Sorbonne, the barricades of May 1968 now seem very distant. Today most radicalisms – not least feminism – are dusted off only occasionally as part of a rallying cry for student demands. The issue is most often the protection of university access for anyone with a *baccalauréat*, a chronic tug of war between governments who are unwilling to finance the swelling numbers of university students and students who consider education a right to which all young middle-class people are entitled. Since 1986, when a schoolboy, Malik Oussekin, was beaten to death by the police, these protests have usually ended in compromise.

LA SORBONNE

47 rue des Ecoles, 75005. Metro St-Michel/Odéon/Maubert-Mutualité/Cluny-La Sorbonne.

Simone de Beauvoir and Simone Weil are just two of the famous women who have graduated from this illustrious institution, which started life as a college for poor theological students. It was founded by Robert de Sorbon, Louis IX's chaplain in 1253; the current buildings date from the turn of the century and replaced those of Richelieu's architect Le Mercier, begun in 1626. The only part of Richelieu's Sorbonne that remains is the chapel, which houses his tomb.

The garish pedestrian streets running northeast from the inter-section of boulevards St-Germain and St-Michel date from this period, as do the Cluny Museum, the church of Saint-Julien le Pauvre – in a surprisingly quiet garden – and the beginnings of Saint-Séverin, with its remarkable eighteenth-century organ. The name of rue de la Parcheminerie ("Parchment") bears witness to its high concentration of copyists and illuminators in the Middle Ages. Following the invention of the printing process, a flurry of new presses sprang up around rue Saint-Jacques. By 1571 there were fourteen bookstores on rue Lanneau, a tradition still maintained; in

September lines stretch around the corner of boulevard St-Michel and rue de l'Ecole de Médecine for Gilbert Joseph, an institution where hordes of mothers descend every year to buy their children's required textbooks.

Haussmann's Legacy

The Latin Quarter could hardly have hoped to escape Haussmann's attention: its streets were medieval and its (all-male) students revolutionary. Today, the avenues he built – boulevards St-Germain and St-Michel, rues des Écoles, Monge, Soufflot, Gay-Lussac – host the only local life that lingers in the Latin Quarter. The medieval streets that remain, squeezed into the rectangle bounded by boulevards St-Michel and St-Germain, rue Dante, and the river, are now overrun with students and tourism. Greek restaurants spill out on to the pavement, waiters heckling for custom and turning their spits of roasting meat. (Curiously, this practice seems to have existed under the *ancien régime*: Mercier claimed that "the Turks in the entourage of the Ottoman ambassador liked the rue de la Huchette best of all, because of the smell of roasting meat and spits turning infinitely!") Rue de la Huchette, however, is known for something other than kebabs: it is home to the tiny Théâtre de la Huchette, where a double bill of one-act plays by Ionesco has been running nonstop

---

SYLVIA BEACH (1887–1962) AND ADRIENNE MONNIER (1892–1955)

Sylvia Beach arrived in Paris from the United States in 1917; she met Adrienne Monnier, owner of the already famous bookshop Maison des Amis des Livres at number 7 rue de l'Odéon. Rather than attempting to make a huge profit from the sale of books, the shop operated as an informal library and reading room where Adrienne encouraged her customers to expand their knowledge of literature. Sylvia Beach soon followed suit by opening Shakespeare and Company which, along with her publication of James Joyce's *Ulysses*, made her name.

The physical contrast between the two women – Sylvia was small and slight; Adrienne was round and motherly – is amusingly presented by Sylvia in her book, *Shakespeare and Company*: in describing the location of her original shop in rue Dupuytren she writes:

> At number 8 – there were only about ten numbers on this hilly little street – was a shop with the shutters up and a sign reading *Boutique à louer*. "It had once been a laundry," said Adrienne, pointing to the words *gros* and *fin*, on either side of the door, meaning they did both sheets and fine linen. Adrienne, who was rather plump, placed herself under the *gros* and told me to stand under the *fin*. "That's you and me," she said.

It was thanks to these two women that rue de l'Odéon (eventual home of Shakespeare and Company) became a literary mecca in the Paris of the 1920s and 1930s – French, English, Irish and Americans flocked there to indulge their literary passions.

ARTISTS & INTELLECTUALS

for over thirty years. This part of the area is at least animated at night, but to watch local students you would do better to head south to the Montagne Sainte-Geneviève, a hill whose summit is marked by the Panthéon.

PANTHÉON

Place du Panthéon, 75005. Metro Luxembourg. Tel. 43 54 34 51. Open 10 a.m.–6 p.m. summer, 10 a.m.–5 p.m. winter. Entrance fee, but free guided tours lasting 45 minutes (French only).

Begun by Louise XV to fulfill a vow to erect a church to the patron saint of Paris, Sainte-Geneviève, if he survived his illness, and completed just before the Revolution, this rather stubby Neoclassical mass had hardly begun to serve as a church before it was seized by the Constituent Assembly in 1885. It was recycled for elaborate reburials of already-dead philosophers whom hindsight had dubbed ancestors of the Revolution; you can still see Rousseau's monument and Voltaire's. Throughout the nineteenth century the building's shifts between Church and state provided an index to political change, but since Victor Hugo's funeral in 1885 the building has remained a site of secular beatification. In a country where the publication of an author's works in Gallimard's prestigious Pléiade series (women include Colette, George Sand, Madame de Sévigné and Marguerite Yourcenar) can furnish newspapers with pages of polemic, *la panthéonisation* tops even the nearby Collège de France (also overwhelmingly male-dominated) as a national stamp of approval for intellectuals and statesmen, in the literal sense of the word. As one might expect in a monument dedicated to *les grands hommes*, only one woman is present: Sophie Berthelot (1837–1907), who, according to one talkative guard, "had done nothing in her life but died on the same day as her husband so that they had to bury them together." In his words: "If you're looking for ladies, you'd better go to Père-Lachaise."

HÉLOÏSE AND ABELARD

Héloïse and Abelard are the protagonists of one of the greatest love stories of all time. Abelard, a philosopher, teacher of theology and Canon of Notre-Dame, seduced his pupil Héloïse, secretly married her, and fathered her son. Her uncle, Fulbert, also a canon, was so incensed by Abelard's behavior that he had him castrated, whereupon he retired to the Abbey of Saint-Denis and Héloïse became a nun.

At the request of his followers, Abelard took up teaching again, but his doctrines were condemned by the Synod in 1121, at which point he founded the monastery of Paraclet, where his wife became abbess and he himself withdrew to another abbey. Héloïse remained in the monastery, but the couple kept up a passionate correspondence all their lives. They were finally able to lie together again in death, buried side by side in Père-Lachaise Cemetery.

The Panthéon itself is undergoing repairs and will be off-limits at least until the end of 1993; for now, the best part of the visit is the 250-step climb to the top of the dome, with a plunging view of the interior and, at the top, a 360-degree panorama of Paris.

BIBLIOTHÈQUE SAINTE-GENEVIÈVE AND SAINT-ÉTIENNE-DU-MONT

The Town Hall opposite the Panthéon housed the original women's library and archives donated by feminist journalist Marguerite Durand – not to be confused with Marguerite Duras – while next door to the Panthéon is the nineteenth-century Bibliothèque Sainte-Geneviève. This building has a magnificent nineteenth-century reading room where young students, dressed in the ubiquitous black, pore over the ancient tomes on long tables lit by attractive individual reading lights and can daydream as they gaze out at the sixteenth-century church of Saint-Étienne-du-Mont.

Marguerite de Valois, first wife of Henri IV, laid the first stone of the church's façade in 1610 and work on the church continued

SIMONE WEIL (1909-43)

The importance of the work of this French philosopher was discovered only after her death, when the posthumous publication *La Pesanteur et la Grâce* revealed her genius. She was hailed as a mystic – Albert Camus described her as one of the greatest spirits of the century; he himself published her unfinished essay *L'Enracinement*.

Feeling deprived of contact with the real world – something she considered vital to her creativity – Weil got a job as a manual worker in 1934 – an experience she describes in *La Condition ouvrière*. A militant revolutionary, she was aware very early on of the Nazi threat and equally suspicious of "Sovietism," for she opposed all forms of military and police rule. Having rejected Judaism, her parents' religion, she turned towards Christianity but, averse to all dogma, refused to be baptized. In the end she tried to draw the best from a mixture of various faiths, including Hinduism. Habitually dressed from head to toe in black, she presented a slightly unnerving figure to the world, even intimidating fellow Sorbonne student Simone de Beauvoir:

I managed to get near her one day. I don't know how the conversation got started; she declared in no uncertain tones that only one thing mattered in the world today: the revolution which would feed all the starving people of the earth. I retorted, no less peremptorily, that the problem was not to make men happy, but to find the reason for their existence. She looked me up and down: "It's easy to see you've never gone hungry," she snapped. Our relationship did not go any further. I realized that she had classified me as a "high-minded little bourgeoise," and this annoyed me . . . (From *Memoirs of a Dutiful Daughter*).

During a spell in London, where she was horrified by the comparative luxury of her compatriots, Simone Weil stopped eating to show solidarity with the French people suffering wartime deprivation. Already weakened by tuberculosis, she died of starvation on August 24, 1943.

throughout the seventeenth century. The church boasts an unusual rood screen, an exceptionally richly decorated organ and a shrine to Sainte Geneviève. The prestigious Lycée Henri-IV has swallowed up the medieval abbey of Sainte-Geneviève, which you can visit on request or glimpse by slipping in the entrance of 23 rue Clovis.

Number 45 rue d'Ulm is the École Normale Supérieure, the breeding-ground for the nation's intellectual elite which admitted women only sixty years ago; this didn't prevent Simone Weil from coming first in the annual examination in the 1930s. Nearby is rue Pierre et Marie Curie, one of the only streets in Paris named after two people; in 1909 it was named after Pierre, and only thirty-four years after her death, in 1967, was Marie's name tacked on to the street of the laboratory where she won two Nobel Prizes. (She was not, however, admitted to the French Academy of Sciences.) All Marie has to herself is a square in the desolate eastern part of the *arrondissement* – the name of her lover, Paul Langevin, is remembered in a far more desirable piece of property at the intersection of rues des Écoles and Monge.

All the streets abound with staircases and slopes. Place Lucien-Herr, named after an anticlerical local librarian who filed theology under fiction, is almost too picturesque to be real. Further up, as rue de la Montagne Sainte-Geneviève becomes rue Descartes and then rue Mouffetard, the atmosphere changes again, and you could almost be back around Saint-Séverin, only here the youth hostels and Greek restaurants are tempered by a lively market and pleasant streets branching off at either side – from the provincial charm of rue Rollin to the animation of the African stalls on rue de l'Arbalète.

AROUND THE JARDIN DES PLANTES

The east of the fifth *arrondissement* is less touristy, yet there are several attractions worth the effort (but avert your eyes from the endless towers of Jussieu, an ugly-looking branch of the University of Paris whose slippery courtyard is said to have been designed to cause students to fall down in case of a riot). In welcome contrast,

SAINTE GENEVIÈVE (422–512)

Sainte Geneviève, patron saint of Paris, seems to have been sanctified not for having endured the usual string of abominable tortures and tests in the name of her faith, but because from birth she was endowed with a saintliness which manifested itself in many ways. From being a shepherdess, she became a nun at the age of fifteen, and by the power of prayer she managed to save the City of Paris twice – once in 451 from invasion by Attila the Hun, the second time from famine during the reign of Clovis. A story about her goes that her mother, having hit the young Geneviève, lost her sight. Geneviève restored her sight by bathing her eyes in water from a certain well in Nanterre. To this day the well is revered for its healing powers.

the neighborhood's first landmark is the Institut du Monde Arabe, and the pseudo-Andalusian Mosquée de Paris, curiously situated in an area with one of the city's lowest Muslim populations.

Institut du Monde Arabe

23 quai Saint-Bernard, 75005. Metro Jussieu/Cardinal Lemoine. Tel. 40 51 38 38. Museum and library open 1–8 p.m. Tuesday–Sunday; temporary exhibitions open 10 a.m.–10 p.m.

This fascinating modern building, with its back to the Seine, has an elegant glass façade covered with thousands of tiny photosensitive shutters that open and close with the sun like the aperture of a camera. Inside, both permanent and short-term exhibitions illustrate developments in art culture and literature from the Arab world. If you are tired, the quickest lift in Paris will take you to the ninth floor for a magnificent view of the Seine while you sip a cup of mint tea, the only Arab item on the rather expensive menu. If you leave the Institute and head away from the river, you'll come to rue Jussieu. Follow this road east, and you'll come to the lush gardens of the Jardin des Plantes.

Jardin des Plantes

Main entrance on place Valhubert. Metro Jussieu/Monge/Gare d'Austerlitz. Tel. 40 79 30 00. Open daily 7:15 a.m.–8 p.m.

This botanical garden teeming with exotic plants, birds and animals started life under Louis XIII in 1626 as a garden for medicinal plants. It was here that tobacco and chocolate were first introduced to France. Today you'll find a mini-zoo, a maze, and various sections of the Natural History Museum – great for children.

As you wander around, you'll see the minaret of Paris's mosque in the distance.

Mosquée de Paris

1–2 place du Puits-de-l'Ermite, 75005. Metro Monge. Tel. 45 35 97 33. Closed Muslim holidays. Hammam: 39 rue Geoffroy-Saint-Hilaire, 75005. Metro Censier Daubenton. Tel. 43 31 18 14. Open to women 10 a.m.–8 p.m. Monday, Wednesday, Thursday, Saturday.

The mosque, built in the 1920s, has its own pleasant gardens with a rose-pink marble colonnade, a library, a Moorish tearoom where you can sip mint tea, an alcohol-free Arab restaurant, a hostel, classrooms and *hammam* (steam baths). This is a good place to meet other women, especially in the final room, where you can rest on mattresses after progressing through the various rooms of hot steam and cold water. The mosque also boasts its own minaret, and a Grand Patio inspired by the Alhambra where the mosaic frieze depicts verses from the Koran.

La Salpêtrière

South of rue Claude Bernard and boulevard Saint-Marcel, the fifth *arrondissement* becomes an ordinary residential area, punctuated only by a string of hospital walls lining boulevard Port-Royal and, on the eastern edge, the construction site of François Mitterrand's final architectural project, a hulking new library – often in the news either as a squatters' site or because of the architect's plan to hide readers in dark basements while exposing books to blinding

MARGUERITE DURAS (BORN 1914)

Marguerite Duras hit the headlines in 1992 when her semi-autobiographical novel *L'Amant* (*The Lover*) was made into a film. Novelist, playwright, filmmaker and journalist, she belongs to that generation of women writers who, like Simone de Beauvoir, have shown their readiness to become involved in the political conflicts and intellectual debates of their time. She was born in what was then French Indochina, but came to Paris at the age of seventeen to study at the Sorbonne. She took part in the Resistance, worked in a publishing house, joined the Communist Party – which she was later to leave – and published her first novel in 1942. But her true literary career began in 1950, with *Barrage contre le pacifique*, which depicts her youthful years in Indochina, and *Les Petits Chevaux de Tarquinia* (1953), which featured a group of characters who spend their vacation vainly seeking to establish authentic relationships with one another. The themes that were to pervade all her future works are already present in these early novels. Words, reduced to a bare minimum, separate individuals rather than bring them together. The characters are thrown back upon their existential solitude, trapped in their own indifference and diminishing vitality.

Fame came to Duras through her association with Alain Resnais in co-authoring the film *Hiroshima mon amour* (1959). The film's ambitions were both political – it is a warning against nuclear danger – and aesthetic – it introduced a new kind of screenwriting in which dialogue determines the visual image, while the image enacts meaning and fills the gaps in the dialogue.

Her subsequent writing was remarkably prolific. Among her most significant works are plays: *Les Viaducs de Seine-et-Oise* (1960), *Le Square* (1962), *La Musica* (1965); films: *Une aussi longue absence* (1961), *India Song* (1973); and novels: *Le Ravissement de Lol V. Stein* (1964), *L'Amante anglaise* (1967). In 1984, her novel *L'Amant* achieved extraordinary success. The apparent banality of her diction miraculously conveys the intense emotional experience of re-creating her Indochinese adolescence, a memory that combines both pain and ecstasy. The honesty and courage of her vision constantly fly in the face of stifling conventions and prejudices. *La Vie Matérielle* is a challenging, at times bleak, collection of conversations with Jérôme Beaujour, its subjects ranging from the TV coverage of Lech Walesa's wife collecting her husband's Nobel Prize, to alcohol: "Living with alcohol is living with death close at hand. What stops you killing yourself when you're intoxicated out of your mind is the thought that once you're dead you won't be able to drink any more."

The same concern for authenticity and sincerity pervades her latest book, *Yann Andrea Steiner* (1992), an autobiographical account of a passionate affair, which claims a woman's right to love whomsoever she chooses, at an age when passion is usually denied by society.

sunlight. Nearby stands the enormous Pitié-Salpêtrière hospital complex, whose distinctive domed silhouette struck terror into the hearts of *ancien régime* prostitutes, who were held and shaved here before being deported. Other women could be put here by their fathers or husbands. Jeanne de la Motte, who was imprisoned for embarrassing Marie-Antoinette, managed to escape only because she disguised herself as a man. After the Revolution, when the prison became an insane asylum, one of the first patients, attacked from both Right and Left, was Théroigne de Méricourt. Later, hysterics were displayed to fascinated intellectuals. Indeed, Freud came to Paris to attend Professor Charcot's famous course on hysteria; his early work on psychoanalysis was greatly influenced by what he had seen at the Salpêtrière. The hospital trained the first woman nurses in France, amidst bitter protests. In 1907 no one could have predicted that the profession was to become 85 percent female, resulting in wages that men know better than to fight over. Today you can walk around the pleasant gardens or the seventeenth-century chapel.

MARIE CURIE (1867–1934)

Born Maria Sklodovska in Warsaw, the daughter of a mathematics and physics professor, the future Marie Curie spoke and read French, Russian and German by the time she left school at the age of sixteen, and participated in the activities of an underground Polish university. In 1891 she went to Paris, where she gained a degree in physics with high honors. Four years later she married Pierre Curie, a professor at the École de Physique et Chimie de Paris; they had two daughters. "I have a great deal of work, what with the housekeeping, the children, the teaching and the laboratory," she wrote, "and I don't know how I shall manage it all." Manage, however, she did.

From early on her research centered on Henri Becquerel's discovery of radioactivity; she used the electrometer invented by her husband to measure the conducting power of rays from uranium compounds. In 1898 they together isolated the first radioactive elements, polonium – named, in Marie's honor, after Poland – and radium. The couple shared the Nobel Prize for Physics with Henri Becquerel in 1903; a year later a Chair of Physics was created for Pierre Curie at the Sorbonne.

When Pierre died in a car accident in 1906, Marie took his place to become the first woman in France to occupy a university Chair. She went on to publish an important *Treaty on Radioactivity* and developed methods of separating radium from radioactive residues, providing the International Radium Standard in 1911, when she became the first person ever to win a second Nobel Prize, this time for chemistry. During World War I Marie Curie set up a physics and chemistry laboratory in the Radium Institute in Paris and, with her daughter Irène, founded a school for radiologist nurses, so developing the medical uses of radium. She also drove an ambulance equipped with X-ray machines to the front lines. In 1929 she was given $50,000 by President Hoover to buy radium for her research. Five years later, after publishing a second *Treaty on Radioactivity*, she died of leukemia.

MUSÉE CLUNY

6 place Paul Painlevé, 75005. Metro Saint-Michel/Odéon.
Tel 43 25 62 00.
Open daily 9:45–12:30 a.m.; 2 p.m.–5:15 p.m. except Tuesday.

This museum, housed in one of the city's finest fifteenth-century mansions, has a treasure trove of exhibits from the Middle Ages: sculptures, bronzes, stained glass and tapestries that are not to be missed.

The building dates as far back as the third century, when it was a Gallo-Roman thermal bath-complex, a part of which still forms the west side of the museum. The house you'll see today was built between 1485 and 1498 by the Amboise family and lived in by Mary Tudor, eldest daughter of Henry VII, married at the age of sixteen to Louis XII, then in his fifties. He died three months later. During her official period of mourning, she was watched anxiously by Louis's cousin, François I, for if she bore a child, it would deprive him of his right to the throne. François was, then, delighted when Mary was discovered one night in the company of the Duke of Suffolk, and forced the couple to marry immediately, and return to England. Some 300 years later, the building was partly destroyed by the Revolution. During the nineteenth century, when the Romantics rediscovered the Middle Ages, it became known as a place steeped in medieval atmosphere. In 1843, a government decree ordered the creation of the Cluny Baths and Museum.

The Exhibits   In the ground-floor galleries are documents on medieval costumes, wooden sculptures and beautiful tapestries from the Netherlands. See especially *The Offering of a Heart*, the oldest tapestry in the museum (early fifteenth century). There are also many fragments of Notre-Dame vandalized during the Revolution, including 21 heads of Kings of Judah, abandoned on the terrace of the cathedral after the sculptures had been mutilated.

In Room 4 is the famous tapestry *La Vie seigneurale*, describing everyday life in a medieval castle. Each of the hangings focuses on a specific theme or activity: embroidery, reading, walking, hunting, bathing and loving. Whether or not you have a passion for tapestry (and these may well convert you), the highlight of the museum is undoubtedly *La Dame à la licorne* (The Lady and the Unicorn) on the first floor. This beautiful series of six tapestries features an exquisite woman, flanked by a lion and a unicorn, surrounded by a woven paradise of tiny flowers, birds and animals on a rich red background. Each tapestry is an allegory of one of the five senses, though no one is quite sure what the sixth symbolizes though it is thought to be the renunciation of self-possession. It depicts a gorgeously dressed noblewoman emerging from a tent while her servant holds out a box, from which she is taking jewelry. The entrance to the tent is held open by a lion on the left and a unicorn on the right.

The museum also contains religious paintings, such as the four-teenth-century English Scenes from the life of the Virgin, and the famous *Pietà de Tarascon* ordered by Jeanne de Laval, wife of King René, for her room in the southern Castle of Tarascon. In Room 15 there are some interesting items from the daily life including chastity belts, shoes, books, tableware, travel objects and children's toys.

Finally, don't miss the great hall of the Roman thermal baths (Room 10), built around 200 AD. This is the only Roman room in France, complete with the vaults on which the hanging garden of the abbots of Cluny rested until 1820. The room was used as the *frigidarium* or cold baths.

MONTPARNASSE

Like Montmartre and St-Germain-des-Prés, Montparnasse is one of the places that has made Paris synonymous with the avant-garde. The area had its heyday between the wars, when the literary and artistic world of Paris – both French and cosmopolitan – would meet in the now famous cafés: the Dôme, the Select, the Rotonde, and the Coupole. You can still, if the mood takes you, go to these cafés and sit musing in the smoky atmosphere over a strong black coffee trying to imagine the conversations of former famous regu-

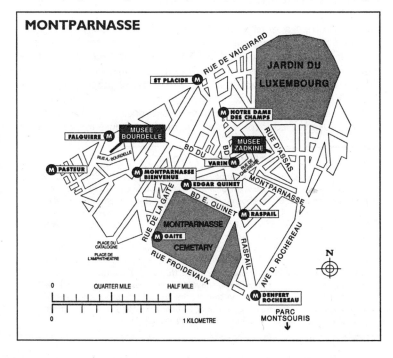

MONTPARNASSE

lars: Utrillo (son of Suzanne Valadon), Modigliani, Chagall, Fujita and Soutine. The most atmospheric is the Coupole, one-time meeting place of Sartre, Simone de Beauvoir, and pro-Communist writers Louis Aragon and Elsa Triolet.

At the beginning of the nineteenth century, Montmartre was painters' territory, not too far from the École des Beaux-Arts and with the advantage of large, affordable studios to rent. But by the 1890s, disenchanted with an increasingly tawdry Montmartre, they began to gravitate towards Montparnasse, and it was here, too, that foreigners settled when they arrived in Paris to study art. One such painter is captured in Jean Rhys's character Lois, for whom Marya occasionally sits in *Quartet*:

> She would often stop painting to talk, and it was evident that she took Montparnasse very seriously indeed. She thought of it as a possible stepping stone to higher things and she liked explaining, classifying, fitting the inhabitants (that is to say, of course, the Anglo-Saxon inhabitants) into their proper places in the scheme of things. The Beautiful Young Men, the Dazzlers, the Middle Westerners, the Down-and-Outs, the Freaks who would never do anything, the Freaks who just possibly might.

WOMEN OF MONTPARNASSE

Of the American painters showing in the *salons* at the turn of the century, more than a third were women, but until 1900 women were excluded from the École des Beaux-Arts (which forced them to pay for expensive private courses) and, if they were "nice girls," they didn't frequent the cafés, where ideas took shape. For many – like Kiki, who posed for Man Ray, and a long list of others – modeling and affairs with male painters were stepping stones to showing one's own work. Elizabeth Mills Reid used her position as wife of the American Ambassador to open a cheap lodging-house for women art

ANAÏS NIN (1903–77)

Anaïs Nin, the celebrated author of *Venus erotica*, published in 1969, and of her diaries (the expurgated passages of which were published only after her husband's death in 1986), was born in 1903 in Havana to the Spanish composer Joaquim Nin, and a Danish mother. Her cosmopolitan childhood took her to France and the United States. At the age of eleven she started writing a diary, which she dedicated to her father. Through her writing she explores her own identity, her relationship with her parents, and the link between femininity and creation. In 1931 she settled at Louveciennes near Paris. Her work provides fascinating glimpses into the literary and artistic world of the time. She made friends with Henry and June Miller, and conducted a passionate affair with both of them. Married to an American banker, she divided her time between writing and taking part in the social round, liking to be admired and proud of her delicate good looks. She died in New York's Greenwich Village in 1977.

students at 4 rue de Chevreuse. There was a special *Salon* for women painters, a few of whom – such as Hermine David or the Russian Marevna Vorobev – managed to make a go of it, but Montparnasse was no exception to the rule that women's main function was to bring men together. Hostesses like Baroness Hélène d'OEttingen, gallery-owners like Berthe Weill (who showed Alice Halicka, Hermine David, Valentine Prax) and motherly restaurateurs like Marie Vassilieff and Rosalie Tobia, all fulfilled this role. Today, drinking and eating are still the main activities on the boulevard du Montparnasse.

Montparnasse attracted a glorious mélange of unconventional women: Isadora Duncan lived here for a time, as did the black American dancer Josephine Baker who had lodgings in rue Campagne Première and *tout Paris* in the worlds of writing and painting passed through the house on rue Fleurus where Gertrude Stein and her lover Alice B. Toklas held frequent gatherings.

Tour Montparnasse
Place du 18 Juin, 75015. Metro Montparnasse. Tel. 45 68 10 00.

For most young Parisians the word Montparnasse conjures up the image of one of Europe's highest modern tower blocks which they

JEAN RHYS (1894–1970)

Born Gwen Williams in Dominica, the daughter of a Welsh doctor and a white Creole mother, novelist Jean Rhys was educated at the Convent of the Faithful Virgin in Roseau. At the age of seventeen she went to England, where she studied briefly in Cambridge and then at London's Royal Academy of Dramatic Art. By the time she was twenty she was playing in vaudeville and musicals such as *Our Miss Gibbs* under the pseudonym Vivian Gray.

In 1919 Rhys left England for the Netherlands, where she married a Dutch poet and translator, Jean Lenglet. Three years later they settled in Paris, where she met James Joyce, Ernest Hemingway, Djuna Barnes and Ford Madox Ford, who became her lover and literary mentor. In 1927 she published a collection of stories, *The Left Bank*, followed by *Quartet*, a fraught *ménage à quatre* in which Madox Ford and his wife are acutely portrayed. In 1931 she divorced, returned to England, and married Leslie Tiklen Smith. Her next three novels – *After Leaving Mr. Mackenzie, Voyage in the Dark*, and *Good Morning Midnight* – all describe women betrayed or duped by the men they love. With the outbreak of war and the failure of *Good Morning Midnight* (1939), her books went out of print and Jean Rhys literally dropped from sight, leaving many to assume that she was dead. In fact, after the death of her second husband, she married Max Haner, and settled into a reclusive life in Cornwall.

She began to write again in 1959 when she was rediscovered, largely due to the enthusiasm of the writer Francis Wyndham. *Wide Sargasso Sea* was published in 1966, the story of Mr. Rochester's first wife, Bertha Antoinetta, the original "mad woman in the attic" in Charlotte Brontë's *Jane Eyre*, partly set in the Caribbean of her childhood. This novel won the Royal Society of Literature Award and the W.H. Smith Award. She later published a collection of stories, *Sleep It Off Lady* (1976) and her unfinished biography, *Smile Please*.

love to hate, and a shopping and office complex plonked over the railway station of the same name. For 36 francs you can ascend the Tour Montparnasse for the view – said to be the best in Paris, partly because you can't see the tower! The small streets surrounding the station still house many artists' workshops. This area is known as the Breton Quarter. There are several bookshops with works in the Breton language, and a good choice of *crêperies* where you can have a pancake meal for a very reasonable price.

Montparnasse Cemetery

3 boulevard Edgar Quinet, 75014. Metro Edgar Quinet.
Tel. 43 20 68 52.Open daily 8 a.m.–5:30 p.m. winter;
6 p.m. summer; from 9 a.m. weekends.

Simone de Beauvoir's tomb, which she shares with Jean-Paul Sartre, is in Montparnasse Cemetery, the smallest of the three Parisian cemeteries. While it's not as picturesque as Père-Lachaise, it contains the mortal remains of a good many artists, writers and famous publishers, among them Charles Baudelaire, Robert Desnos, Tristan Tzara (father of Dadaism), Leconte de Lisle, Guy de Maupassant and the composer César Franck. Among the few illustrious women are the nineteenth-century actress Marie Dorval, pilot Maryse Bastie, artist Sylvia Lopez and actresses Maria Montez and Delphine Seyrig.

Closerie des Lilas

The old cafés are still very much alive, and its worth installing yourself in one for a couple of hours to drink in the spirit of the former *habitués*. The Closerie des Lilas on the corner of the boulevard du Montparnasse and the boulevard Saint-Michel was another popular meeting place for the literati, and played host to some scandalous

KIKI (1901–53)

Alice Prin, nicknamed Kiki, was born in Bourgogne. She and her five illegitimate brothers and sisters were educated by their grandmother. While she was living in Chatillon-sur-Seine she entertained people by singing in bars with her godfather until her mother summoned her to Paris, where she did a series of odd jobs. At the age of sixteen, jobless and homeless, she made friends with artists from Montparnasse, among them the painter Mendjisky, who became her first lover. In 1921 she met Man Ray and modeled for him as odalisque or *femme fatale* until 1937. It's Kiki's rear, with f-holes daubed on her back, in Man Ray's notorious *Violincello*. When he went to New York she began to mix with the Surrealist poets Soupault, Tzara and Robert Desnos.

Kiki lived part of her life in a cheap hotel, looking after her lover Henri Broca, who gradually went mad, and eventually died, during the war in a concentration camp. After the war, having lost many of her friends, she destroyed her health through drink and drug abuse. She died alone in 1953 at the Laennec Hospital leaving behind only a book of *Souvenirs*, published in 1929.

scenes between partisans of different artistic and literary schools. Trotsky and Lenin frequented the café while they were in exile, and much later Hemingway, in his book *A Movable Feast*, recalls his first meeting here with Scott Fitzgerald. Some tables even have copper plaques in memory of more celebrated regulars, though there's not a single woman's name among them.

One name you might expect to see is that of Anaïs Nin, whose love of Parisian cafés is expressed in a passage from her famous *Journals*. Returning to the city in 1954 after fifteen years' absence, she describes spotting a tiny café on the way from the airport:

> But as I passed I saw a café on the street, with an open door, and one small round table outside, just big enough for two persons, two glasses of wine, a diminutive café like the café in Utrillo streets, shabby with a faded sign, a dull window, lopsided walls, uneven roof. The smallness of it, the intimacy of it, the humanity of its proportion, the absence of American arrogance, the absence of gloss and glitter touched me and once again opened me to tenderness as Paris has always done.

GERTRUDE STEIN (1874-1946) AND ALICE B. TOKLAS (1877-1967)

She was a golden brown presence, burned by the Tuscan sun and with a golden glint in her warm brown hair. She was dressed in a warm brown corduroy suit. She wore a large round coral brooch and when she talked, very little, or laughed, a great deal, I thought her voice came from this brooch. It was unlike anyone else's voice – deep, full, velvety like a great contralto's, like two voices. She was large and heavy with delicate small hands and a beautifully modeled and unique head.

So Alice B. Toklas described her first impressions of her lifelong lover, the American writer Gertrude Stein.

Born into an Austro-Israeli family in 1874, Stein moved from the United States to Paris at the age of nineteen where, at number 20 rue de Fleurus, she and Toklas held some of the most famous literary gatherings of the twentieth century. James Joyce, Scott Fitzgerald, Anaïs Nin, Ernest Hemingway, not to mention painters such as Picasso, Gris and Cézanne, all would come to imbibe an atmosphere of unrivaled creativity along with Alice's delicious cakes and tea.

A prolific writer, Stein was constantly irritated by a lack of recognition of her own work. Success finally came with the publication of the amusing and lively *Autobiography of Alice B. Toklas* in 1933, followed by other books, all of which reveal her very individual style, usually written in the present tense and often as not devoid of punctuation. Toklas also published the famous *Alice B. Toklas Cook Book* and a volume of reminiscences entitled *What is Remembered*.

When Gertrude Stein died in 1946, she left everything, including her formidable art collection, to Toklas, on whose death in 1967 it was finally dispersed.

Rue de la Gaité

Montparnasse is liveliest at night, when the bars and cinemas, the music hall theaters and a scattering of fringe venues, pull the crowds. A typical night-time haunt is the rather seedy rue de la Gaité – best avoided alone on account of the sex shops and almost laughably tacky pornographic movie theaters, but not particularly dangerous. It was at the Gaité Montparnasse that Colette performed (almost) naked in the 1920s; in the 1950s, under the directorship of Marguerite Jamois, Anouilh chose to stage at least two productions at the Théâtre Montparnasse. Recently renovated, the theater now incorporates an 1886 café with the original decor preserved.

Parc Montsouris

During the day the boulevard du Montparnasse is dirty and noisy. A more interesting place to wander is to the south around place du Catalogne and place de l'Amphithéâtre, where there's a playground for children. Opposite is a curious old church, Notre-Dame-du-Travail (35 rue Guilleminot), built at the turn of the century and optimistically dedicated to the "reconciliation of Capital with Labor." Alternatively, if you're looking for greenery, a little oxygen, and somewhere to stroll or sit, you should head for the Parc Montsouris. Paris is very short of green parks, and this small space – complete with a hill, trees, lawns, flowers, a pond, a grotto, and

JOSEPHINE BAKER (1906–75)

The black American singer and dancer Josephine Baker was not only a great performer. She was also a courageous woman who dared to challenge the racial prejudices of her time.

Born in 1906 in St. Louis, Missouri, she left home to try her luck on Broadway via Philadelphia, where she performed in theaters and music halls. A grand tour of Europe changed her career. She was an instant success, as well as causing unprecedented outrage, as the star of the music-hall show Revue Nègre and the chief priestess at the Ebony Venus cabaret, performing naked except for a banana girdle. She also gained immense popularity with her song "J'ai deux amours" ("Two loves I have, My country and Paris"), and was partly responsible for acclimatizing Parisian tastes to the melodies and rhythms of American blacks.

Horrified by the rise of Nazism, she was not content with entertaining the Allied troops, but actually enrolled in the army to become the most famous sub-lieutenant in the French air force, where she was awarded the Croix de Guerre and the Légion d'Honneur.

After the war, she and her husband founded a "Home for Human Brotherhood" and adopted twelve children from various countries, whom she called her "rainbow tribe." She supported Martin Luther King's struggle for civil rights in the States. Her last years were marred by financial crises. To repay her debts, she gave many shows and "farewell performances" until 1975, when, during a show at the Bobino music hall in Paris, she collapsed on stage with a fatal heart attack.

even a small waterfall – is delightful. Frequented by international students from the nearby Cité Universitaire, and flocks of children playing around the pond, it's a very welcome restingplace.

Further southeast is a crumbling neighborhood known, appropriately, as Plaisance, where old streets like Pernety and Gergovie house a working-class population, and the grocery shops and cafés feel surprisingly convivial. Finally, before you leave Montparnasse, take the time to visit two small museums.

Musée Zadkine and Musée Bourdelle
100bis rue d'Assas, 75006. Metro Port-Royal. Tel. 43 26 91 90. Open daily 10 a.m.–5:30 p.m.; closed Monday; and 16 rue Antoine-Bourdelle, 75015. Tel. 45 48 67 27. Metro Falguière/Montparnasse. Open daily 10 a.m.–5:40 p.m.; closed Monday.

Musée Zadkine is situated in the studio occupied by the Cubist sculptor Ossip Zadkine from 1928 until his death in 1967. He is said to have been enchanted by this little house, where you can see over 300 of his works, including drawings and gouaches, all donated to the City of Paris by his wife.

The second museum celebrates another sculptor, Antoine Bourdelle, who had his studio here from 1884, the year he entered the Ecole des Beaux-Arts, until his death in 1929. The Musée Bourdelle, based around the family home, was inaugurated in 1949

ISADORA DUNCAN (1878-1927)

The American dancer Isadora Duncan was born in San Francisco, where her Irish mother, abandoned by her husband with four children, gave piano lessons to make ends meet. From the start Isadora was a free spirit, rejecting school in favor of teaching movement and dance to the children around her. She received no lessons herself until she was about eleven.

In 1898 – having already achieved some fame for her free and sensual barefoot performances (often to readings by her brother and sister) – the family lost everything in a fire in New York's Windsor Hotel. Urged by Isadora, they moved to London. Her career took off, with private performances in *salons* and galleries all over Europe, including the Princesse de Polignac's *salon* in Paris, where she danced before the composer Fauré, the painter Eugène Carrière, and Rodin. Her love life was as wild as her dancing. Her two children were tragically drowned in 1913.

Isadora's last performance was in Paris in 1927, when she danced to Schubert's Unfinished *Symphony* and *Ave Maria*. Among her admirers was Janet Flanner, who remarked in her 1920s journal:

> A Paris couturier once said woman's modern freedom in dress is largely due to Isadora. She was the first artist to appear unlincuctured, barefooted and free. She arrived like a glorious bounding Minerva in the midst of a cautious corseted decade.

She too, like her children, died in an accident: strangled by her silk scarf, which caught in the wheel of her open car.

ARTISTS & INTELLECTUALS

and has since been considerably enlarged to accommodate around 900 works by the artist, among them several family portraits in oil, 62 portraits of Beethoven (done from his death mask) and a bas-relief inspired by Isadora Duncan from the Théâtre des Champs-Elysées. The garden also contains some monumental bronzes.

MONTMARTRE

The ghosts of artists and intellectuals from the recent past continue to linger in the cafés, bars and streets of Montparnasse; Montmartre is haunted by their predecessors. Be warned, however: to arrive here, on the opposite side of town – a good Metro ride away, then a short walk – is to enter one of the most commercialized corners of Paris.

Montmartre will not disappoint anyone looking for bus-loads of people with cameras slung around their necks. The bereted daubers at place du Tertre would be equally at home in EuroDisney, and the "reserved for prayer" signs labeling half of the basilica of Sacré-Cœur's benches suggest – rightly – that the rest have been sur-rendered to tourists tuckered out by the climb up Montmartre hill.

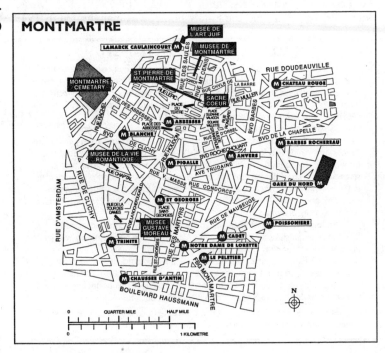

So, a word of advice: if you don't want to bump into other tourists, don't come to Montmartre. It's that simple.

But it would be missing the point: entertainment has always been part of Montmartre's history. In the eighteenth century there was already a street of fifty-eight houses which boasted twenty-five taverns, and in 1814 Russian troops descended on local bars shouting "bistro" – meaning quick! – for a hasty drink. Indeed, the French word *bistro* is now used to denote a café where you can eat a good simple meal quickly and without fuss. While in most of Paris, cafés are named after their street, conversely, the rue de la Goutte d'Or and the place du Château Rouge are named after cabarets – so that gives you an indication of the area's priorities!

Some women enjoyed slumming it – like the duchess who pretended to be a model in order to catch a glimpse of Degas's studio – others worked as prostitutes, often doubling as models; while some worked as dancers, such as Toulouse-Lautrec's favorite Jane Avril (see below) – all have been part of the hurly-burly of street life.

And so has art. The Impressionists painted the open-air restaurants and balls where Parisian workers flocked for a taste of the suburbs. Even today there is always a crowd of caricaturists and pseudo-Impressionists at place du Tertre. Towards the end of the nineteenth century this square became a haven for many poor – but now famous – artists, though it seems doubtful that any of their modern-day replacements will make it into the history books.

Bâteau-Lavoir

In the Bâteau-Lavoir, diminutive wooden artists' studios on place Emile Goudeau, artists such as Picasso, Braque and Juan Gris created their first Cubist paintings in 1900. At the same time, not far away, both Mary Cassatt and Suzanne Valadon went about their painting. The Bâteau-Lavoir burnt down in 1970, but has been replaced by a complex of artists' studios.

LOUISE MICHEL (1830–1905)

Louise Michel, anarchist and founder of the International League of Revolutionary Women, was born the illegitimate child of a servant. Nevertheless she received a good education and became a teacher. She shared her liberal and revolutionary ideas with the opponents of Napoleon III, and joined the Communards soon after the proclamation of the Republic in 1870. The following year, on April 3, 1871, she joined the federal troops and, wearing a black dress and a red scarf, took part in riots and demonstrations at the barricades in defense of Paris. Also known as the "Red Virgin," she was finally arrested and deported to New Caledonia, where she took part in that island's nationalist struggles.

An amnesty allowed her to return to France in 1880, only to be twice imprisoned for revolutionary activities before writing her *Mémoires* and *La Commune: Histoire et Souvenirs*. She died on a lecture tour in Marseille in 1905.

Montmartre has always attracted the avant-garde: the Paris Commune had its origins here; the Romantics created "New Athens" to the south in the ninth *arrondissement*; Impressionists worked at place Clichy when it was still the countryside; and in 1871, 120 women died defending the barricades on the place Blanche.

Today the radical and artistic life of Montmartre is behind rather than ahead of the times, and Bohemia is truly dead and buried.

Montmartre Cemetery
20 rue Rachel, 75018. Metro place de Clichy.
Tel. 43 87 64 24. Open 8 a.m.–7:30 p.m. Monday–Friday;
8:30 a.m.–5:30 p.m. Saturday; 9 a.m.– 5:30 p.m. Sunday. Map
available at the gatehouse.

This cemetery, unlike Père-Lachaise, is genuinely gloomy, not helped by the shadow of rue de Caulaincourt looming on metal stilts overhead. Here lie many of those women who contributed to the popularity of Montmartre: the dancer Marie Taglioni, whose fragile body exemplified the Romantic ideal of femininity; the actress Alphonsine Plessis, model for Dumas's consumptive heroine in *La Dame aux Camélias*; the songwriter Marguerite Carrère; the poet Marceline Desbordes-Valmore; the singer Pauline Viardot; the hostess Madame Récamier; the writer Louise Colet, better known as Flaubert's lover and correspondent; and Thérèse Aubry, who played the goddess Reason in a revolutionary pageant – to name but a few.

There are many faces to Montmartre, the best being the least unmarked by tourism. A recommended option is to stick to the village-like western half of the slope. From the station at place Blanche you can climb the market street rue Lepic to the white-washed place des Abbesses, embellished by Art Nouveau Metro exits and an early-twentieth-century brick and cement church, Saint-Jean-de-Montmartre. Rue Ravignan takes you through the shady place Emile Goudeau. From here on up, windy streets such as rues Orchampt, Berthe, Cortot, and de l'Abreuvoir (painted into stereotype by Utrillo) alternate with elegant avenues like the Art Nouveau avenue Junot and the romantically named and wooded allée des Brouillards (Misty Alley). Square Suzanne Buisson, named after the secretary of the National Socialist Women's Committee who was killed in a concentration camp in 1943, is a peaceful place to sit. Further up, on rue des Saules, Aristide Bruant's cabaret, the Lapin Agile, still stands at number 22.

Place du Tertre and Place Calvaire
At this point, the aptly named rue Saint-Rustique will take you to the place du Tertre, bordered by pretty houses and cafés where you can sit out and watch the many caricaturists and portraitists making

a quick buck by producing a flattering chocolate-boxy likeness of the tourist seated before them. This hardly amounts to art, but it's the only remaining vestige of an illustrious artistic community. Leading off is the place du Calvaire, the smallest square in Paris, with a magnificent view over the capital. Further on up the hill you come to the church of Sacré-Cœur, but the best way to approach this tourist attraction is head-on with everyone else. The first leg of the itinerary (Metro Pigalle) is the garish rue de Steinkerque – the approach from the northeast, via rue Muller, is prettier, but dilutes the full effect. If you're allergic to steps, catch the funicular at place Suzanne Valadon. Otherwise you climb on to terraced Square Willette (whose eastern outcropping is surprisingly romantic), where you can take a rest before trudging onward.

SACRÉ-CŒUR
Rue Chevalier de la Barre, 75018. Metro Blanche/Pigalle.
Tel. 42 51 17 02. Open: dome 8 a.m.–11 p.m.; church 10 a.m.–
5 p.m. summer 9 a.m.–6 p.m.; crypt Saturday 10 a.m.–5 p.m.

This bulbous neo-Byzantine wedding cake, built over a fifty-year period to expiate the crimes of the Paris Commune, is a useful landmark from a distance. Close up, it's ugly. The hilltop location and hulking size were designed to make the church a sinister reminder of the repression for the radical east of Paris, although now, fortunately, the omnipresent tower blocks do make it possible to get away from the sight. The church has taken advantage of tourist numbers to proselytize, and coin-operated doctrinal recordings compete with multilingual leaflets informing non-Christians that it's the answer to all their doubts, and reassuring Protestants that "here in the basilica there is no superstition." Unfortunately, the address on the letterhead is rue Chevalier de la Barre, named after a nineteen-year-old broken on the wheel in 1766 because he hadn't doffed his hat to a religious procession.

Saint-Pierre de Montmartre
2 rue du Mont-Cenis, 75018. Tel. 46 06 57 63

Next door is Saint-Pierre de Montmartre, a twelfth-century church which gains from the contrast with its neighbor; in fact it was saved from demolition only by a lobby of local artists, some actively anticlerical, who wanted to prove their loathing for Sacré-Cœur. The church gives an impression of age: the marble columns come from the original Gallo-Roman temple it replaced, and its simpler Romanesque style is a welcome respite from the fussiness of Sacré-Cœur. Inside are the tombstones of important abbesses, including Queen Adelaide of Savoy, who founded the Abbey of which the church of Saint-Pierre is all that survives. Women in religious

ARTISTS & INTELLECTUALS

Orders, not being subjected to the yoke of men, had considerable power, and were allowed the right to vote until the Revolution. Another casualty of the Revolution was the last abbess, Louise-Marie de Montmorency-Laval, who was guillotined in 1794 and buried in Saint-Pierre.

Musée de Montmartre
12 rue Cortot, 75018. Metro Lamarck-Caulicourt.
Tel. 46 06 61 11. Open daily 2:30–6 p.m.;
Monday, Sunday 11 a.m.–6 p.m.

Located in a beautiful white house, once lived in by Suzanne Valadon, this museum is nevertheless disappointing. Somehow the motley assembly of mementoes – most notably some original cabaret posters by Toulouse-Lautrec – and the reconstruction of "l'Abreuvoir," the café frequented by painters such as Utrillo, don't manage to capture the spirit of bohemian life. The museum organizes temporary exhibitions featuring local artists and writers, and you can also walk around the nearby Montmartre vineyard (entrance on rue des Saules) which still yields a good crop of grapes every year.

At the bottom of the hill known as the Butte de Montmartre, real life takes over. The stretch of boulevards that change their name from Clichy to Rochechouart to La Chapelle is always lively, with bins of cheap clothes in front of stores. Surprising snatches of greenery can be glimpsed in alleys like Cité Veron and quiet courtyards like Cité du Midi. Occasionally, there's an old-fashioned carnival, complete with sword-swallowers and enormous dolls to win, along the boulevard Rochechouart.

GOUTTE D'OR AND PIGALLE

To the east, north of the intersection between boulevard Barbès and boulevard de la Chapelle, is the Goutte d'Or, mentioned in Zola's novel *L'Assommoir*, whose heroine, Gervaise, washes other women's laundry. The area also has its place among Marya's memories in Jean Rhys's *Quartet*:

> Marya had often wandered about that part of Paris with Stephan when they lived in Montmartre, and she remembered the dingy streets, the vegetable shops kept by sleek-haired women, the bars haunted by gaily dressed little prostitutes who seemed to be perpetually making the gesture of opening their bags to powder their noses. Over the whole of the quarter the sinister and rakish atmosphere of the Faubourg Montmartre spread like some perfume.

Nowadays this is the heart of West Indian Paris. Streets like Goutte d'Or and d'Orsel, though in decline, are still something of a commercial center for fabric. But above all you'll notice the area's culture, pulsating with a rhythm all its own, from restaurants serv-

JANE AVRIL (1868–1923)

Jane Avril, born into the Italian nobility, defied her strict upbringing and boarding-school education by becoming a dancer at the age of eighteen. It was four years later, at the Moulin Rouge, that she first caught the eye of Toulouse-Lautrec. Renowned for her wild and supple improvisation, she was also hired by all the other leading cabaret venues of the time, including the Hippodrome and the Chat Noir, where she captured the heart of Alphonse Allais, who is said to have pursued her one evening with a revolver while desperately declaring his love.

In later years she danced and sang at the Jardins de Paris and the Folies Bergères before marrying and very much settling down with the painter Maurice Biais, by whom she had a son. This marked the end of her stage career; after her husband's death, she spent her last years quietly writing and knitting in an old people's home at Jouay-en-Josas.

ing Creole food and galleries specializing in black artists to clubs where the music is loud and the beat is strong. It's not the most comfortable place to wander around at night, but the level of stares and comments is hardly higher than it is in the center of town.

The same is true of Pigalle, the notorious red-light district where sex is as available as soap. If you must visit this patch of the city, it's best seen by night; during the day, litter from last night's festivities and the dreary shop fronts look tired and dispiriting, reminiscent of an aging night-club hostess seen in the cold light of day without her make-up or sequined costume. This is where the young Edith Piaf first sang after running away to Paris with her lover at the age of fifteen. It's the site, too, of the famous Moulin Rouge immortalized by Toulouse-Lautrec in his posters featuring the dancer Jane Avril, the fiery redhead who, with her partner La Goulue, delighted and scandalized audiences with her cancan.

The thrills evoked by the prospect of a glimpse of flesh in the nineteenth century have been replaced by a tired cabaret that seems tame in comparison to the "live sex of all kinds" offered in any number of seedy strip joints along the boulevard de Clichy.

Musée Gustave Moreau

14 rue de la Rochefoucauld, 75009. Metro Trinité.
Tel. 48 74 38 50. Open 10 a.m.–12:45 p.m., 2–5:15 p.m.;
Wednesday 11 a.m.–5:15 p.m.

Abandoning the seediness of Pigalle in search of culture, you might well turn towards number 14 rue de la Rochefoucauld, where the Symbolist painter Gustave Moreau lived until his death in 1898. The museum has been referred to as the temple of Symbolism; it contains over 8000 examples of Moreau's work which is generally recognized as a precursor to the Fauve, Surrealist and Abstract movements. Certainly he numbered Matisse among his pupils.

NOUVELLE ATHÈNES

As you head south of the boulevard, the neon fades away. The "New Athens" around place Saint-Georges was rather grandly developed in the 1820s, when Romantics made it their meeting place. Some streets, like rue de l'Agent Bailly or Cité Charles-Godon, are quiet and almost provincial; others, like rue du Faubourg Montmartre and rue des Martyrs, have lively food markets.

The ninth *arrondissement* must have one of the highest proportions of streets named after women: apart from the passage des Deux-Sœurs, named after two sisters who owned the land, a handful of streets (rues de Bellefonds, de Rochechouart, de la Tour d'Auvergne, and de la Rochefoucauld) were named after the abbesses of a convent located near present-day rue de Clichy. The rue de la Tour des Dames, named after the sister's windmill, is full of 1820s mansions, several built for actresses like Mademoiselle Mars (number 1) and Mademoiselle Duchesnois (number 3). In the nineteenth century this part of Paris was favored by women entertainers of all kinds, whether they were actresses or courtesans, and wealthy men liked to rent grand apartments for their mistresses here, even if they refused cash payments to match. The church of Notre-Dame-de-Lorette gave its name to *lorettes*, a euphemism for upscale courtesans. "The first thing that met my eyes upon arriving in this neighborhood," wrote the painter Delacroix in 1822, "was a

---

LA GOULUE (1866–1929)

Among the girls performing their saucy acrobatics on the stages of Pigalle, none was more agile, more pretty or curvaceous than Louise-Josephine Weber, nicknamed La Goulue (The Glutton) because of her zest for life. She was the daughter of a laundrywoman; her background couldn't have been more different from the aristocratic upbringing of Toulouse-Lautrec's other favorite model, Jame Avril. But by 1890, thanks to some sound financial advice, at the height of her fame, she had become a woman of some means, with a large house and garden in Montmartre.

Unfortunately, she lacked the same judgment in the matters of the heart. Her lover Charles Tazzani, a good-for-nothing ex-convict who fleeced her, was followed by an alcoholic English jockey. As her thirties approached she began to lose her figure and her enthusiasm for dance, turning instead to animal taming, which she learned with the tamer Pezon. In 1900 she married a conjuror called Joseph-Nicolas Droxler, with whom she toured the fairs with her menagerie. Fiery-natured and somewhat trigger-happy, she shot at both men at one time or another, but in spite of his bullet wounds, her husband bore her no ill will.

Things went from bad to worse and Louise had to sell her menagerie to pay for the care of her ailing son Simon, who died in 1920. She eventually became a flower-seller, moving into a caravan decorated with sketches by Toulouse-Lautrec. She died at Lariboisière on January 21, 1929, at the age of sixty-three, apparently with no regrets!

magnificent *lorette* of the grand style, all decked out in black velvet and satin. In stepping out of the carriage she showed me her leg up to the navel." During the Second Empire, materialistic *lorettes* were contrasted with their predecessors, *grisettes*, who were looked upon with nostalgia. Simple seamstresses or flower-makers, they would live with students eager to sow their wild oats before returning to the provinces and finding a wife. *Grisettes*, it was claimed, sat quietly at home darning their lovers' socks to save them money, while *lorettes* sucked men dry to buy gaudy dresses.

A pilgrimage should be made to 14 rue Saint-Georges, where from 1897 to 1903 the feminist newspaper *La Fronde* was published. The all-women staff was not legally allowed to print a daily, since labor laws forbade women to work at night, but they refused to admit male employees who, they predicted, would be suspected of ghostwriting the articles. At the time, the laws setting the hours for each sex were fraught with contradictions: industrial night work was considered a health hazard, although women were expected to cook and clean after they arrived home exhausted from day work; and their afternoons were lengthened by the law which gave them a break at noon, so that they could go home to cook their husbands' midday meals.

Not far away, in rue Chaptal, is a museum created to honor another woman who refused to conform to the strictures imposed on women by men: George Sand.

GEORGE SAND (1804–76)

Aurore Dupin, alias George Sand, left a distinctive mark on cultural history – not only through her talent as a writer, but also through her freedom of spirit, generosity and passionate commitment to socialist and humanitarian ideals.

She was already deeply concerned about the condition of men and women in society when her unhappy marriage to Baron Dudevant eventually prompted her to strike out on her own. After obtaining a legal separation in 1835, she adopted a masculine pen name, and from then on she often dressed as a man. In Paris Sand lived in the Left Bank's rue de Seine and rues Pigalle and Taitbout in Nouvelle Athènes, where she gathered around her many of the century's most important artists: musicians such as Berlioz, Liszt and Chopin (with whom she had a ten-year relationship), writers such as Balzac and de Musset, and the painter Delacroix.

Having written several novels preoccupied with utopian ideals, she became bitter at the failure of the 1848 Revolution and withdrew to her country house in Nohant, where she wrote a series of rural novels, as well as puppet plays for her son and the local village children. Her benevolent attitude to her dependents and country people soon gained her the title "*la bonne dame de Nohant*" ("the good lady of Nohant").

Not only was she largely responsible for the development of the socially conscious novel in Europe, but her literary influence extended further – as far as Russia, where she was highly rated by Turgenev.

Musée de la Vie Romantique
(Maison Renan-Scheffer)

16 rue Chaptal, 75009. Metro Saint-Georges/Pigalle.
Tel. 48 74 95 38. Open 10 a.m.–5:40 p.m; closed Monday and public holidays.

This museum situated at the very end of a small lane, was once the house of the painter Ary Scheffer. It is reminiscent of the Romanticist movement of 1820–50 – one of the most interesting literary and artistic periods in Paris. The Musée de la Vie Romantique pays homage to George Sand whose granddaughter donated all the writer's belongings to the museum. There are also memorabilia from Flaubert, Chopin, Liszt, Lamennais, Rossini and Delacroix.

The George Sand Rooms on the ground floor were decorated by the architect J. Garcia according to descriptions of the writer's private apartment. Adding to this authentic atmosphere are hundreds of items that belonged to Sand – portraits, furnishing, drawings and jewels. Of note are two paintings by Delacroix, master of Romanticist painting, who was a friend of Chopin and George Sand: *L'Education de la Vierge* and *Lélia*. There are also some paintings of Nohant, a place to which Delacroix had often been invited. Other works to look out for are Ingres's *Portrait de Calametta*, a bust of Sand's daughter Claudine by the sculptor Houdon, and numerous portraits of the writer herself by Charpentier and Blaize. On the first floor are portraits and landscapes from her own collection.

AWAY FROM THE CENTER

Finally we reach the lesser-known parts of the city, the outer *arrondissements* that wouldn't be included on a whistle-stop tour but represent the more intriguing, unexpected side of Paris as well as offering plenty to do, especially with children eager to run outdoors on an empty weekend. This is the time when hundreds of Parisians head for the Bois de Boulogne, to cycle, ride horses, jog, go boating, play ball or simply spread out a sumptuous Sunday picnic before lying back to watch others use up all their energy. For a very different experience you can visit Chinatown, with its overwhelming choice of Asian restaurants and exotic supermarkets piled high with spices and great sacks of rice, or discover the hidden qualities of Belleville. One of these is Père-Lachaise Cemetery, also a beautiful park, where people come to wander, contemplate the inscriptions of famous names, and remind themselves of their own mortality. If you're feeling lazy or looking for a way to entertain the children, hop on a boat to La Bastille and chug gently down the canals bordered by leafy paths, a favorite with French families for a post-prandial stroll, where the children will wave to you from the bridges, past the rotunda of the place Stalingrad, formerly a toll gate for merchants entering the city, and on towards the high-tech ultramodern complex of La Villette.

Once you've acquired a taste for the ultramodern, you'll have to make your pilgrimage out to La Défense for a look at the great vast sugar cube of the Grande Arche. Breathtaking in the bright sunlight, it is awesome at any time of year; its sheer size can even have a therapeutic, calming effect after a day being abused by travel agents, scorned by store clerks, and ignored by waiters, reassuring you, in the face of such monumental proportions, that despite the attempts of certain people to make others feel smaller, in the end we are all only *this* high.

THE 16TH ARRONDISSEMENT, THE BOIS DE BOULOGNE AND LA DÉFENSE

The sixteenth *arrondissement* is the large expanse of Paris that stretches away to the west of the Champs Elysées on the Right Bank and is neatly sandwiched between the Seine and the Bois de

Boulogne. Home to rich, bourgeois families, this *quartier* is the habitat of the "BCBG" [*bon chic, bon genre*], distinguishable by her Hermès scarf, pearl necklace and Gucci loafers tapping irritably while a miniature dog on the end of a Cartier leash squats in the gutter, before being hauled back to some palatial apartment. This area, though it's full of imposing nineteenth-century buildings, has to be one of the least lively in Paris, and parts of it – notably avenue Foch and around Porte Dauphine – are made positively unsavory by the rent boys who hang around. If you're alone, don't expect to be able to hail a taxi on the avenue Foch late at night – if anyone stops, it won't be a cab driver.

The main reason for the area's dubious nighttime reputation is the presence of the Bois de Boulogne. Despite a recent clean-up campaign by the police, including cordoning off and patrolling certain areas, the Brazilian transvestites who ply their trade in the wood are drifting back, and the place's renown as a sort of open-air brothel still seems justified. The day time, however, is a different matter.

If you're looking for a large expanse of green or somewhere to let your children loose without leaving Paris, head for the Bois de Boulogne. Since it covers over 2000 acres, it's best to go by car; otherwise, pick your destination, travel by public transportation, then walk.

BOIS DE BOULOGNE

Metro Porte d'Auteuil/Port Dauphine/Porte Maillot.
Open daily dawn till dusk.

Stretching from Neuilly to Boulogne and bordered by the old city fortifications on one side and the Seine on the other, this was a royal park for many centuries. It was Louis XIV who first opened it to the public, and Haussmann who did much of the present-day landscaping, including the racecourses and the main approach road, avenue Foch – encouraged by Emperor Napoleon III, who had developed a taste for English-style parks, such as Hyde Park, during his exile in London. The Bois later became popular with the *demi-mode* of the Left-Bank – Natalie Barney would ride there dressed in men's clothes.

The best place to take children is the Jardin d'Acclimatation in the northeastern corner or the Musée en Herbe, created ten years ago by three women archeologists, which aims to introduce children to various aspects of their heritage through displays, activities, games and specially devised workshops. Past themes include Astérix and the era of the Gauls, the Australian Aborigines, and Mammoths and Elephants. To the southeast of the Jardin d'Acclimatation, adults might prefer to head for the château and gardens of Bagatelle.

Bagatelle

Metro Pont de Neuilly. Tel. 47 47 47 10.
Open 8:30–9 a.m., 6–8 p.m. according to the season.

The château, built in 1775 and considerably modified in 1835 by the then owner, Lord Seymour Duke of Hertford, has passed through many hands, including those of Sir Richard Wallace, owner of London's Wallace Collection. It was originally built by the Comte d'Artois, who bet that he could have the castle built in two months, in time for a visit from his sister-in-law Marie-Antoinette. (The work was actually completed in 63 days.) One hundred and fifty years on, Wallace's wife left it to her secretary and lover Sir Murray Scott, whose estate sold it in 1915 to the City of Paris, which has owned it ever since.

Even more popular than the château are the grounds. The rose garden was the brainchild of Jean-Claude-Nicolas Forestier, Curator of the city's parks and gardens and friend of the Impressionists, particularly Monet. It was largely the Impressionists' influence that inspired him to plant the flowers in large groups to provide a mass of color. The rose garden contains 9000 rose bushes, and is a dream to visit in June. Other superb collections, according to season, are the spring bulbs, rhododendrons, dahlias and, in winter, the snowdrops.

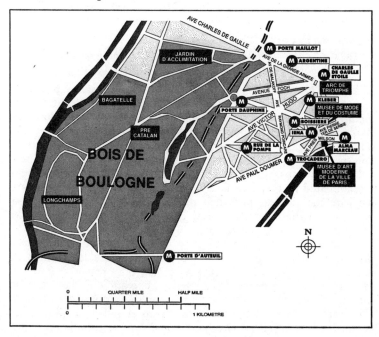

Sports

For something a little more active than a stroll around the garden and tea at the terrace café, the Bois de Boulogne offers a good choice of sporting facilities. Bicycles can be hired at the entrance of the Jardin d'Acclimatation; pedal boats on the Petit Lac; or boats on the Grand Lac, where you can row yourself across to the chalet-style café-restaurant on the bigger of the two islands – a real Swiss chalet brought here during the Second Empire to please the Empress Eugénie. This passion for all things Swiss also manifests itself in the Grand Cascade (near the Carrefour de Longchamp), a ten-meter-high artificial waterfall built out of rocks from the forest of Fontainebleau.

As the headquarters of the Racing Club de France, the Bois boasts two racecourses, one for the flat and one for steeplechases, as well as hosting polo matches and showjumping events. Longchamp, of course, is the home of the famous Prix de L'Arc de Triomphe, one of the biggest events in the sporting calendar. Another is the Roland Garros tennis tournament held at the stadium at the southern end of the Bois, which attracts as many big names as Wimbledon.

For bucolic pleasures the Pré Catalan in the southeast of the park has some of the oldest and biggest trees, including an oak nearly seven meters round. You will also find the Shakespeare garden, where you can examine all the plants mentioned in his plays while – if you're lucky – hearing the great author being declaimed on the grass of the open-air theater – in French, of course.

Musée de la Femme et de l'Automate

12 rue du Center. Metro Pont Neuilly. Tel. 47 45 29 40.
Open 2:30–5:30 p.m; closed Tuesday.

This is an extraordinary name for a very strange museum. If you can, borrow a French speaking child and try to make it out to Neuilly-sur-Seine (a twenty-minute walk from the Bois de Boulogne, or fifteen minutes from Metro Pont de Neuilly) for this oddity which is really two museums. The understandable half – and the only part that attracts more than a handful of visitors – is a collection of musical automatons. Every afternoon at 3 p.m. these are animated by the charming guide, who keeps up a quick repartee with the children and their parents in a room copied from a ballroom in the Château de Rambouillet, complete with Rococo swirls and fake gilded chandeliers.

The other half of the collection is the "Musée de la Femme" proper, encompassing the lifelong dream of its founder, a mysterious and evidently rich collector who died only recently. A quick look at the bizarre displays is enough to explain why the sole visitors are those who arrived too early for the automatons. In one glass case a photo of Brigitte Bardot rubs shoulders with a mannequin wearing a Juliette Greco mask and American-Indian cooking implements; in another a Spanish shawl is draped around a badly blown-up photo of a woman's body out of which protrudes a three-dimensional plastic hand holding a fan. The most coherent exhibits are probably the porcelain and wax models of Joan of Arc. There's also a roomful of signed letters replying to requests for autographs – some, like Margaret Thatcher's and Indira Gandhi's, boast signed or unsigned photographs too – and a box of royalist relics, including Marie-Antoinette's corset and a book opened *in medias res* to a discussion of Charlotte Corday's trial. The visit ends with a framed color postcard of a statue of Marie Harel, inventor of Camembert cheese, donated in 1956 by the cheese-producing center of Van Wer, Ohio, and a photo of a Metro station plastered with advertisements for the museum.

Back in the heart of the sixteenth, a stone's throw from the chic area surrounding the avenue George V, are two more conventional museums which in many ways combine two of the things with which Paris has been synonymous for years: modern art and *haute couture*. Well worth visiting, even if you feel you've slaked your thirst at the Pompidou Center, is the Musée d'Art Moderne de la Ville de Paris, while in an adjacent street you can treat yourself to a fashion show featuring some of Paris's greatest designers in the Musée de la Mode et du Costume.

Musée d'Art Moderne de la Ville de Paris

11 avenue du President Wilson, 75016. Metro Iéna/Alma Marceau. Tel. 47 23 61 27. Open 10 a.m.–5:30 p.m. Tuesday–Sunday (8 p.m. Wednesday); closed Monday.

The museum is in the east wing of the Palais de Tokyo; the other wing houses the National Center of Photography and the Simone de Beauvoir audiovisual center. The building was erected in 1937 for the World Exhibition, but the art museum opened only in 1962, despite having long been earmarked for the display of modern paintings. It's a bit of a mess – it's been neglected as a result of competition from the Pompidou Center (since 1977) – but it's still worth visiting for the strong selection of Cubist and Fauvist paintings, as well as a large sample of postwar art.

Above the main entrance hall, the Salle Dufy houses outsize works such as Dufy's *La Fée Electricité*, painted in 250 panels to decorate the main entrance hall of the Pavillon de la Lumière (Light Pavilion) during the World Exhibition. Measuring about 60 meters by 10 meters it is said to be the largest painting in the world. Other large canvases are on show two floors below, including Matisse's *La Danse* – the first version of the world-famous painting now on display in Pennsylvania. This room also contains four colorful, swirling abstracts titled *Rythmes* – three by Robert Delaunay, the last by Sonia Delaunay.

The rest of the collection, representing most of twentieth-century-art's key movements, is displayed on the lower ground floor with works by Derain, Vlaminck, Matisse, Picasso, Braque, Modigliani and Rouault. Suzanne Valadon, famous for her vigorous, realistic and individual style, stands out yet again as one of the few recognized women painters of her time. The upper floors are reserved for a variety of contemporary and experimental works, including music and photography.

Centre Audiovisuel Simone de Beauvoir
Palais de Tokyo, 75016. Tel. 47 23 67 48. Metro Alma-Marceau.

Named after the celebrated French writer, author of *Le Deuxième Sexe* (*The Second Sex*) (1948) among other notable works, this audiovisual center was founded in 1982 by Carole Roussopoulos, Delphine Seyrig and Ioana Wieder, with the aim of promoting audiovisual works executed by women and about women.

Since its conception ten years ago, the center has evolved into a library, a production center complete with film unit where workshops are held, and a venue for courses.

The center also organizes competitions to encourage new works and promote unknown filmmakers, and also biannual festivals and retrospectives – for example, under the patronage of the actress Isabelle Huppert and the Secretary of State for the Rights of Women, as a tribute to the actress Delphine Seyrig it is showing a wide selection of new short films in French and English, with debates and round-table discussions.

For details of membership or a list of events phone the center.

Musée de la Mode et du Costume
Palais Galliera, 10 avenue Pierre Ier de Serbie. Metro Iéna/Alma Marceau. Tel. 47 20 85 23. Open 10 a.m.–5:45 p.m. (opening hours may change during exhibitions); closed Monday.

This beautiful Renaissance-style mansion, just on the other side of avenue President Wilson, was built in 1880 for the Duchesse de Galliera. Today it houses about 40,000 items of clothing and fashion accessories dating from the eighteenth century to the present, originally displayed in the Musée Carnavalet. The collection has increased over the years, thanks to donations from the likes of la Baronne Guy de Rothschild and Princess Grace of Monaco.

If you're interested in the evolution of fashion, you'll find it fascinating just to wander around looking at the individual interpretations that top couturiers – present and past – have given to the distinctive trends of each decade: to watch, for instance, the way in which the pendulum swung from the demureness of the 1950s, when girls dressed like their mothers, through the excesses of the

1960s back to the cover-all skirts of the 1970s back again to the micro of the 1980s and into the 1990s where, like an overexposed film, all the styles of the preceding fifty years seem to have become superimposed.

Lack of space, and the danger of exposing fabrics for too long means that the collections are presented in about three temporary thematic exhibitions. There's also a library, which incudes a very rich fashion prints collection.

LA DÉFENSE

Grande Arche. Metro La Défense/RER La Défense. Tel. 47 78 13 33. Open April–September 9 a.m.–6 p.m. Sunday 9:30 a.m.–midnight; October–March 10 a.m.–6 p.m; Sunday 10 a.m.–midnight.

Two kilometers to the west of Paris on a straight axis from Place de la Concorde through the Arc de Triomphe is the area known as La Défense, a commercial and financial district equipped with a huge shopping complex and an international conference center, and dominated by La Grande Arche. From central Paris, you can distinguish La Défense by its cluster of sleek, dark towers poking up into the sky. In the middle of these modern skyscraper blocks, inhabited by multinationals like Elf, Fiat and Honeywell Bull, slightly turned away at an oblique angle to the central axis, stands the sparkling, white edifice of the immense Grande Arche de La Défense.

Designed by Danish architect Otto von Spreckelsen, the building, unveiled in the summer of 1989, was yet another of the government's contributions to the bicentennial celebrations. It's built mainly of white marble, with a bank of death-defying glass elevator capsules that haul you up through a central void into the roof space, from which you can go out on to a parapet for a brilliant view of Paris. The legs of the arch are pierced with hundreds of windows, small glass squares geometrically and symmetrically arranged to echo the cube of the arch itself, signaling floor upon floor of offices. On a bright sunny day the glare thrown up by the marble steps leading up to the central platform – so wide that you feel as though you're entering some vast temple to a gargantuan god – is absolutely dazzling.

To your left, standing under the arch, is the hemispherical CNIT (Centre Nationale des Industries et des Techniques) building, which combines shops with a top-ranking conference center; to your right is a huge modern shopping complex. Stretching away before you is the Esplanade de la Défense, peppered with modern sculptures in an attempt to break up the severity of the modern building materials, and with a multicolored fountain that spouts in time to music. Finally, straight ahead, there's a clear, unbroken view to Paris's other arch, built some 150 years before: the Arc de Triomphe.

GARE DE LYON TO VINCENNES

Almost directly across Paris lies the twelfth *arrondissement*, which you'll pass through on the way to Vincennes. Besides the handsome classic Gare de Lyon, the twelfth is not very appealing. It's no coincidence that two of its most important buildings are modern, forming part of the massive redevelopment project to which the *quartier* continues to be subjected. Out have gone the Bercy wine warehouses and tiny leafy streets, all named after the best wines of France.

Until 1860 the wine merchants transported their wine by barge up the Seine and installed themselves just outside Paris on the banks of the river at Bercy, so that they could sell their wine to Parisians but avoid the wine tax imposed on those living within the city boundaries. At that time many restaurants and open-air dance halls were established next to what was to become France's first wine market, drawing Parisians in their droves to have fun, as well as taking advantage of the lower wine prices. All this stopped when the Commune de Bercy became officially attached to the city in 1860. Since then, decades of decline have led to the current redevelopment in the next stage of a project which has already produced the Palais des Omnisports at Bercy and the Ministère des Finances, between avenue de Deaumesnil and the Seine.

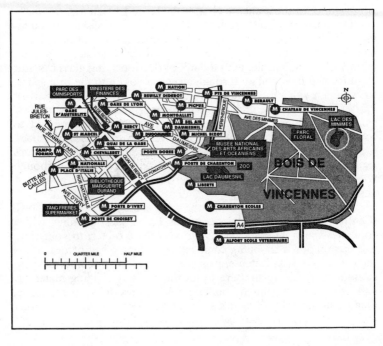

The concrete Palais des Omnisports was completed in 1983 and houses a stadium that can accommodate 17,000 people, an ice rink, an athletics track and two cycling circuits. The whole complex can be covered over, and the stadium is a popular venue for big rock concerts.

Immediately opposite, the Ministère des Finances is hardly more aesthetically pleasing. Built in 1986, mainly of glass and steel, to house the Ministry of Finance after its eviction from the Louvre, this vast building stretches 400 meters along the river bank and at one point juts over the road running along the Seine to plant its feet right on the bank. Home to 6500 employees from the various different departments of the Ministry which were formerly scattered throughout Paris, the building resembles a cross between the Starship *Enterprise* and what you might imagine to be the Ministry of Information in Orwell's *Nineteen Eighty-four*.

GARE DE LYON
75012. Metro Gare de Lyon.

The twelfth *arrondissement* is at least partly redeemed by the Gare de Lyon. This gorgeous building, with its imposing clock tower, was built in 1899 and enlarged in 1929. The ticket counters are housed in the Galérie des Fresques, a long gallery painted with landscapes across France from Paris to the Côte d'Azur. Perhaps more astonishing, however, is the station restaurant, "Le Train Bleu." Classified as a historic monument and regarded as one of the most beautiful restaurants in Paris, this eating place has retained all its original turn-of-the-century decor, reminiscent of the *belle-époque* era, when train travel was at its most luxurious. You dine surrounded by scenes painted and signed by the most celebrated artists of the time. Most evoke large towns like Nice on the PLM (Paris-Lyon-Mediterranée) line, and all are extravagantly framed in gilt. The combination of waiters whisking around in the traditional long white aprons and details like the brass racks for balancing your hatbox makes you feel, as you glance through the window, that it would be quite natural to see a steam train puffing into the station.

BOIS DE VINCENNES
Metro Château de Vincennes/Porte Dorée. Open dawn till dusk.

The southeast corner of the twelfth *arrondissement* borders on the Bois de Vincennes, a popular spot with Parisians looking for a bit of green to spread out on during a warm summer Sunday. Formerly a royal hunting ground like its famous cousin, the Bois de Boulogne, this vast expanse of park – complete with château, lakes, a flower garden and a zoo – was handed over to the City of Paris by Napoleon in 1860 on the assumption that the authorities would have it landscaped into a park for the people.

If you start at the closest entrance to Paris, the Porte Dorée, and head clockwise, you come first to the Lac Daumesnil which, though smaller than the lakes in the Bois de Boulogne, had its own Swiss chalet built on one of the islands for the Universal Exhibition of 1867. You'll also find an eighteenth-century folly, a small rotunda graced with Doric columns above a grotto reminiscent of the Parc des Buttes-Chaumont. The zoo beside the lake created a sensation when it opened in 1931 – people had never before seen wild animals wandering in the relative freedom of surroundings close to their natural habitats. It's said that the first Sunday alone attracted 50,000 visitors.

CHÂTEAU DE VINCENNES

Metro Château de Vincennes. Tel. 43 28 15 48. Guided tours daily 10 a.m.–5 p.m. winter; 9:30 a.m.–7 p.m. summer.

North of the zoo is the chateau, surrounded by a moat with a drawbridge. Less pretty French château than fortified castle, the building has had a checkered history – it has served as prison, armory, royal residence and porcelain factory – and all that remains of the medieval castle is an impressive turreted tower. Henry V of England died of dysentery in 1422 in the main room on the first floor. His body was allegedly boiled in the kitchen below to preserve it for transportation to England.

While it was a prison, the château hid a number of illustrious people, among them the future Henri IV, imprisoned by Catherine de' Medici in the sixteenth century; Diderot in 1749; Latude, sentenced to thirty-five years for plotting against Madame de Pompadour; and in 1777, the Marquis de Sade. Louis XVI abolished the prison, which was prevented from being reopened only by the will of the people during the Revolution. Instead it was turned into a home for women of ill repute who were later transferred to La Salpêtrière.

Also worth visiting is the château's chapel, the Sainte-Chapelle, completed in 1520 and almost pure Gothic apart from five rose windows with Renaissance stained glass. If you look closely you'll be able to distinguish the monograms of Henri II, Catherine de' Medici and Charles IX on the vaulting. South of the chapel are the remains of the seventeenth-century royal residence, restored since suffering considerable damage in the Second World War. The Queen's Pavilion was built for Louis XIV and Marie-Thérèse to honeymoon in; the King's Pavilion was erected for Anne of Austria and Cardinal Mazarin.

Parc Floral and Lac des Minimes

To the south of the château, this huge flower garden, packed with hundreds of species, manages to be lovely all year round. Paths lined with modern sculptures lead to a children's adventure playground near the Lac des Minimes. The most attractive of the park's four lakes, it has a trio of islands, one of which carries the remains of the Convent of the Minimes, founded in 1155. The same island also boasts the only known surviving tree from the time of Louis XV. Beside the lake is a tropical garden where a series of Indochinese, Moroccan, Tunisian and Congolese pavilions house the Institute for Agronomical and Tropical research. The pavilions were transported here from the World Fair in Marseille in 1906.

Other attractions include a Buddhist center, containing a sixteen-and-a-half foot gold leaf effigy of Buddha, which can be visited only at certain times; a high-speed cycling track, a racecourse and an arboretum. Before you leave you should also take a look at the Musée National des Arts Africains et Océaniens, located by the entrance you started from.

Musée National des Arts Africains et Océaniens

293 avenue Daumesnil, 75012. Metro Porte Dorée. Tel. 43 43 14 54. Open 10 a.m.–12 p.m., 1:30–5:20 p.m., 12:30–6 p.m. Saturday and Sunday; closed Tuesday.

The building, made for the 1931 Colonial Exhibition, is quintessential Art Deco, embellished with great sculptured friezes that attempt to make Imperialism seem benevolent. The huge range of artifacts inside includes jewelry, masks, statues, ceramics and headdresses from Australia and the Pacific, as well as many former African colonies. These exhibits take up the top three floors; downstairs there's a large tropical aquarium with ninety-two tanks, a terrarium for terrapins and even a large crocodile pit.

CHINATOWN AND THE 13TH ARRONDISSEMENT

The arrival of refugees from Cambodia, Vietnam, Laos, Thailand and even China decided the fate of the monstrous concrete towers built between the place d'Italie and the Porte de Choisy in the thirteenth *arrondissement*. Originally built as a hygienic, cost-effective way of solving the housing problem, the towers were still largely uninhabited in the 1970s when the arriving refugees were promptly installed, originally on a temporary basis. But with increasing numbers coming to join their families and friends a strong Asiatic community, which expanded to include ten different nationalities, started to grow up. In 1982 the first ten Chinese shops opened in Porte de Choisy, and Chinatown was born. Nowadays you can see Chinese characters on the neon shop signs flashing on every street corner. No transactions are carried out in French, and you can have your hair and laundry done, do your week's shopping and eat out without ever setting foot outside the community. On Sundays, when

AWAY FROM THE CENTER

Asians from all over the capital come to do their shopping in the open markets and massive Chinese supermarkets, it's hardly like being in Paris at all.

The attraction is the sheer exoticism of the place – the ability to step off the Metro and into another land. The streets are crammed with Chinese and Vietnamese restaurants, but it's perhaps more exciting to explore the enormous Tang Frères supermarket at 48 avenue d'Ivry (Metro Tolbiac). This vast emporium is the clearinghouse for tons of vegetables, fruit, dry goods and fish, brought in from Thailand, Sri Lanka and Taiwan by boat and plane; you'll see bamboo baskets piled high with exotic fruits and vegetables, walls of bottles of soy sauce and huge sacks of rice, as well as many unidentifiable – sometimes even unmentionable – items. Put away your phrasebook, take a deep breath of the exotic aromas, and you will be transported to the other side of the world.

To think, however, that the thirteenth is nothing but Chinatown would be to make a grave error. Théroigne de Méricourt died here in the infamous Hôspital de la Salpêtrière, built under Louis XIV to house the insane. More recently the Bibliothèque Marguerite Durand was moved here from its original location in the Latin Quarter.

Bibliothèque Marguerite Durand
79 rue Nationale, 75013. Metro Nationale.
Tel. 45 70 80 30.
Open 2 p.m.–6 p.m. Tuesday–Saturday.

Throughout her life, Marguerite Durand – journalist and founder of the feminist newspaper *La Fronde* – collected books, press cuttings, tracts, invitations, prospectuses, papers and law texts by and about women, all of which she carefully classified in biographical and thematic files. She donated these books and archives to the City of Paris in 1931; the following year a small library, bearing her name and opened to the public, was established in the town hall opposite the Panthéon in the fifth *arrondissement*. The continual addition of new material necessitated a transfer to the new modern premises on rue Nationale in 1989.

A further contrast, by virtue of its Frenchness, is provided by the area known as the Butte-aux-Cailles. Centered around the street of the same name, this area has escaped the renovators' zeal and retains the picturesque quality of old Paris, with the added advantage that book and food shops, bars and bistros stay open until midnight. Look out for one of the green Art Nouveau fountains designed and paid for by the Englishman Sir Richard Wallace.

Before leaving the district you might like to pay a visit to the Gobelins tapestry workshops, where they have been making tapestries for four centuries and still employ very much the same methods as they used hundreds of years ago (42 avenue des Gobelins, Metro Gobelins. Guided visits Tuesday, Wednesday and Thursday 2–3 p.m.).

Last but by no means least, if the idea of women from the distant past weaving tapestries while waiting for their menfolk to come home sends shivers down your spine, take a look at the building at 5 rue Jules-Breton, where the following is writ large on its façade: "In humanity woman has the same duties as man. She must have the same rights in the family and society."

BELLEVILLE

When Simone de Beauvoir came to Belleville as a bourgeois adolescent to do charity work, she described herself as a clandestine immigrant. The hill stretching from rue de Belleville to rue de Ménilmontant continues to fascinate intellectuals from the wealthier west of Paris, and Belleville shows all the signs of an area on the verge of gentrification. Unfortunately, it is undergoing some serious development at the same time. Unlike in some parts of Paris, where luxury apartments shoot up as the area increases in prestige, most of the demolition in Belleville is intended to make way for affordable and comfortable public housing. But the advertisements for lofts and tiny houses in the windows of local agents suggest that even if current residents aren't being chased out, they're being forced to move *up* in a vertical segregation that allots people from the west of Paris quaint old houses ready to renovate and everyone else cheap new apartments already starting to crumble.

On the "plain" of Belleville to the west of the boulevards that mark the boundaries of the actual hill, the busy markets and bars of rue du Faubourg du Temple, lined with intriguing alleyways on either side, form a lively Turkish and North African neighborhood. The population of Belleville proper is more mixed: young arty types, the working-class and a wide range of recent immigrants. In fact, the wealthy have long enjoyed "slumming" it in Belleville: by the eighteenth century, excursions to the country taverns of La Courtille were extremely fashionable among aristocrats eager for exoticism and excess. One observer complained that on Mondays he couldn't walk through Belleville without stumbling over piles of empty wine casks. The songwriter Vadé, who dubbed a Bellevilloise his muse, claimed that "to leave Paris without seeing La Courtille is like leaving Rome without seeing the Pope. Those in the know often leave the Luxembourg for an inn in the suburbs." In Vadé's time Belleville still boasted fresh air and bucolic pleasures; although the name place des Fêtes lingers on a Metro station, the image changed when a rural exodus and political upheavals brought successive waves of immigrants: Auvergnats from central France, Jews from Eastern Europe, Armenians, Greeks, North Africans and Vietnamese. The elite soon lost its fondness for excursions to Belleville, but entertainment has remained a constant feature, from local singers like Edith Piaf to the unbroken strip of Asian and North African restaurants running along rue de Belleville.

To wander around Belleville, you need a sense of leisure. The buildings are a hodgepodge of periods and heights, as different from a well-preserved *quartier* like the Marais as they are from an entirely new development like La Défense. The slope and the low roofs are reminiscent of Montmartre, but the picturesque qualities are less consistent here: country streets like the rue de l'Ermitage or the gardens carved out of the abandoned lot on rue des Savies are hidden behind tall new buildings. With cranes everywhere reminding you that buildings are going up while others are coming down,

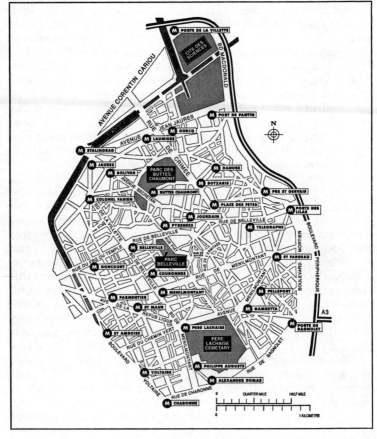

you'll never see the same street twice. Stranger still, Belleville has something in common with the more traditional tourist landmarks like the Eiffel Tower and the Arc de Triomphe: the views. Walking down rue de Ménilmontant or rue de Belleville reveals glimpses of the city below; and at nightfall you can climb rue Piat (or descend rue Jouye-Rouve) to the Parc de Belleville, a bleak new terraced garden crowned by a colonnade from which you see – not Belleville itself, which is blocked by the nearby apartment towers, but the Eiffel Tower, the Panthéon and (inevitably) the Tour Montparnasse.

It is worth stopping to look at the street art on the corner of rue de Belleville and rue Julien-Lacroix; you might also want to drop in on La Bellevilleuse, a neighborhood preservation group that occasionally sponsors photography exhibitions relating to local history. Though many of the restaurants on rue du Faubourg du Temple are too overwhelmingly male for women alone to feel at ease, the Kurdish restaurants you'll find if you head south towards rue Oberkampf and the Asian restaurants that line rue de Belleville allow you to share the culinary exoticism that is often the only aspect of so-called immigrants' culture for which the French can summon up much enthusiasm.

South of Belleville is another neighborhood whose eponymous main street, rue de Ménilmontant, runs parallel to the street that gives Belleville its name. There are fewer Asians and more West Indians here, but still the same bustle and the same startling views. No sooner was Notre-Dame-de-la-Croix completed than the Commune appropriated it for meetings, and a women's club met there before defeat returned the church to its original purpose.

To indulge in a little bucolic fantasy, head north from rue de Belleville to the Parc Buttes-Chaumont, a Haussmannian extravaganza of cliffs and lakes carved out of an old quarry. North of the place de la République at the western end of the rue du Faubourg du Temple is the Canal Saint-Martin, whose tree-lined banks are peaceful during the week but a favorite family promenade on Sundays, when children fight to get a good view of the working drawbridges and couples sunbathe by the water. You can follow the canal up to place Stalingrad, past Ledoux's Neoclassical rotunda, and straight into the park of La Villette. South of Belleville lies the most famous cemetery in Paris, Père-Lachaise.

PÈRE-LACHAISE CEMETERY

Main entrance boulevard de Ménilmontant, 75020. Metro Pére-Lachaise/Gambetta/Alexandre Dumas; bus 61, 69.
Open March 16–November 5, 7:30 a.m.–6 p.m. November 6–March 15, 8 a.m.–5:30 p.m. (8:30 a.m. Saturday; 9 a.m. Sunday and public holidays).

The meeting point of three former villages of the twentieth *arrondissement*, Belleville, Ménilmontant and Charonne, is a hill on which is situated Paris's largest and most visited cemetery. Here marshals, politicians, writers, painters, composers, philosophers and rock stars rub shoulders with ordinary French people.

The cemetery extends over more than 100 acres and the trees and statues, coupled with winding paths and alleyways, make it a pleasant and picturesque park to wander in during the summer. You'll need a map (10 francs at the gate), since the cemetery is arranged into numbered divisions which, while not entirely random, are not exactly systematic either. Also, the most famous people do not necessarily have the largest tombs. Quite the opposite: the most elaborate sepulchers probably contain the least-known people, while Delacroix and Colette, for instance, have only simple slabs.

Many famous women are buried here. Besides writers Colette and Gertrude Stein you will find the tombs of Edith Piaf, actresses Sarah Bernhardt and Simone Signoret, the mathematician Sophie Germain, the violinist Maria Milanohlo and the painter Rosa Bonheur, to name but a few. The ashes of Isadora Duncan are in the Columbarium, the final repository for those who prefer to be cremated.

Some tombs conceal a story of tragic love – that of Héloïse and Abelard, who died in the twelfth century and whose remains were finally reunited at the request of the Duchesse de la Rochefoucauld in 1701 and brought to Père-Lachaise over a century later when the tomb was erected by the City of Paris. An equally tragic story surrounds the grave of Jeanne Hébuterne, girlfriend of Modigliani and mother of his daughter. When Modigliani died in 1920 at the age of thirty-six, a victim of his excessive lifestyle, the story goes that she rushed to the morgue and covered his face with kisses. Still distraught, she went to her parent's house, from which she had been expelled some years before, and, after an argument, went up to the roof and threw herself off, despite being heavily pregnant with a second child.

The rest of the famous dead are too many to enumerate: Molière, La Fontaine, Bellini, Chopin, de Musset, Balzac, Victor Hugo, Oscar Wilde and Jim Morrison. The last two attract their own distinctive devotees. Wilde's tomb is one of the most dramatic, executed by Epstein and commissioned, it is said, by an anonymous lady admirer. The tomb of Jim Morrison, ex-lead singer of The Doors, has long been a place of pilgrimage for aging rockers who scrawl multilingual declarations of love and admiration, both on his tomb and on others nearby. While you're visiting this shrine in the southeastern corner you'll also see plenty of monuments to people involved in political conflict: concentration camp victims, Resistance fighters, Communist Party members and the Mur des Fédérés (Wall of the Federates) against which the survivors of the Paris Commune were shot in 1871, after making a last-ditch attempt to defend themselves amongst the graves of the cemetery.

LA VILLETTE

Up in the northeast of Paris, bordering on Belleville, this part of the nineteenth *arrondissement* was vineyards and fields in the nineteenth century. The area began to develop with the creation of the waterways (Canal de l'Ourq, Canal Saint-Denis and Canal Saint-Martin); industries were set up, jobs were created, and La Villette rapidly became one of the most important industrial sectors of Paris: the population boomed from 2628 in 1829 to 12,180 less than twenty years later. In 1867, further employment was created with the establishment of an enormous cattle market, alongside slaughterhouses, which were intended to supply all the meat Paris would need. In 1955 the authorities decided to rebuild and modernize these iron-frame buildings, designed by Blatard, but work was eventually abandoned in favor of turning the whole site into a gigantic cultural complex dedicated to science and industry.

The resulting Parc de la Villette now stretches from the Porte de la Villette to the Porte de Pantin, an area of 136 acres; the former cattle market has been transformed into La Grande Hall, dedicated to exhibitions, festivals and theater. Just near the Porte de Pantin, La Cité de la Musique houses a movie theater, a theater, the Conservatoire National de Musique, a museum of musical instruments and a concert hall. The main extravagance, however, is a vast science museum, La Cité des Sciences et de l'Industrie.

La Cité des Sciences et de l'Industrie
Parc de la Villette, 75019. Metro Corentin Cariou/Porte de la Villette. Tel. 40 05 72 72.
Open 10 a.m.–6 p.m. Tuesday to Sunday; closed Monday.

The Museum of Science and Industry, opened in 1986, is the best science museum in France. The stainless steel and glass building alone – three times the size of the Pompidou Center – is worth seeing purely from an architectural point of view. Through the main entrance hall, housing a couple of giant domes, two futuristic escalators take you up to the permanent exhibition called Explora, divided into four sections. The accent, as the name implies, is very much on exploring; from Planet Earth to the wider scope of the Universe, where satellites, spacecraft and computers await your instructions, to the Adventure of Life, where children and adults alike can investigate the secrets of life, including the enemies we humans have to fight in order simply to survive in our everyday environment. The third section, entitled Matter and Human Labor, looks at sources of energy by means of interaction with computers, while the last is dedicated to Language and Communication.

Temporary exhibitions cover various aspects of science, technology and industry in more detail, including the economic, social and artistic effects these developments have on our cultures. There is also a planetarium (open 2–8 p.m. Tuesday–Sunday) where a map of the sky at night is reproduced on a giant hemispherical screen on which you can identify all the stars around our planet while you listen to an informative commentary on the latest news from the world of astronomy.

The ground floor of this futuristic museum houses a movie theater, the Cinéma Louis-Lumière, which screens scientific films from 2 to 7 p.m. Tuesday–Friday and from 1 p.m. at weekends and on public holidays. Far more impressive, however, is the vast projection screen contained within the Géode.

The Géode
26 avenue Corentin Cariou. Metro Porte de Pantin.
Tel 40 05 06 07. Open 11 a.m.–9 p.m. Wednesday, Friday,
Saturday, Sunday; 11 a.m.–6 p.m. Tuesday and Thursday.

This massive silver sphere contains a huge OMNIMAX projection screen, at over 100 feet high the biggest in the world, with room for just 357 people in the cinema where nature, documentary and action films are shown – preferably with panoramic views and wildlife that feels close enough to touch. Once inside, the spectator becomes literally part of the film, completely absorbed by the six-track multidirectional stereo sound and the special effects.

Finally the Zenith, a giant canvas stadium holding 6500 people – easy to spot, with its red aeroplace logo – is the second biggest pop and rock venue in Paris, after the Palais des Omnisports at Bercy.

La Villette by boat
For further information, tel. Quiztour, 19 rue d'Athènes 75009: 48 74 75 30. Canauxrama cruises provide a shorter journey; the boat leaves from the Port de l'Arsenal near the place de la Bastille. For prices and departure times contact Canauxrama, 13 quai de la Loire 75019. Tel. 46 07 13 13.

If you're sick of traveling on the Metro, you can go to La Villette by boat. It takes much longer – three hours instead of twenty minutes – but the landscape makes up for the extra time, especially if you leave from the Quai Anatole France, just by the Musée d'Orsay in the seventh *arrondissement*. Also, the trip saves you a journey on a crowded *bâteau-mouche* without missing out on the Louvre and Notre-Dame and with the added bonus of traveling through several locks down the Canal Saint-Martin to La Villette. An English commentary is provided on board.

GETAWAYS

You may never tire of Paris's attractions, but if you feel like a breather from narrow pavements, traffic and crowded streets there are glorious opportunities for combining country air with sightseeing. The impressive châteaux of Fontainebleau, Versailles, Malmaison and Anet are each set among gardens and parks with plenty of space to roam around. Monet's garden at Giverny on the way to Rouen is especially beautiful in May and June when the rhododendrons are out while the château Chantilly is a must for horse lovers. Though easiest reached by car, all these destinations are accessible by public transportation. Try to go midweek if you want to avoid the hordes of Parisians who head out of town on weekends.

FONTAINEBLEAU

By train: take the Fontainebleau–Avon line from Gare de Lyon (50 minutes), then bus A or B.
By car: A6 to Fontainebleau exit, then N7. About 40 miles.
Open 9:30 a.m.–12:30 p.m., 2–5 p.m. Monday, Wednesday–Sunday.

Set among acres of forest, perfect for cycling, riding and exploring on foot, this former royal hunting lodge owes most of·its present form to François I. Famous as a collector of fine art (the *Mona Lisa* was amongst his prize possessions), he assembled a special army of Italian artists and craftsmen to rebuild and decorate the château in 1528. Successive royals continued to add their own touches, such as the Galerie de Diane and "jeu de paume" tennis court installed under Henri IV. Further renovation was carried out on the wishes of Napoleon who, understandably preferring it to Versailles, furnished the interior in Empire style for himself and Josephine. It was from here that he abdicated as Emperor on April 6, 1814.

The outcome of all these changes is a vast rambling place comprised of the first-floor and ground-floor state rooms (*Les Grands et Petits Appartements*) (especially worth noting are the François I Gallery, decorated with frescoes by the Florentine artist Rosso, and Philippe Delorme's huge Renaissance-style ballroom); the Musée Napoleon; and the gardens, part of which were laid out by the famous landscape artist Le Nôtre.

Among the state rooms are the Apartments of Madame de Maintenon, the secret wife of Louis XIV who lived here between 1686 and 1714; the "Chambre de L'Impératrice" where, by tradition, every queen from 1600 onwards slept – except for Marie-Antoinette who, despite having a bed specially made for her, never had the chance to sleep in it! Josephine did, though, in 1805!

If, after the formality of the château and its gardens, you're looking for something bucolic, take a long walk in the vast Forest of

Fontainebleau, or better still, hire a bicycle from the Tourist Office (31 place Napoléon Tel. 64 22 25 68 Monday–Saturday 9 a.m.–7 p.m., Sunday 10 a.m.–noon, 3–7 p.m. From October–April closed 12–2 p.m. and Sunday afternoon).

VERSAILLES

By train: RER line C from Gare d'Austerlitz, Quai d'Orsay or Pont de l'Alma to Versailles-Rive Gauche (40 minutes).
By car: Follow the N185 from Porte de Saint Cloud.
Open: Château October–April 9 a.m.–5:30 p.m; May–September till 7 p.m. Gardens usually open daily from dawn till dusk.

Gazing at this enormous – some say monstrous – pile, it's hard to believe that the Château de Versailles started life as a simple hunting lodge. Transformed into a small château by Louis XIII, it was "the Sun King," Louis XIV, who decided to make it a lasting monument to his reign employing the genius of the architect Le Vau, gardener Le Nôtre and the painter Le Brun. From 1664 to 1670, Le Vau restored and embellished the old building around the Cour de Marbre, Le Nôtre designed the gardens and Le Brun supervised the interior while more than 30,000 workmen toiled under their orders. In 1682 the king moved his court here from Saint Germain. Successive kings added a series of royal apartments, one of the colonnaded pavilions in the entrance court, the interior of the opera house and the Petit Trianon. Louis XVI's *pièce de résistance* was the Hameau, the hamlet or toy farm, he had built for Marie-Antoinette.

Marie-Antoinette's idyll at Versailles was rudely interrupted by one of the most dramatic scenes of the Revolution, as symbolic as the storming of the Bastille – the March of Women on Versailles. On October 5, 1789, driven into protest by hunger and soaring prices, a huge crowd of women gathered outside the capital's Hôtel de Ville in preparation for a great march on the king's palace.

JOSEPHINE BONAPARTE (1763–1814)

Empress of the French from 1804 to 1809, Josephine was born in Martinique, the daughter of a sugar planter. She was educated in the convent of Fort-de-France, and married the Vicomte Alexandre de Beauharnais in France in 1779. She had a son, Eugène, in 1780 and a daughter, Hortense in 1783, but demanded a separation in 1785.

She briefly became the mistress of Barras, a member of the Directory, who introduced her to Napoleon Bonaparte. Attracted by his boundless ambition and energy, she married him on March 9, 1796. When he returned from his Egyptian expeditions in October 1799 – enraged by rumors of her extravagance and infidelities – he demanded a separation. In 1804 she persuaded him to remarry her with full religious rites. Napoleon finally divorced her in 1809, but she kept the title and honors of Empress, and the châteaux of Malmaison, Navarre and Laeken near Brussels. She spent the rest of her life in Malmaison, where the Emperor would sometimes visit her. She died at the age of fifty-one.

Armed with powder, guns and cannon, some 6,000 set off, among them men in women's clothing, to demand bread and the transfer of government to Paris. By the time they arrived, drenched after six hours on the road in pouring rain, the king had heard news of their approach and given orders to barricade the palace. However, unable to keep out the swarming mob, among them the famous Théroigne de Méricourt, King and Queen fled, never to return.

Today, wandering among fellow tourists in the peace of the château's formal gardens, with their fountains, orangerie and great sweep of lawn, such dramatic events seem almost unimaginable. The château's interior is so vast that you'll need to know where you're aiming for. Or, better still, take a private guided tour (limited to 30 people and available in English) since they lead you through the State Apartments and other rooms otherwise closed to the public. Look out especially for the Hall of Mirrors and Marie-Antoinette's bedchamber where custom permitted that anyone who wished could watch the Queen give birth thus ensuring the baby could not be switched for another! Apparently the attending crowd was once so great that people had to stand on furniture to get a better view.

The Grand and Petit Trianons were built as retreats from the château, the second being the favorite residence of Marie-Antoinette whose love of play-acting inspired the installation of a small theater, all white and blue with gilded cherubs. The same passion for performance lay behind the creation of the Hameau in the grounds of the Petit Trianon. You can still see the remains of this miniature farm where the Queen used to dress up with her friends as shepherdesses and milkmaids to tend a herd of perfumed and beribboned sheep!

Take time to appreciate the beauty of the gardens with their fountains, the Orangerie and the enormous vistas of lawn.

GIVERNY

By train: travel to Vernon from Gare Saint Lazare, followed by a three-mile bus or taxi ride to Giverny.

By car: take the D5 past Roche-Guyon and Gasny. The village is famous as the home of the French Impressionist painter, Claude Monet, who lived here from 1883 until his death in 1926. He is buried in Giverny cemetery.

House open April 1–October 31, Tuesday–Sunday 10 a.m.–noon, 2–6 p.m. Gardens open all year round, Tuesday–Sunday 10 a.m.–6 p.m., but the best time to visit is May/June and in the autumn.

This expedition is a real treat and worth combining with a trip to Anet (below).

Claude Monet's house contains none of the artist's original paintings, but as you wander through the rooms, glimpsing the brilliant colors and greenery of his garden, you see so vividly the sources of his inspiration. The interior of the house is simple; it is as if the artist put all his decorative efforts into the garden, with the occasional dash of brilliance inside – in the sunshine-yellow and sky-blue dining room and the blue and white-tiled kitchen, complete with the old cooking range. The large studio, covered in Monet reproductions, includes a photo of the painter at work. His private collection of Japanese engravings by Hokusai, Utamaro, Hiroshige and Korin line the walls.

In spring, summer and autumn, the garden in front of the house is an explosion of color. The famous water-lily pond, located on the other side of the road, is reached by a tunnel at the back of the garden. Be warned, the tranquillity of your stroll may be rudely interrupted by any number of people trying to capture their own impression of the lily pond on film, preferably with as many friends and relations crowded on to that familiar curved green bridge as possible! But, despite the crowds, the house and garden are a joy to visit.

ANET

By car: N12 to Dreux. At Houdan, turn right onto D 923 to Anet.

Open November 1–March 31, Saturday 2–5 p.m, Sunday 10–11:30 a.m. and 2–5 p.m. April 1–October 31, every day except Tuesday 2:30–6:30 p.m; Sunday 10–11:30 a.m. and 2:30–6:30 p.m.

Diane de Poitiers was born in 1499 and died in the château of Anet in 1566. In 1538, at the age of nineteen, the Dauphin and future Henri II, already married to Catherine de' Medici, fell in love with thirty-eight-year-old Diane. When the Dauphin became king in 1547, Diane began to restore the château with the aid of Philibert de l'Orme. In four years, between 1548 and 1552, the famous architect built one of the most impressive Renaissance marvels. Diane's influence over the king was so great that he offered her the château of Chenonceaux and the jewels of the crown. Luckily, she hung on to the château of Anet for, as soon as the king died, Catherine de' Medici, who had borne the humiliation of being second string to her husband's mistress, was able to get her own back by demanding the return of Chenonceaux.

The château was decorated by famous Renaissance artists, including Jean Goujon, Benvenuto Cellini and Germain Pilon. When Henri II died in 1559, Diane retired to Anet and died after she fell off her horse in 1566. After the Revolution, the château was looted and, of the original château, only the entrance façade, the left aisle of the Cour d'honneur, the chapel and certain small buildings erected in the seventeenth century by the Duc de Vendôme remain.

The main entrance, built in 1552, is one of the most notable examples of a Renaissance gateway. The central arch is decorated with a copy of *Lying Diane* by Benvenuto Cellini. It used to be embellished with a statue by Jean Goujon, *Huntress Diane*, which is now on display in the Louvre. The gateway is surmounted by a deer and two dogs, once part of a clockwork mechanism that was activated every time the clock struck the hour.

The ground floor, containing the hall, the Dauphin's bedroom, the cabinet des Céramiques, and Diane's bedroom affords a view of the magnificent park through the windows.

The chapel adjoining the château, built by Diane's grandson to house her tomb, took ten years to complete. Diane's tomb, constructed in black marble on which she is seen praying, is decorated with bas-reliefs of the *Adoration of the Magi*.

MALMAISON
By train: RER A 1 line direct to Rueil-Malmaison.
By car: roughly five miles by the N13 from the Pont de Neuilly.

Open 10:30 a.m.–1 p.m., 2–6 p.m. daily.

Again situated to the west of Paris, the château of Malmaison became home to Empress Josephine after 1798. Lovingly restored, it is an absolute delight to visit and a fitting monument to the Empire style. After Josephine was unceremoniously dumped by Napoleon in favor of a younger women who could give him an heir, she retired here and devoted her time to gardening. Josephine died in 1814 of a chill. A year later Napoleon spent five days at Malmaison between Waterloo and his departure for Sainte Hélène. The château was later bought by Maria Christina of Spain and by Napoléon III in 1861. In 1896, it was sold to Daniel Osiris (1828–1907) who decorated it and presented it to the nation as a Napoleonic Museum.

As you wander through the château it feels surprisingly like a home and the presence of its two most famous occupants is tangible everywhere. Napoleon's memory is evoked in the billiard room by his throne (previously at Fontainebleau), his insignia woven into the Savonnerie carpet, and his image woven into a Gobelins tapestry. The tented Council Chamber reminds us of his status as a military leader.

Josephine's presence is conveyed by what remains of her possessions and the furnishings chosen for her apartments. The music room contains some of her instruments presided over by a marble bust of the Empress. Upstairs the "salle des atours" is hung with silk and there are watercolors of Malmaison by Garnerey and portraits of Josephine along with her knicknacks. You can also visit her boudoir, her bathroom, and her bedroom.

Outside, pause to appreciate the magnificent rose garden planted by Josephine, as well as the coach house containing the "Opal" in which the empress drove to Malmaison after her divorce and the emperor's *dormeuse* (sleeper) used at Waterloo. The park also contains the Pavillon Osiris (with a portrait of Tsar Alexander I drawn by Gérard) and a summerhouse. The ticket that allows you entry to the château also gives access to the Bois-Préau museum containing more items from the same Empire period.

CHANTILLY

By train: direct from the Gare du Nord.
By car: take the N16; also accessible by the N17 and D924A (26 miles).

Open: 10 a.m.–5 p.m. Wednesday–Monday; till 6 p.m. in summer.

Horse races, impressive stables and an equine museum make Chantilly a horse-lover's dream. In addition the chateau has a massive collection of paintings, tapestries, and other antiquities and there's a pleasant park and forest for walking in.

The town of Chantilly takes its name from a Gallo-Roman man, Cantillius, who liked the place and so built the first house. Like the nineteenth-century building you see today, the original château was effectively two edifices, the smaller of which – the Petit Château or Capitainerie – was built by Jean Bullant in 1560 for the Constable Anne de Montmorency and decorated by artists such as François Clouet, Bernard Palissy and Jean Goujon. In 1632, it passed on to the Grand Condé, head of the powerful Condé family. The park, laid out yet again by Le Nôtre, was apparently renowned for its sumptuous open-air banquets. In her letters, Madame de Sévigné describes one such feast, attended by Louis XIV, when the famous chef Vatel, on discovering that there hadn't been enough meat to go round, committed suicide by running on to a sword. He was the first known chef ever to serve whipped cream, hence the term *crème Chantilly*. (These days, unless specified as home-made [*fait maison*] 90 percent of *crème Chantilly* comes out of an aerosol can!)

After being looted and demolished during the Revolution, between 1876 and 1883 the château was entirely rebuilt in the Renaissance style by the Duc d'Aumale who bequeathed the domain and its art collections to the Institut de France. Today the larger half contains the Musée Condé with its huge display of antiquities while the smaller château exhibits the living quarters of the Condé family.

The Duc's collection is impressive – in many ways unparalleled in volume, worth and diversity. The problem is that everything has been crammed together in much too small a space with the result that it's hard to pick out the highlights without getting indigestion. Not to be missed are some magnificent sixteenth-century portraits in the Galerie du Logis, the Galerie de Psyche with forty-two sepia stained-glass windows representing the loves of Cupid and Psyche and, in the so-called Santuario, outstanding works by Raphael and Filippino Lippi, together with reproductions of 40 miniatures from Jean Fouquet's *Book of Hours of Etienne Chevalier*. There are also some wonderful precious stones in the Cabinet des Gemmes, including a reproduction of the famous Grand Condé pink diamond.

The pride of the château, however, is the library of rare books located in the Apartments among which you can admire the magnificently illuminated *Très Riches Heures du duc de Berri*, executed in 1410 by Pol de Limborg and brothers. The Apartments also house many Gobelins and Beauvais tapestries and notable furniture, such as a Reisner chest of drawers designed for Louis XVI's bedroom at Versailles.

When you've tired of indoors, the gently rolling park has a castle moat swarming with fish, two *allées des philosophes*, where visiting philosophers used to stroll and talk under the plane trees, an English garden and the Maison de Sylvie where the Duchesse de Montmorency hid the poet Théophile de Viau when he was condemned to death in 1623 for his licentious verses.

Finally (or depending on your priorities, perhaps first) only five minutes' walk from the château stand the vast stables built by the duc de Bourbon, great-grandson to the Grand Condé, and still in use. Convinced there was a good chance that he might be reincarnated as a horse, he had the stables built in suitable style and comfort for his return. Here you'll also find the Musée Vivant du Cheval complete with wooden models of horses and various equestrian exhibits. The racecourse adjoining the stables still hosts two of the most prestigious events of the French racing season.

ACCOMMODATIONS

Paris has every kind of hotel, ranging from the top-class, marble-and-gilt-clad Hôtel Crillon, favored by visiting dignitaries, to the tiny Hôtel Henri IV, tucked away in the place Dauphine, where the price of a room would just about buy you a gin and tonic at the Crillon. Generally speaking you get what you pay for, although prices for hotels of similar standard will vary a little according to the *arrondissement*: the eighth houses some of the smartest and priciest hotels, closely followed by the sixth, which is a particularly desirable area to stay in.

The small size of Paris means that it's not too inconvenient to stay in one of the cheaper *arrondissements*, a little further out but usually no more than 15 minutes' Metro ride from the center. However, women on their own are advised to stay centrally, since the extra money spent on getting taxis home to a place where you feel uneasy walking around late will probably make up the difference in the price of your room. Also, you'll have the benefit of being able to pop back to the hotel to rest weary limbs, change before going out, or take a break to write a few postcards in the comfort of your own room.

It cannot be stressed too much what a difference it makes staying in an area in which you feel secure if you are alone. This can affect your whole stay, giving you the confidence to venture out after dark to taste café life instead of kidding yourself that you really wanted an early night. The Left Bank fifth and sixth *arrondissements* are especially recommended. Les Halles, although central, can be intimidating on the Metro late at night, and definitely avoid the area around Pigalle, stretching from the east of the seventeenth *arrondissement* to the west of the eighteenth.

Reservations

If the thought of making a reservation fills you with horror, don't panic; all but the very cheapest hotels are likely to have someone at the front desk with enough English to take a reservation. Otherwise the French Tourist Office will do it for you. If you're particularly fussy about the area and type of hotel you stay in, you are strongly advised to reserve ahead, whatever the time of year. Paris is sufficiently appealing to attract tourists all the year round. Christmas and Easter are obvious peak times; otherwise June right through to October are the busiest months. Hotels also get very booked up during autumn and spring trade fairs.

Hotels that come under the auspices of the Office du Tourisme are obliged to display their prices both at the front desk and on the back of room doors. Breakfast is not always included, so check first, and remember it's fun to try breakfast in a different cafe every morning. If possible, ask to see the room or one similar before you accept it. If the hotel refuses, just walk out. Either they have something to hide, or they are so uninterested in customer relations that you probably wouldn't want to stay there anyway. Some may explain that the rooms are occupied, and suggest that you return at around 1 p.m., when the previous guests will have vacated them.

Children are generally welcome in hotels, though few can offer babysitters, so if this is a priority, be sure to check in advance. Many hotels have cribs, for which you'll probably be charged the same as for an extra bed – roughly 35% of the room price.

Staying Alone

Unfortunately, as with hotels virtually everywhere, staying alone has its disadvantages. Single rooms are all too often small and stuffy, and not likely to cost very much less than a double. The best advice, once you've have seen what's available, may well be to grit your teeth and go for a double. Remember that smaller hotels tend to be much cozier and less impersonal. Also, the people at the desk will soon get to know you.

Alternatives

Hotels are not your only option. Bed-and-breakfast accommodations, though not as common as in the provinces, are nevertheless available. If the idea of staying in a Parisian home appeals, contact the organization "Bed and Breakfast," 73 rue Notre-Dame-des-Champs, 75006, tel. 43 25 43 97; Metro Notre-Dame-des-Champs, open 9 a.m. – 1 p.m., 2 p.m. – 7 p.m.

Student and youth accommodations are both cheap and plentiful in Paris. Some places require an internationally recognized student card, but others are open to all. Rooms are usually shared; singles, when available, may not work out any cheaper than a small hotel. For details contact Acceuil des Jeunes en France, 12 rue des Barres, 75004, tel. 42 72 72 09; Metro Pont Marie (18–30 age range) or Union des Centres de Rencontres Internationales de France, 4 rue Jean-Jacques Rousseau, 75001, tel. 42 60 42 40; Metro Louvre. The latter's Centre International de Paris/Louvre at no 20 (tel. 42 36 88 18) is the largest, with some single rooms. It's also very central, and has an encouragingly smart, newly decorated, coral-pink foyer.

A C C O M M O D A T I O N S

If you're in search of all-female accommodations, the YWCA (22 rue de Naples, 75008. Metro Europe/Villiers, tel. 45 22 23 49) caters for women only and will accept guests for a minimum of three days' stay during the summer. The drawback is the curfew. For longer stays, the Association des Foyers de Jeunes: Foyer des Jeunes Filles (234 rue de Tolbiac, 75013, tel. 45 89 06 42. Metro Tolbiac) has large single rooms for women aged 18–25 for a one-month minimum stay, except during July and August, when shorter reservations are taken.

The other option, if you are intending to stay longer than a few days, is to rent an apartment. The cost needn't be astronomical; indeed, with two of you sharing this can offer the advantages of self-catering and independence – the sense of having your own place that you do not get in a hotel. Contact Rothray, 10 rue Nicolas-Flamel, 75004, tel. 48 87 13 37; Metro Pont Marie.

HOTELS

Paris hotels are classified by stars. At the top of the list is four-star deluxe, followed by the less glamorous plain four-star down to one- and no-star hotels at the bottom of the scale. Two- and three-star places usually offer good reliable accommodations for a reasonable price, especially compared to London or New York. Some require a deposit when you make your reservations. All but budget hotels take major credit cards and traveler's checks, unless otherwise stated.

Hôtel le Crillon ★★★★ (deluxe)
10 place de la Concorde, 75008,
tel. 42 65 24 24, fax 47 42 72 10, telex 290204.

For ostentatious luxury, this eighteenth-century palace hotel is hard to beat. Dowagers in furs perch on Louis XV chairs in the vast, marble-lined reception hall; Japanese beauties waft silently down the thickly carpeted corridors. The King of Morocco took up a whole floor overlooking the place de la Concorde, whereas Madonna preferred the rooftop suite designed by Sonia Rykiel. Humbler guests won't be disappointed with the sumptuous singles. If the two-Michelin-star restaurant is a bit overwhelming, there's L'Obélisque bistro for more informal lunching and dining. Even the laundry price list is revealing, itemizing silk underwear and cocktail dresses.

163 rooms (120 rooms, 43 suites). Single 2100F–2600F, Double 2600F–3150F, deluxe and suites up to 7000F. Breakfast 120F. Facilities: direct-dial phone, TV, satellite, radio, minibar, hair dryer, room service, laundry/dry-cleaning service, 7 conference rooms, full business services, car/limo hire, helicopter service, sauna and gym.

Hôtel Montalembert ★★★★ (deluxe)
3 rue de Montalembert, 75007, tel. 45 48 68 11, fax 42 22 58 19, telex 200132.

The Montalembert combines Asian minimalism with French flair; owner Grace Leo-Andrieu is from Hong Kong, and her designer was responsible for Kenzo's Paris headquarters. Contemporary details such as primitivist bronze door handles and light fittings blend with restored pieces from the original 1920s hotel. The open-plan restaurant, bar and lounge areas are pleasantly informal, and service is friendly. Hedonists will enjoy the fluffy striped duvets, enveloping bathrobes and peach bubble bath. A sophisticated hotel, the Montalembert has welcomed the likes of Paloma Picasso and Philippe Starck.

51 rooms (5 suites).

1450F–1859F, 1 or 2 people, suite 2400F–3000F. Breakfast 90F.

Facilities include: direct-dial phone, wake-up and message recording, air-conditioning, radio and TV, satellite, VCR and video library, minibar, personal safe, hair dryer, room service (breakfast 6:30 – 10:30 a.m., dinner 4 – 11 p.m., light snacks 24 hours), laundry/dry-cleaning service, car/limo hire, 2 conference rooms for 30 and 12 people but no comprehensive business facilities, adjacent underground parking.

Lancaster Hôtel ★★★ (deluxe)
7 rue de Berri, Champs Elysées, 75008,
tel. 43 59 90 43, fax 42 89 22 71, telex LOYNE 640991.

The Lancaster has the feel of a discreet eighteenth-century town house, impeccably elegant yet small enough for personal service. Just off the Champs Elysées, it's a world away from the fast-food joints spilling down the rue de Berri. The bright, cozy rooms are individually decorated, and boast Persian rugs and antique porcelain. For entirely civilized breakfasts there's a pretty courtyard draped in honeysuckle that used to be the stables of the private mansion. The two bronze fawns peeping out of the greenery were given by a countess in payment for her bill.

66 rooms (15 singles, 10 suites).

Single 1590F–1890F, Double 2150F–2500F, suites 3500F–7200F.

Facilities: direct-dial phone, TV, satellite, radio, some rooms air-conditioned, minibar, hair dryer on request, full room service till midnight, light snacks 24 hours, laundry/dry-cleaning, 2 meeting rooms for 12 and 20 people, full business services, car/limo service.

Hôtel Left Bank ★★★
9 rue de L'Ancienne Comédie, 75006,
tel. 43 54 01 70, fax 43 26 17 14, telex 200502.

Right at the heart of the bustling sixth *arrondissement*, this beautifully decorated hotel exudes a cushioned aura of well-heeled gentility. A tiny interior courtyard is stuffed with lush green vegetation, and you can have breakfast in the cozy dining room. Perfectly located and highly recommended.

31 bedrooms, 1 suite ("All our rooms are large").

Double or twin 950F, single 850F. Breakfast 25F.

Facilities: direct-dial phone, TV (English channels), air-conditioning, minibar, personal safe, soundproofed rooms, hair dryer, laundry service.

Hôtel de Seine ★★★
52 rue de Seine, St-Germain-des-Prés, 75006, tel. 46 34 22 80, fax 46 34 04 74.

Recently refurbished, smart country-house-style hotel in a great location, a stone's throw from the colorful rue de Buci food market and with the whole of the sixth *arrondissement* right on your doorstep. Breakfast is served in the dining room on the ground floor, which has the feel of a private drawing room in a rather affluent household. Warm and friendly welcome.

Double 800–900F, Single 800F. Breakfast 45F. 30 rooms, all with bathroom.

Facilities: direct-dial phone, satellite TV, hair dryer, safe at reception desk for customer's use. No air-conditioning. No laundry or dry-cleaning service, but there's a dry cleaner's across the street.

Hôtel de L'Odéon ★★★★
13, rue Saint-Sulpice, 75006, tel. 43 25 70 11, fax 43 29 97 34, telex 206731.

Located in the heart of the sixth *arrondissement* within easy distance to the lively place de l'Odéon and numerous cafés and bars, this family-run hotel has an Old World charm. Wooden beams and exposed stone walls are much in evidence, and the terracotta hues of the lobby give it a warm, cozy feel. All the bedrooms are decorated differently in a country style, some with special features like a four-poster. The tiny flowery interior courtyard adds to the attractions.

29 rooms (4 singles). Double 710F–830F, Single 580F. Breakfast 42F.

Facilities: direct-dial phone, cable TV, air-conditioning, personal safe.

Hôtel Saint-Merry ★★★
78 rue de la Verrerie, 75004, tel. 42 78 14 15, fax 40 29 06 82.

This unusual little hotel represents the labor of love of owner Monsieur Crabbe, who, bit by bit over thirty years, has been creating his own Gothic fantasy. Once a brothel, the rambling Saint-Merry clings to the walls of the neighboring Gothic church of the same name. Every room is different, but all are done up in medieval style with an ornately carved confessional made into a headboard here, a church pew there. One room even has a pair of flying buttresses from the church arching over the bed. M. Crabbe is building a suite up in the roof, which promises to be spectacular when he finally finishes it: "I don't know when, I'm not in a hurry, maybe three years . . . ." There's no elevator or TV, but what you're paying for is atmosphere, laid on with a trowel. This plus the central Beaubourg location makes it an extremely popular place to stay, so reserve two or three months in advance.

12 rooms. 380F–800F. Breakfast 40F.

Facilities: direct-dial phone. No credit cards.

Hôtel Saint-Paul le Marais ★★★
8 rue de Sévigné, 75004, tel. 48 04 97 27, fax 48 87 37 04.

This comfortable, reassuring hotel is a good base for exploring the Marais. Professional staff welcome you at the front desk at one end of a spacious lounge bar with leather armchairs where you can relax with a drink before heading out for the evening. A leafy private patio opens out to the back. The contemporary rooms are done in pastel shades, and all bathrooms have quality fittings. Breakfast is served in the vaulted stone basement, there's a small meeting room for informal gatherings, and fax and photocopying can be arranged.

27 rooms. 480–580F. Breakfast 40F, supplementary bed 100F.

Facilities: direct-dial phone, TV, hair dryer.

Hôtel Louis II ★★★
2 rue Saint-Sulpice, 75006, tel. 46 33 13 80, fax 46 33 17 29.

Don't be put off by the rather shabby exterior. The building dates from the eighteenth century and the rooms, all different, are decorated in keeping. Rose-patterned wallpaper and lace bedspreads and tablecloths add to the charm of the irregularly shaped rooms up in the eaves; others lower down are more compact and intimate, with bed canopies and dark greens and purples.

22 rooms. 495F–750F.

Facilities: direct-dial phone, TV, minibar, hair dryer.

Hôtel Louvre Saint-Honoré ★★★
141 rue Saint-Honoré, 75001, tel. 42 96 23 23, fax 42 96 21 61.

Housed in an elegant building with recently cleaned sculpted moldings, this totally modernized hotel attracts mainly upscale tourists and businesspeople. Rooms are furnished in bold colors and abstract patterned fabrics; double-glazing keeps out noise from busy rue St-Honoré. Extras like cable TV are laid on, and you're right in the middle of Paris with the Louvre only two minutes' walk away.

40 rooms.

470F–735F.

Facilities: direct-dial phone, TV, satellite, minibar, personal safe, hair dryer, telex and fax service, small meeting room for up to 15 people.

Grand Hôtel de Malte ★★★
93 rue de Richelieu, 75002, tel. 42 96 58 06, fax 42 86 88 19.

The area may not be anything special and the rooms in this large hotel could do with refurbishing, but it's quiet and may be a good bet for last-minute reservations. The bathrooms are all new and sparkling, and the airy breakfast room, a large conservatory full of plants, is a pleasant feature.

59 rooms. 480F–600F. Breakfast 72F, supplementary bed 180F.

Facilities: direct-dial phone, TV, satellite, radio, minibar, hair dryer, laundry service, exchange.

Hôtel Agora Saint-Germain ★★★
42 rue des Bernardins 75005, tel. 46 34 13 00, fax 46 34 75 05.

Well cared for and very comfortable. The rooms have sturdy reproduction furniture with good large desks; the bathrooms boast new fixtures, and some have marble sinks. Tapestry-upholstered chairs and stone walls give a homey feel to the breakfast room. Streetside windows are double-glazed, which is just as well, as the bells from the neighboring church are pretty loud.

39 rooms. 500F–610F, Breakfast 35F, supplementary bed 150F.

Facilities: direct-dial phone, wake-up, TV, satellite, radio, minibar, hair dryer, personal safe.

Hôtel du Panthéon ★★★
19 place du Panthéon, 75005, tel. 43 54 32 95, fax 43 26 64 65.

Mirrors, wrought iron, palms and pillars greet you in the lobby, but the rooms – many decorated in blue, with beamed ceilings – are simpler. The corner rooms are particularly spacious, and those overlooking the square give a great view of the imposing dome of the Panthéon. The leafy shades of the Jardin du Luxembourg are only three minutes away.

42 rooms. 450F–660F. Breakfast 30F, supplementary bed 100F.

Facilities: direct-dial phone, TV, satellite, minibar, dry-cleaning and babysitting service, meeting room for ten people.

Hôtel Molière ★★★
21 rue Molière, 75001, tel. 42 96 22 01, fax 42 60 48 68.

The eighteenth-century façade is currently being renewed to complete the renovation of this excellent, conveniently located hotel. The rooms have a traditional feel and staff are attentive and friendly.

32 rooms. 420F–650F. Breakfast 35F, supplementary bed 100F.

Facilities: direct-dial phone, TV, satellite, video service, minibar.

Hôtel Concortel ★★★
19–21 rue Pasquier, 75008, tel. 42 65 45 44, fax 42 65 18 33.

One of the best things about staying here is the welcome you get from the helpful, friendly staff. The back building has no elevator, so check the location of your room when making a reservation. All street-facing windows are double-glazed. The hotel is well placed for Galeries Lafayette and Printemps, as well as some of the main sights.

46 rooms. 580F–620F. Breakfast 35F, supplementary bed 100F.

Facilities: direct-dial phone, TV, radio, minibar, some rooms have personal safes, fax and photocopying, laundry and dry-cleaning, meeting room for ten people.

Hôtel de la Bretonnerie ★★★
22 rue Sainte-Croix-de-la Bretonnerie, 75004, tel. 48 87 77 63, fax 42, 77 26, 78. Closed last week in July and during August.

Monsieur and Madame Sagot have renovated a seventeenth-century Marais town house to create this wonderful hotel. The dark wood and tapestries in reception give a country-house feel, and the pleasant staff make you feel welcome. All the rooms are different, but echo the Old World style with Louis XIII furnishing, thick floral fabrics, bed curtains or four-posters and sturdy beams. Take care to book at least a month in advance.

31 rooms. 500F–700F. Supplementary bed 100F.

Facilities: direct-dial phone, TV, minibar; hair dryer, laundry/dry-cleaning service.

Tonic Hôtel ★★★
12–14 rue du Roule, 75001, tel. 42 33 00 71, fax 40 26 06 86.

The lobby may not inspire you to check in, but the rooms themselves are pretty, spacious and airy. All are decorated in pink, with rose-patterned upholstery and curtains, but the main attraction is the bathroom. Each has a steambath and pulsating massage shower to ease tired legs after a hard day's sightseeing or a long night's dancing. The staff can be a bit curt.

20 rooms. 470F–700F. Breakfast 30F, supplementary bed 100F.

Facilities: direct-dial phone, TV, satellite, minibar, personal safe, hair dryer, massage shower, steambath, fax and photocopying service.

No travelers' checks.

Hôtel Lido ★★★
4 passage de la Madeleine, 75008, tel. 42 66 27 37, fax 42 66 61 23.

Rich-colored tapestries against bare stone walls and classical music welcome you into the Lido's attractive lobby. The rooms themselves are pleasant, too: some are decorated in warm reds, others in gold, with lace bedspreads. You can eat breakfast in your room or in the stone cellar where the red leather chairs and solid wood tables look fit for a banquet.

32 rooms. 730F–830F. Breakfast included, supplementary bed 100F.

Facilities: direct-dial phone, TV, satellite, radio, minibar, hair dryer.

Hôtel le Saint-Grégoire ★★★
43 rue de l'Abbé-Grégoire, 75006, tel. 45 48 23 23, fax 45 48 33 95.

Stylish little hotel entirely suited to its area, just south of the designer boutiques of St-Germain. While it lacks the services offered by four- and five-star establishments, the Saint-Grégoire has the decor, the easy confidence and the clientele to allow it to be mistaken for a relaxed business hotel. The front desk is off a lounge area furnished with kelims, and baby bay trees topping an open fire. Lovely antiques have been matched with well-chosen modern pieces in the rooms; bathrooms have an abundance of marble, and fluffy towels as well as a bathrobe. Basket chairs and fresh flowers lighten the stone cellar breakfast room. The effect is all cosmopolitan sophistication, and although prices are steep for the three-star category, the added style and comfort make it worth it.

20 rooms. 690F–830F. Breakfast 55F.

Facilities: direct-dial phone, TV, satellite, radio, minibar on request, hair dryer.

Hôtel du Bois ★★
11 rue du Dôme, 75116, tel. 45 00 31 96, fax 45 00 90 05, telex 615453F.

The window boxes and shutters of this English-run hotel, ten minutes from l'Etoile, look on to a little cobblestoned street off avenue Victor Hugo. There's no language problem, staff are friendly and there's a soothing, wholesome atmosphere, perfect for anyone who feels diffident about the big city. The rooms, recently refurbished in peach or flowery wallpaper, are comfortable and very spacious. Scrupulously clean white bathrooms with new fittings live up to the standard of cheerful quality appreciated by the mainly British clientele.

41 rooms (6 single/shower, 19 double/ shower, 12 double bath, 13 twin/bath).

Low season single/shower, 375F, double/shower 435F, double/bath 485F; high season single/shower 385F, double/shower 465F, double/bath 535F, supplementary bed 100F, children under 4 free. Breakfast 38F.

Facilities: direct-dial phone, TV with video channel (films in English), minibar, breakfast in room 7:30–10 a.m.

Hôtel des Grandes Ecoles ★★
75 rue du Cardinal Lemoine, 75005, tel. 43 26 79 23, fax 43 25 28 15 (phone reservations 2–6 p.m.)

Entering this unique hotel is like stepping out of the Latin Quarter into a country village. It occupies a group of low buildings around a courtyard and flower-filled garden down a cobblestoned lane off rue Cardinal Lemoine. Rooms vary in size and standard of decor, as the management wants to provide accommodations for most budgets, but all have an attractive, cottagey feel. The airy breakfast room has a piano, and a nostalgic scent of polish rises from the parquet floor and the gleaming tables. In fine weather breakfast is served in the courtyard. Not surprisingly, it's essential to book well in advance.

48 rooms (most single or double occupancy, 39 with bath or shower and toilet; 9 with washbasin).

Bath/shower and toilet 400F–550F, washbasin 260F–330F. Breakfast 100F, supplementary bed 100F.

Facilities: upper-price: direct-dial phone, hair dryer; lower-price: phone.

Credit cards: Visa and MasterCard.

Familia Hôtel ★★
11 rue des Ecoles, 75005, tel. 43 54 55 27, fax 43 29 61 77.

The rooms of this family-run hotel have handy extras, such as satellite TV and hair dryers, which make it great value for money. The modern decor in blues and grays is inoffensive enough; the bathrooms are new and immaculate. Several of the rooms have balconies. Well placed for the sights of the Latin Quarter, the Familia is one of the better bets for unpretentious comfort.

30 rooms (15 bath, 15 bath and shower). Single occupancy 370F–440F, double 440F–500F. Breakfast included.

Facilities: direct-dial phone with wake-up, TV, satellite (BBC, CNN, MTV, etc.), minibar, hair dryer. French franc travelers' checks only.

Hôtel Esmeralda ★★
4 rue St-Julien-le-Pauvre, 75005, tel. 43 54 19 20, fax 40 51 00 68, telex 270105F.

Just opposite Notre-Dame, the Esmeralda oozes character. The low-ceilinged reception has dark wood paneling and ancient red armchairs and every bedroom is different, though all share a certain shabby chic. You pay for the atmosphere and the central location rather than immaculate facilities, and some of the bathrooms are rather dilapidated.

19 rooms (16 bath/shower and toilet), all double. 290F–420F.

Facilities: direct-dial phone.

Cash only.

Le Jardin des Plantes ★★
5 rue Linné, 75005, tel. 47 07 06 20, fax 47 07 62 74, telex PLANTEL 203684F.

Situated right opposite the Jardin des Plantes, this hotel follows a garden theme with leafy motifs, fresh cotton fabrics and modern white cane furniture. Street-facing bedrooms tend to be lightest, and double-glazing eliminates traffic noise. Lounge chairs and breakfast tables are put out on a roof terrace when the weather's fine, and there's even a sauna.

33 rooms, double or twin. Double/ shower/toilet 390F (1 person)–440F (2 people), double/twin/bath/shower/toilet 450F (1 person)–500F (2 people), larger rooms, terrace level 510F–640F. Breakfast 40F, a supplementary bed 100F, sauna 70F.

Facilities: direct-dial phone, TV, minibar, hair dryer, ironing room.

French franc travelers' checks, Visa, MasterCard and American Express.

Hôtel du Marais ★★
2bis rue des Commines, 75003, tel. 48 87 78 27, fax 48 87 09 01, telex 260717.
While it's not particularly atmospheric, this is one of the cheaper hotels in the Marais. The rooms are simply furnished in modern brown veneer, with plain cream bedspreads and flowery curtains. Some are a little cramped, but all are comfortable and clean.

39 rooms (9 single/shower, 12 double/shower, 6 twin/shower, 6 double/bath, 6 twin/bath).

Single/shower 290F, double/shower 320F, twin/shower, double/bath 360F, twin/bath 420F. Breakfast 28F, supplementary bed 100F, crib free.

Facilities: direct-dial phone, TV, minibar, telex, radio.

French franc travelers' checks, Visa, MasterCard and American Express.

Grand Hôtel Jeanne d'Arc ★★
3 rue Jarente, 75004, tel. 48 87 62 11, fax 48 87 37 31.
On a quiet street right in the middle of the Marais, the idiosyncratic Jeanne d'Arc is booked up well in advance, usually by regulars. The lobby and lounge are full of Thirties and Forties furniture draped in doilies crocheted by the proprietess. The rooms themselves are large, mainly blue, with solid reproduction Louis XV beds and wardrobes. An unflappable husband-and-wife team take justified pride in their hotel, which feels more like a home.

37 rooms, double or twin. Double 320F (1/2 people), twin 390F. Breakfast 30F.

Facilities: direct-dial phone, wake-up, TV.

French franc travelers' checks only.

Timhôtel la Bourse ★★
3 rue de la Banque, 75002, tel. 42 61 53 90, fax 40 47 01 49.
The Timhôtel chain aims to provide reliable accommodations without frills at affordable prices. The Bourse hotel is no exception, and although the rooms can be cramped, they are clean and comfortable.

46 rooms (14 single/bath/shower, 32 double). 408F–508F. Breakfast 45F.

Facilities: direct-dial phone, TV, satellite.

French franc travelers' checks only.

Hôtel Marigny ★★
11 rue de l'Arcade, 75008, tel. 42 66 42 71, fax 47 42 06 76.
Within easy walking distance of the Tuileries, Garnier's Opéra and other such Right Bank attractions. The rooms are simply furnished, but clean.

32 rooms. 430F–460F (195F for basic rooms aimed at students). Breakfast 30F, supplementary bed 150F.

Facilities: direct-dial phone, TV, minibar.

Credit cards: MasterCard only.

Hôtel du Collège de France ★★
7 rue Thénard, 75005, tel. 43 26 78 36, fax 46 34 58 29.
Quiet peaceful hotel, well located for the Latin Quarter and Île de la Cité. The staff are welcoming and the rooms, some of which are comparatively spacious, are solidly furnished.

29 rooms (all double). 480F–500F, Breakfast 30F, supplementary bed 100F.

Facilities: direct-dial phone, TV, radio, hair dryer.

French franc travelers' checks only. Credit cards: American Express only.

Hôtel le Pavillon ★★
54 rue Saint-Dominique, 75007, tel. 45 51 42 87.

Situated in a former convent at the end of a quiet alley just off rue Saint-Dominique, a few minutes from the Musée d'Orsay. The rooms vary, and the furnishings in some are a little shabby. But bath or shower rooms are solid and clean, and the unusual decor – florid carpets twinned with clashing wallpaper – has a certain eccentric appeal. The cheapest rooms are at basement level, and though they're quite bearable, they're a bit dark. There's a pretty courtyard where guests can have breakfast in summer.

18 rooms. 380F–429F.

Facilities: direct-dial phone, TV. French franc travelers' checks only.

Hôtel Prince ★★
66 avenue Bosquet, 75007, tel. 47 05 40 90.

Recently renovated and now popular with French businessmen as well as tourists, the Prince occupies a typically Parisian apartment block on broad avenue Bosquet between the Eiffel Tower and Les Invalides. The gray-and-maroon decor is muted and contemporary, and double-glazed windows keep out traffic noise. Good if you're in search of respectable peace and quiet.

30 rooms. 300F (singles which must be reserved well in advance,) 450F. Supplementary bed 70F.

Facilities: direct-dial phone, TV, minibar.

Hôtel Castex ★
5 rue Castex, 75004, tel. 42 72 31 52, fax 42 72 57 91.

This cheerful family-run hotel was refurbished two years ago, and the owner is justly proud of his achievement. The rooms, each with bouquets of dried flowers, are bright and welcoming. Staff are friendly and the hotel is right on the doorstep of the Marais, as well as within walking distance of most Bastille nightspots. The doors close at midnight, and guests are given an entry code.

24 rooms. 170F–400F. Breakfast 25F, supplementary bed 70F (Please Note: most rooms up to 280F).

Facilities: direct-dial phone.

French franc travelers' checks only.

Hôtel Floridor ★
28 place Denfert-Rochereau, 75014, tel. 43 21 35 53, fax 43 27 65 81.

A no-nonsense hotel that offers excellent value for money, just south of Montparnasse. Rooms are scrupulously clean, and those overlooking the place Denfert-Rochereau have the advantage of a good view out over the square, plus double-glazing to shut out traffic noise. Refurbishment in the form of new flowery wallpaper and soft carpets is currently underway.

48 rooms. 239F–308F. Breakfast included, supplementary bed 60F.

Facilities: direct-dial phone, TV.

French franc travelers' checks only. No credit cards.

Grand Hôtel Lévêque ★
29 rue Cler, 75007, tel. 47 05 49 15, fax 45 50 49 36.

Bustling rue Cler is one of the nicest streets in the area between the Eiffel Tower and Les Invalides, and the unpretentious Grand Hôtel Lévêque is right in the middle. Stall-holders call out their prices; shoppers with baskets hurry by under streetside windows. All rooms are clean, and the staff are pleasant.

50 rooms. 190F–295F. Breakfast included, supplementary bed 80F.

Facilities: direct-dial phone.

French franc travelers' checks only. No credit cards.

Hôtel Richelieu Mazarin ★
51 rue de Richelieu, 75001, tel. 42 97 46 20.

This functional but very central hotel is usually full of *habitués*, so be sure to reserve several months in advance. There are strictly no frills, but it's clean and very convenient.

40 rooms. 200F–300F. Breakfast 25F, supplementary bed 60F, shower 10F (for rooms with basin only).

Facilities: direct-dial phones.

Cash only.

Delhy's Hôtel ★
22 rue de l'Hirondelle, 75006, tel. 43 26 58 25.

The lobby of this ancient hotel tends to be packed with rucksacks belonging to budget travelers who know a bargain when they see one. Right on lively place St-Michel, it couldn't be better situated for exploring St-Germain and the Latin Quarter. Up the creaking stairs you'll find a selection of basic, irregularly shaped rooms, all of which are clean, if not beautifully designed. Rooms are less difficult to come by than they are in other cheap, central hotels, but don't wait too long to make a reservation.

21 rooms. 200F–300F. Breakfast 25F.

Facilities: direct-dial phone.

Cash only.

Henry IV ★
25 place Dauphine, 75001, tel. 43 54 44 53.

The "Henri quat," as it's known, is famous, and reserving months in advance is recommended. It's easy to see why so many budget travelers want to stay in this little hotel, which overlooks one of the prettiest squares in Paris. Rooms are basic, with basin only, flowered wallpaper and battered old furniture – perfect if you have ever hankered after a bohemian garret.

22 rooms. 165F–180F. Breakfast 20F.

Cash only.

Hôtel Marignan ★
13 rue du Sommerard, 75005, tel. 43 54 63 81.

This family-run hotel has attracted hordes of students and budget travelers to its simple, clean rooms for years. There may only be showers on the land-

A
C
C
O
M
M
O
D
A
T
I
O
N
S

ings, but place St-Michel is three minutes' walk away, and the prices are very reasonable. There's also a laundry and an eating room for the guests' use.

30 rooms. 170F–300F, shower 15F. Breakfast included.

Cash only.

Hôtel Récamier ★

3bis place Saint-Sulpice, 75006, tel. 43 26 04 89.

Place Saint-Sulpice is peaceful at night despite being on the doorstep of St-Germain-des-Prés, and you get the best of both worlds in this pretty, well-cared-for little hotel. The furnishings may be worn, but the rooms have a certain charm.

30 rooms. 260F–360F. Breakfast 35F.

Cash only.

APARTMENT RENTAL

Rothray

10 rue Nicolas-Flamel, 75004, tel. 48 87 13 37, fax 40 26 34 33.

Ray Lampard, an Englishman based in Paris, and his partner Roth provide furnished private apartments for short- or long-term rent, ranging from studios to two-bedroom apartments that sleep four. All are central, nicely furnished and equipped with stereo, cable color TV and phone. When you arrive you'll find fresh flowers, a bottle of wine, and fruit juices and beer in the fridge. Many apartments have open fireplaces and beamed ceilings. If you're considering a longer stay, all this – plus a caring personal service from Ray and Roth – should make it a pleasant one.

Apartments range from 550F–1100F per day, depending on size, location, and length of stay.

HOSTELS

For those on a limited budget and interested in meeting other travelers, there are seven youth hostels in Paris. You need to be a member of the 70-nation International Youth Hostel Federation.

Le D'Artagnan; 80 rue Vitruve, 75020; tel. 43 61 08 75

Jules Ferry; 8 Boulevard Jules Ferry, 75011; tel. 43 57 55 60

Auberge d'Eté; Auberge d'Eté; tel. 43 57 02 60

Cité des Sciences; 1 Rue Jean-Baptiste Clement, 93310

Rue Marcel Duhamel; Rue Marcel Duhamel, 91290;
   tel. 64 90 28 85

Relais Européen de la Jeunesse; 52 avenue Robert Schumann,
   91200; tel. 69 84 81 39

To obtain additional information about the French facilities, contact the American Youth Hostels (AYH); 202-783-6161. The main number in Paris is 46 70 00 01.

EATING AND
DRINKING

A woman drinking a cup of coffee or lunching alone in a café or brasserie in Paris is totally unremarkable. The French take eating tremendously seriously. Lunch during the working day is not a hasty sandwich to be stuffed down between panic phone calls and writing a fax. The very ida of having anything less than an hour in which to have a proper meal gives them indigestion. For this reason, it is perfectly normal to see women out alone at lunchtime.

In the evenings you'll be a lot more conspicuous. Parisian women don't tend to dine out on their own, so to help you avoid feeling too self-conscious, we recommend at least two options. Either pick a busy café and make for a table crammed in with everyone else, where you will quickly become absorbed by the crowd, or go for a middling-priced restaurant with linen tablecloths where the waiters are unlikely to give you more than a passing glance and the clientele are too absorbed in their food or conversations to notice you.

The brasserie falls between the two. The waiters will probably be younger and livelier, and you may well be subjected to some gentle banter as they rush between tables. Equally, you stand a greater chance of becoming involved in conversations with neighboring diners, for the atmosphere is noticeably more relaxed than it is in a restaurant.

Breakfast is one of the least intimidating meals, and in many ways the nicest to have in a café. This is where women and men alike stop to collect their thoughts and organize their ideas in peace over a solitary coffee and croissants before starting their day. From the moment the café opens to the moment when the long-aproned waiter goes outside to wind down the shutters, people will be popping in and out between meetings, for a meeting, or after a particularly tough work session for their obligatory shot of caffeine. Take a book or some postcards for reassurance, install yourself, and contemplate the passing tide of humanity.

DRINKING

Unless you want to cripple yourself financially, it's best to follow the French example and drink coffee, soft drinks, beer or a kir – a popular alcoholic drink, often made with cheap white wine disguised by the addition of blackcurrant, which costs much the same as a beer. When ordering the latter, either choose one of the named beers or ask for *un demi*, effectively a half-pint of light draft lager.

SOFT DRINKS

The usual range of soft drinks is available, and will again cost about the same as a beer or kir. Water is either fizzy [*gazeuse*] or still [*non-gazeuse*], but people have a tendency to ask for their water by name as well. Badoit (slightly salty) is among the most widely available of the fizzy waters; Evian is still very popular. If you ask for a *jus d'orange* you will get the kind in a bottle, probably sweetened. If you want freshly squeezed juice, order an *orange pressée*.

LIQUOR

If you do decide to drink spirits in a café, be warned. A gin, vodka, whisky or similar can easily cost three to four times the price of a beer, and if you order them in a popular upscale café like the Deux Magots you will need a second drink to recover from the shock of seeing the bill for the first. A similar warning about aperitif in restaurants. When you sit down, a waiter will always ask if you would like an aperitif with your meal. The French don't usually, so in no way feel obliged to say yes – it's perfectly acceptable to wait until your wine arrives. If you do decide to have an aperitif, a decent restaurant should make a good kir made with a drinkable white wine and often a choice of raspberry, blackcurrant or strawberry liqueur to flavor it. Anything else will again add a hefty chunk to your bill. When you order water in a restaurant you are perfectly within your rights to order a jug of tap water, *une carafe d'eau*, for which you will not be charged.

COFFEE AND TEA

Coffee is not had with meals in France but reserved for afterwards or at any other moment of the day when the urge for caffeine takes you. When you're ordering, there are several options: *un café* is black and strong, served in a small cup and often drunk with a couple of lumps of sugar; *un café crème* is essentially a large cup of milky coffee (if you want it frothy, ask for a *cappuccino)*; *une noisette* is a black coffee with just a dash of milk; and *un déca* is a decaffeinated version of any of the above. *Un thé* is a cup of hot water with a teabag floating in it. *Un thé au lait* is the same, with a small jug of milk next to it; *un thé au citron* is tea with a slice of lemon.

EATING

SNACKS

The fast-food joints that do exist are either American or French imitations and in no way reflect anything typical of French cuisine. If you feel like picnicking in Paris, you will find that, almost all bakeries do a range of sandwiches made of half a fresh *baguette* liberally stuffed with a choice of fillings: *rillettes* (fatty pork pâté), pâté, Camembert, and ham and cheese are among the staples. If you want something healthier, the *traiteurs*, who specialize in ready-prepared dishes, will sell you plastic boxes of all different kinds of mixed salads, alongside precooked dishes such as stuffed tomatoes, veal escalope in a wine sauce, slices of roast chicken, homemade pâté, quiche and pizza. If you're looking for a light lunch, most cafés will do a *croque monsieur*: a delicious toasted cheese and ham sandwich that can be consumed with a salad and a glass of wine.

RESERVATIONS

If you prefer not to take pot luck, aren't prepared to wait for a table, or are going to be deeply disappointed at being turned away, it's definitely wise to make reservations in advance. Since the introduction of new anti-smoking legislation, some restaurants are beginning to separate smoking from nonsmoking areas, so you might wish to specify *non-fumeur*. Beware, however; this could be met with a derisory laugh, since some restaurateurs are making it a point of honor to pander to their regular clientele in flouting the law. If you're dining out midweek it's usually enough to reserve a day or two in advance or, in off-peak season, the same morning. For Friday and Saturday nights or Sunday lunchtimes, reserve your table at least a couple of days ahead.

SPECIALITIES

There is no such thing as typical Parisian cuisine. One of the advantages of Paris is that you can sample all the regional specialities, and just as the French are proud of their individual regions, that region will always be justly proud of its particular culinary offerings. Parts

OPENING TIMES

Cafés open early to catch the breakfasters, while brasseries and restaurants cater to the lunch crowd just before noon, then have a lull before preparing for the evening meal. Regular restaurants are unlikely to accept customers after 11 p.m., so it's wise to arrive by 10:30 p.m. Brasseries tend to stay open later, as do cafés, although these are unlikely to serve more than a sandwich after 10:30 p.m. These are general rules; a lot depends on how lively a particular *quartier* is after dark. Night owls who head for the first, fourth, fifth and sixth arrondissements won't be disappointed.

EATING AND DRINKING

THE MENU

The French word for menu, meaning the list of dishes available, is *la carte*. The *menu* refers to a fixed-price menu, generally offering a starter, main course and dessert. There will be a choice of at least two dishes at each stage, sometimes with a quarter of a liter of wine thrown in. The *menu* is nearly always excellent value for money, and works out much cheaper than eating *à la carte*, so bringing otherwise unaffordable restaurants into range. For instance, if you have an urge to be cosseted in the plush surroundings of one of the capital's pricier restaurants, opting for the *menu* at lunchtime could save burning a hole in your pocket. Watch out, however, for indifferent restaurants or brasseries that capitalize on the *menu* system to offer you a disappointing selection of poor-quality food and wine under the guise of value for money.

of the country are especially well known for a certain dish – for instance, *bœuf bourguignon, saucisson de Lyon* or *tarte normande* – and there are plenty of restaurants dedicated to producing only regional specialities. For example, in an *Alsacienne* restaurant you will be treated to plates of steaming *choucroute:* cabbage on which nestle large slabs of bacon, spicy sausage or hunks of boiled ham. A restaurant that specializes in Normandy cooking will serve up calorie-laden dishes laced with cream, topped off with a glass of fiery apple liqueur known as Calvados. Brittany is famous for its sweet *crêpes* and *galettes*, the savory kind of pancake stuffed with anything: cheese, ham, mushrooms, spinach and egg, washed down with Breton cider. The list is endless, and the specialities are by no means only French. At least part of the country's colonial history is reflected in the diversity of national dishes available throughout Paris – from Vietnamese, Chinese and Thai to North African, Turkish, West Indian, Senegalese, Japanese and Greek, not to mention the range of Jewish food available in and around the Marais. That said, the following selection concentrates mainly on French cuisine.

Whatever the pitfalls – the complexities of the system, the brusqueness of the waiters, the terror of negotiating the wine list – dining out in Paris is always an experience, and often one of the most enjoyable ways of spending a couple of hours.

TIPPING

French law obliges every restaurant, café and brasserie automatically to include the service charge in your bill, so technically speaking you needn't leave anything. Nevertheless, custom has it that if you especially enjoyed your meal and the service was good, you can leave an extra few francs to show your appreciation.

BRASSERIES

Chez Jenny

39 boulevard du Temple, 75003, tel. 42 74 75 75. Metro République.
Open 11:30 a.m.–1 a.m. daily. 150F–200F.

Waitresses in Alsatian national costumes serve up steaming plates of *choucroute paysanne* (sauerkraut with bratwurst, frankfurters, slab bacon and potatoes) in this large friendly old brasserie. Popular with families and older couples; the menu features special dishes for children.

Brasserie de l'ile St-Louis

55 quai de Bourbon, 75004, tel. 43 54 02 59. Metro Pont-Marie.
Open 11:30 a.m. – 1:30 a.m.; closed Thursday lunchtime, Wednesday, August. 150F.

Small, lively brasserie overlooking Notre-Dame; fills up quickly with locals and tourists at night. Desserts include the famous and delicious ice cream from Berthillon, based on the Ile St-Louis.

Bofinger

3–7 rue de la Bastille, 75004, tel. 42 72 87 82. Metro Bastille.
Open noon–3 p.m.; 7:30 p.m.–1:00 a.m. daily. 200F.

Paris's oldest brasserie, with its stunning glass dome, is a popular haunt with post-opera diners. The decor is authentic 1919, and you might well think some of the waiters are too. Delicious seafood is favored by the regular clientele whose loyalty make it essential to make reservations.

Brasserie Lipp

151 boulevard St-Germain, 75006, tel. 45 48 53 91. Metro St-Germain.
Open Tuesday–Sunday until 12:45 a.m. 180F–200F.

One of the most traditional old brasseries, with decor to match. Formerly the watering-hole of such notables as Picasso and Sartre, now frequented by an equally elitist crowd but worth braving the disdain of waiters and clientele alike for a good brasserie staple like a *pot au feu* or *steak au poivre*.

Wepler

14 place Clichy, 75018, tel. 45 22 53 24. Metro place Clichy.
Open 8 a.m.– 1 a.m. daily. 200F.

Unpretentious place, renowned for some of the best shellfish in Paris. Head for the section without tablecloths and order an inexpensive plate of oysters and a glass of dry white wine. Solitary eaters should feel completely at home.

La Coupole

102 boulevard du Montparnasse, 75014, tel. 43 20 14 20. Metro Vavin.
Open 8 a.m.–2 a.m. daily. 200F–250F.

This huge brasserie, founded in 1927, is a Paris institution. The original 1930s decor and frescoes were recently rejuvenated, and the place bustles with life as waiters skid round corners, appearing with menus and lighters as if by magic. Good for people-watching and eating alone.

Brasserie Flo

7 cour des Petites-Ecuries, 75010, tel. 47 70 13 59. Metro Château d'Eau.
Open 12–3 p.m.; 7 p.m.–1:30 a.m. daily. 250F–300F.

Under the same management as La Coupole, but the long, low dark-paneled dining room gives a more intimate feel. Exuberant flower displays, splendid mirrors and silver seafood stands heaped with ice and moist shellfish all add to the rather sumptuous atmosphere. Try a *plateau de fruits de mer* (mixed seafood platter). The waiters will happily explain how to use the obscure tools designed for eating snails and crab – a good way of keeping busy if you have qualms about eating alone. Finish with a refreshing fruit sorbet.

Au Pied de Cochon

6 rue Coquillière, 75001, tel. 42 36 11 75. Metro Les Halles.
Open 24 hours daily. 250F–300F.

Perhaps a bit unappealing with its brash neon sign and jostling lines, but recommended for reasonable food at any hour. If you're into kitsch you'll also appreciate the decor of pink and glowing orange cherubs tumbling across the walls amid a froth of fluffy clouds and looping garlands. Specialities are *plat royale*, a mixed plate of shellfish, or pigs' feet. No outstanding dishes, but if you're searching for a traditional bowl of onion soup at 5 a.m. you could do a lot worse.

BISTROS

Perraudin

157 rue St-Jacques, 75005, tel. 46 33 15 75. Metro Odéon.
Open noon–2:30 p.m.; 7:30–10:15 p.m. Closed Saturday, Sunday dinner,
Monday a.m. 100F.

Good home cooking is dished up in this welcoming Latin Quarter bistro that attracts locals and visitors alike. While waiting for a place at the red-and-white-checked tables, you'll be given the menu (English translation available) to study and served complimentary kir and olives by the *patronne*. Enjoy a warming *confit de canard* (duck cooked and preserved in its own fat) or *bœuf bourguignon* in cheerful surroundings.

La Pomme

18 place Dauphine, 75001, tel. 43 25 74 93. Metro Pont Neuf.
Open noon–2 p.m.; 7–10:30 p.m. Closed Sunday dinner, Thursday, December
20–February 1. 120F–180F.

With only eight tables La Pomme, situated in pretty place Dauphine on Ile de la Cité, has the feel of a village café. The food, prepared and served by the *patronne*, is simple and good, especially the *salade tiède de lentilles* (warm lentil salad).

Le Scheffer

22 rue Scheffer, 72016, tel. 47 27 81 11. Metro Trocadéro.
Open noon–2:30 p.m.; 7:30–10:30 p.m. Closed Sunday and holidays. 150F.

Recommended for a revitalizing lunch once you've exhausted yourself in the museums of the Trocadéro. The food is good, the service quick and efficient. Try the *plat du jour*, written on the mirror at the side, or the *faux-filet au poivre* (peppered sirloin steak).

La Chaumière
10 rue du Pot de Fer, 75005, tel. 45 87 10 60.
Open noon–2 p.m. 7–11 p.m. Closed Sunday, December. 150F carte, 75F menu.

A few minutes' walk from the market in rue Mouffetard, La Chaumière is a local institution. By 1 p.m. regulars are pouring into the low-ceilinged dining rooms where orders, chosen from a series of small blackboards, are yelled back into the kitchen. The robust cooking is very much meat-oriented, featuring dishes such as *andouillette* with rice and *merguez* (spicy sausage) served with a fried egg.

Bistro de la Grille
14 rue Mabillon, 75006, tel. 43 54 16 87. Metro Mabillon.
Open noon–5:30 p.m.; 7:30–midnight daily. 150F.

A squashy old leather *banquette* lines one wall: people sit under authentic old photos of stars in this dark, cozy restaurant where the tables are so close together that you sometimes have the impression that you've joined a private dinner party. Waiters jolly, *menu* excellent value and food delicious, particularly the aromatic *bœuf bourguignon*, reposing in its own copper pot in a rich gravy.

Chardenoux
1 rue Jules-Valles, 75011, tel. 43 71 49 52, Metro Charonne.
Open noon–2 p.m. 8 p.m.–1:30 a.m. Closed Saturday lunch, Sunday, August.
180F–200F carte, 150F menu.

A traditional bistro with authentic 1900s decor, including a long zinc bar embellished with multicolored marble. Choose from the well-prepared salads, followed by a typical provincial bistro dish (strictly for carnivores) such as *andouillette grillée AAAAA* (grilled sausage made of pig intestines, endorsed by the Association Amicale des Authentiques Amateurs d'Andouillettes), *confit de canard* or delicious *boudin noir* (black pudding). Attracts lunchtime workers and a younger, livelier clientele at night.

Chez Paul
13 rue de Charonne, 75011, tel. 47 00 34 57. Metro Charonne.
Open noon–2:30 p.m. 7 p.m.–12:30 a.m. Closed Sunday. 150F.

A former workers' café where nowadays arty types crowd round the downstairs bar or pack on to the haphazard tables, drinking and loudly swapping news. The seating upstairs is more comfortable, though the boisterous atmosphere could prove disconcerting on your own. The *gigot d'agneau* (leg of lamb) and *rillettes de lapin* (minced rabbit) are both delicious and reasonably priced.

Aux Charpentiers
10 rue Mabillon, 75006, tel. 43 26 30 05. Metro Mabillon.
Open noon–2:30 p.m. 7 p.m.–11:30 p.m. Closed Sunday, and holidays. 180F.

This friendly St-Germain bistro is named after the *compagnons charpentiers*, master-carpenters and cabinetmakers whose organization stemmed from the medieval guilds. Scale models for architectural construction and photos of guild members adorn the walls. As so often, a different dish is served every day of the week, from *petit salé aux lentilles* (salt pork with lentils) on Wednesdays to *chou farci* (stuffed cabbage) on Saturdays. The avuncular waiters will make you feel at home among the local regulars. There are two floors but the ground floor is the most pleasant.

Le Maquis

69 rue Caulaincourt, 75018, tel. 42 59 76 07. Metro Lamarck Caulaincourt.
Open noon–2 p.m.; 7:30–10 p.m. Closed Sunday, Monday.
200F carte, 70F menu.

Just down the hill from Sacré-Cœur, this popular local bistro is a much better bet than the many tourist restaurants up on the Butte. Simple, delicious dishes made from fresh market produce are served in the modern dining room, or a glassed-in terrace in summer.

Le Caméléon

6 rue de Chevreuse, 75006, tel. 43 20 63 43. Metro Vavin.
Open noon–2 p.m.; 8–10:15 p.m. Closed Sunday, Monday, August. 200F.

You can be sure of a warm welcome at this traditional Parisian bistro in Montparnasse. It is very popular, so make sure you get reservations, even if you're eating alone. By 9 p.m. the marble-topped tables are packed with noisy groups of regulars enjoying the hearty bourgeois cuisine. Service is informal, quick and friendly.

RESTAURANTS

BUDGET

Chartier

7 rue du Faubourg Montmartre, 75009, tel. 47 70 86 29. Metro rue Montmartre. Open 11 a.m.–3 p.m.; 6–9:30 p.m. daily. 60F–80F.

This huge, inexpensive eatery is justly famous and great for people-watching. The splendid decor features high ceilings, huge wall mirrors, fancy moldings and brass luggage racks. The simpler dishes, such as grilled *entrecôte* or *steak au poivre* with *frites*, are best.

Le Drouot

103 rue de Richelieu, 75002, tel. 42 96 68 23. Metro Richelieu-Drouot.
Open 11:30 a.m.–3 p.m., 6:30–10 p.m. daily. 50F–80F.

This sister restaurant to Chartier is less atmospheric and rather stark, but still excellent value.

Le Polidor

41 rue Monsieur-le-Prince, 75006, tel. 43 26 95 34. Metro Odéon.
Open noon–2:30 p.m.; 7 p.m.–12:30 a.m. daily (Sunday 11 p.m.) 80F–100F.

Polidor has been serving up home-cooked food to students, artists and would-be bohemians since 1845. Period posters decorate the narrow dining room where people squeeze together at long tables, making it quite easy to strike up a conversation with your neighbors. The waitresses are quick and efficient, and the steak with crisp *frites* is very good.

La Lozère

4 rue Hautefeuille, 75006, tel. 43 54 26 64. Metro St-Michel.
Open noon–2 p.m.; 7:30–10:30 p.m. Closed Sunday, Monday, August, Christmas. 130F carte, 75F menu.

This small, rustic restaurant, attached to the tourist agency for the rugged Lozère region in central France, is perfect for a warming meal on a cold day. Customers sit at wooden tables and carve a hunk of brown bread from the basket before filling up with regional specialities such as *aligot* (mashed potato with melted Cantal cheese) or *jambon cru* (cured country ham).

Le Petit St-Benoît
4 rue St-Benoît, 75006, tel. 42 60 27 92. Metro St-Germain-des-Prés.
Open noon–2:30 p.m.; 7–10 p.m. Closed Saturday, Sunday. 80F.

In warm weather crowds pack the terrace of this small bistro, just off boulevard St-Germain; in winter they crowd into the narrow dining area, which feels a bit like a private living room. Bags and coats are stowed in luggage racks, as there is no space elsewhere. Budget travelers and students share tables, and the motherly waitresses bring steaming plates of plain food, such as *hachis parmentier* (chopped meat and potatoes) or *potée aux choux* (thick cabbage soup).

La Fresque
100 rue Rambuteau, 75001, tel. 42 33 17 56. Metro Les Halles.
Open noon–2:30 p.m.; 7 p.m.–midnight. Closed Sunday lunch.
150F carte, 70F menu (lunch only).

Housed in an ex-snail-seller's shop in Les Halles, this funky little restaurant – now all exposed pipes, iron pillars and displays of original art – attracts a cosmopolitan, alternative crowd. Children run around, dodging the ebullient waiters and waitresses bringing a mix of French bourgeois and vegetarian food, with interesting ideas like the Gorbachev platter, thick slabs of smoked salmon served with blinis and chilled vodka. Good restaurants in this area are few and far between, and although the cuisine may not be *haute*, it will satisfy your appetite in a relaxed, friendly setting.

L'Incroyable
26 rue de Richelieu, 75001, tel. 42 96 24 64. Metro Palais-Royal.
Open 11:45 a.m.–2:15 p.m.; 6:30–8:30 p.m. daily. 60F.

Situated in a tiny passage off the rue de Richelieu, the most *incroyable* (unbelievable) thing about this place is the sight of the waitresses dashing across the cobblestones into the second dining room located on the other side of the passage. Tiny and authentic, with quirky decor, the simple home-cooked fare is served at rock-bottom prices. This is where to go for a genuine slice of France.

Le Potiron
16 rue du Roule, 75001, tel. 42 33 35 68. Metro Louvre.
Open till 11:00 p.m. Closed Sunday, Monday. 80F.

Run by women, with art exhibitions by women, with imaginative nouvelle-cuisine-type cooking and inexpensive into the bargain. Worth a stopoff on your way to or from the Louvre.

Le Petit Vatel
5 rue Lobineau, 75006, tel. 43 54 28 49. Metro Mabillon.
Open noon–3 p.m.; 7 p.m.–midnight. Closed Sunday lunch. 90F.

Tucked away in St-Germain, this tiny restaurant probably seats no more than ten, but all food is available for takeout and it's a real find. Dishes are simple, including a choice of vegetarian main courses and the service warm and welcoming. For dessert, the *fromage blanc* with chestnut purée is delicious.

Restaurant les Beaux-Arts

11 rue Bonaparte, 75006, tel. 43 26 92 64. Metro St-Germain-des-Prés.
Open noon–2 p.m.; 7 p.m.–10:45 p.m. daily. 100F carte, 63F menu.

A mixed crowd of locals and visitors crowd elbow to elbow for this cheap, reliable fare. The three-course menu at 63F is great value for money. Eat on the ground floor – the room upstairs is rather soulless.

Thoumieux

79 rue St-Dominique, 75007, tel. 47 05 49 75. Metro Invalides.
Open noon–3 p.m; 7–11:30 p.m. Closed Monday. 150F carte, 52F menu.

Good home cooking in rather plush surroundings considering the price. The waiters can get a bit harassed – perhaps understandably, as business is brisk. At lunchtime workers from the surrounding government offices down large portions of *cassoulet, confit* and other such hefty dishes. If you've got room, the strawberry crêpes are definitely worth trying.

Café de Mars

11 rue Augereau, 75007, tel. 47 05 05 91. Metro Ecole Militaire.
Open noon–2:30 p.m.; 8–11:30 p.m. Closed Saturday lunch, Sunday dinner.
Sunday brunch 11:30 a.m.–4:30 p.m. 150F.

Trendy media types from surrounding production companies tend to flock here for a light lunch served by waitresses who look as if they've stepped out of fashion pages. The decor is simple and clean; pasta dishes and crunchy salads are popular.

Ferme Sainte-Suzanne

4 rue des Fossés St-Jacques, 75005, tel. 43 54 90 02. RER Luxembourg. Open
11:30 a.m.–2:30 p.m. 7:30–9:30 p.m. Closed Saturday, Sunday. 100F–150F.

Cheese is a speciality, served with an interesting range of salads. The *chèvre* (goat's cheese) and orange salad is recommended. Stone walls, a beamed ceiling and cool marble tables. Unpretentious decor.

Le Roi du Pot-au-Feu

34 rue Vignon, 75009, tel. 47 42 37 10. Metro Madeleine.
Open noon–9 p.m. daily. Closed Sun, July. 150F.

Cozy, cheerful place, famous – as the name suggests – for its *pot-au-feu*. Snug booths provide an ideal setting for savoring this hearty traditional French dish which comes in two parts: a bowl of broth, followed by a hunk of meat on the bone (complete with marrow) accompanied by roughly chopped vegetables. Washed down with a glass of Gamay d'Anjou, this makes a perfect meal for cold days.

MODERATE (200F PLUS)

Chez Georges

1 rue du Mail, 75002, tel. 42 60 07 11. Metro Sentier.
Open noon–2:30 p.m.; 7–9:45 p.m. Closed Sunday, holidays. 250F–300F.

Upscale version of a traditional Parisian bistro with a very pretty dining room lined with arching mirrors. The clientele tends to range from Parisian gourmets to foreign businessmen. The food is wonderful: the *steak de canard* (pan-fried duck breast) a real treat.

L'Assommoir

12 rue Girardon, 75018, tel. 42 64 55 01. Metro Lamarck Caulaincourt.
Open noon–2:30 p.m.; 7–11 p.m. Closed Sunday dinner, Monday. 280F.

This charming restaurant, hidden on the north slope of Montmartre, used to be a café-cum-grocery and a certain bohemian informality still prevails. The decor is eclectic; an ice box shaped like an owl, African sculptures, china cats, a model yacht and two alarm clocks jostle for space around the counter. The jovial *patron* welcomes all alike to his red-and-white-checked tables, sitting with customers while they choose. Worth trying are the *salade Joséphine* (colorful mixed salad) and the *coquilles Saint-Jacques* (scallops) cooked in champagne. Try to leave room for excellent desserts like the huge, sticky *rhum baba*.

Ambassade d'Auvergne

22 rue du Grenier Saint-Lazare, 75003, tel. 42 72 31 22. Metro Etienne
Marcel/Rambuteau. Open noon–2:30 p.m.; 7:30–11 p.m. daily. 250F–300F.

Hearty food from the Auvergne is served on two floors. Downstairs cured hams and copper pans dangle from the beamed ceiling, and wooden sideboards line the walls. Among the specialities are the spicy *boudin noir* (black pudding sausage), *chou farci* (stuffed cabbage) and their own *pot-au-feu*, which includes poultry. Service is quick and professional.

Chez Pauline

5 rue Villedo, 75001, tel. 42 96 20 70. Metro Pyramides. Open noon–2:15 p.m.;
7:30–10:30 p.m. Closed Saturday lunch, Sunday. 350F–400F.

Another Parisian bistro that has gone upscale over the years. If you're in the mood for soft lamplight and the wafting scent of fresh flowers, Chez Pauline is a treat. Three or more people can reserve one of the comfortable curved booths upstairs. Traditional bistro dishes with a difference are served alongside more contemporary creations like *huîtres chaudes à la crème de caviar* (warm oysters in caviar sauce). Dress up and indulge yourself.

Le Procope

13 rue de l'Ancienne Comédie, 75006, tel. 43 26 99 20. Metro Odéon.
Open noon–12 a.m. daily. Set menus from 72F–289F.

Open until the early hours, this place merits a mention more for its historical associations than anything else. It's supposedly the oldest café in the world (it dates from the late seventeenth century): you can come here and rub shoulders with the ghosts of Balzac, Voltaire, Rousseau and Napoleon, all of whom are said to have frequented it at one time or another. During the winter you can sit in the brightly lit interior along with the well-heeled middle-aged clientele and be gawked at by the students, looking trendily down-at-heel, lining up outside for entry to the late-night pub next door. In the summer, if you are extremely lucky, you might be seated at one of the tables on the balcony on the first floor, protected by a smart red umbrella and surrounded by geraniums, for a pigeon's-eye view of the throng in the rue de l'Ancienne Comédie below.

Le Vagenende

142 boulevard St-Germain, 75006, tel. 43 26 19 14. Metro Odéon.
Open noon–3 p.m.; 7 p.m.–1 a.m. daily. 200F.

This turn-of-the-century brasserie has the most spectacular Art Nouveau decor, complete with stained-glass oval in the ceiling, dark wood, and tulip-shaped lampshades. It's off the boulevard St-Germain; in summer you can sit out – or half-out – on the pavement, but the inside is particularly beautiful in the evenings. Food carefully prepared, waiters very friendly.

Le Train Bleu
20 boulevard Diderot, Gare de Lyon, 75012, tel. 43 43 09 06. Metro Gare de Lyon. Open noon–2 p.m.; 7–10 p.m. daily. 250F plus.

Unmissable for anyone who wants to steep themselves in French turn-of-the-century atmosphere, while eating traditional French cuisine. Prices can be on the high side.

La Timonerie
35 quai de la Tournelle, 75005, tel. 43 25 44 42. Metro Maubert-Mutualité. Open noon–2:30 p.m; 7:45–10:30 p.m. Closed Sunday, Monday. 230F–300F carte, 195F lunch menu.

Elegant modern restaurant decorated with pine paneling, potted miniature rose plants and prints from old cookery books. Hostess Françoise de Givenchy (married to the chef) welcomes her fairly well-heeled customers, and sets an informal but professional tone. Interesting *à la carte* options include ravioli with aubergine, or try the more traditional roast *foie gras* served with potatoes. The lunch menu is delicious, and very good value.

La Table d'Anvers
2 place d'Anvers, 75009, tel. 48 78 35 21. Metro Anvers. Open noon–2 p.m.; 7:15–11 p.m. Closed Saturday lunch, Sunday, August. 500F carte, 190F, 350F lunch menus.

You need to dress smartly for a meal at this sophisticated restaurant, situated in an attractive square just south of Montmartre, where the contemporary yellow and cream furnishings provide a neutral backdrop for the rather yuppyish clientele. Delicious starter salads combine bitter herbs and delicate sweet dressings. Stick to fish or something light to follow, as the biggest treat is dessert. The pastries are famous, and even the humble *tarte aux pommes* is exceptionally mouthwatering. If you're having the lunch menu, beware: wine by the glass is not available, and half a bottle could double your bill.

HAUTE CUISINE

Jacques Cagna
32 rue des Grands-Augustins, 75006, tel. 43 26 49 39. Metro St-Michel. Open noon–2 p.m.; 7–10:30 p.m. Closed Saturday, Sunday. Reserve 5–6 days in advance for dinner, 2 days in advance for lunch. 500F–700F carte, 250F menu (lunch only).

Skilful blend of classic and contemporary cuisine served on the first floor of a beautiful seventeenth-century house. The food – such as *filet de bar farci d'huîtres* (bass stuffed with oysters) or *côté de bœuf poêlée* (pan-fried rib of beef) from Aberdeen – is fairly simple but high-quality.

Guy Savoy
18 rue Troyon, 75017, tel. 43 80 40 61. Metro Charles de Gaulle/Etoile. Open noon–2 p.m.; 7:30–10:30 p.m. Monday–Friday; 7:30–10:30 p.m. Saturday. Closed Sunday, August. 350F–800F carte, 540F menu.

Reserve 10–15 days in advance for dinner, 5 days for lunch. Boasting two Michelin stars, this is again classic cuisine combined with the light and inventive touch of contemporary cooking. Consistently high quality attracts a loyal clientele for dishes such as *langoustines à la crème de lentilles* (giant prawns with lentil sauce) and *lapereau a l'ancienne et gratin de légumes* (baby rabbit cooked in the traditional way, with vegetable gratin).

Jules Verne

Second floor, Eiffel Tower, 75007, tel. 45 55 61 44. Metro Bir Hakeim. Ecole Militaire/Trocadéro. Open 12:30–2:30 p.m.; 7:30–10:15 p.m. daily. Average 650F, menu 270F (lunch only, Monday–Friday).

A combination of excellent food and breathtaking views of the city make this one of the most sought-after restaurants in Paris. Reserving for lunch is less difficult.

ITALIAN

Casa Bini

36 rue Grégoire-de-Tours, 75006, tel. 46 34 05 60. Metro Odéon. Open 12:30–2:30 p.m.; 7–10:30 p.m. Closed Saturday lunch, Sunday, August. 300F.

Chef Anna Bini creates delicious pasta and sauces in her airy restaurant in St-Germain. The best dishes combine fresh, simple ingredients, like the Casa Bini with parma ham and wafer-thin slices of parmesan. Or try a plate of lightly steamed vegetables served with lemon and olive oil. The friendly waiters tell you what pasta and sauces are available. House wines are served by the pitcher, and a range of traditional Italian desserts provide a good finish.

JAPANESE

Matsuri Sushi

36 rue de Richelieu, 75001, tel. 42 61 05 73. Metro Palais-Royal. Open noon– 2:30 p.m.; 7–10:30 p.m. 7–11:30 p.m. Friday, Saturday. Closed Saturday lunch, Sunday. Sushi 22F per portion, main courses 100F–150F.

Matsuri Sushi claims to be the first moving sushi counter in Europe. Plates of salmon topped with colorful caviar, or rice wrapped up in seaweed, are prepared in the central kitchen and placed on a conveyor belt that revolves before customers sitting on low wooden stools. Choice of two main courses. Eat as much as you want, and the plates are counted when you've finished. Lots of people eat alone here, accompanying their meal with *sake* or Japanese beer.

JEWISH/CENTRAL EUROPEAN

Jo Goldenberg

7 rue des Rosiers, 75004, tel. 48 87 29 16/48 87 70 39. Metro St-Paul. Open noon–2:30 p.m.; 7 p.m.–2 a.m. daily. 200F.

Kitsch decor and rather haphazard service characterize this famous busy, restaurant. You can either make reservations or just arrive and eat at the bar, although you may feel conspicuous taking the latter option. A range of traditional dishes are available at reasonable prices.

Chez Marianne

2 rue des Hospitalières-Saint-Gervais, 75004, tel. 42 72 18 86. Metro St-Paul. Open 11 a.m.–5 p.m.; 5:30 p.m.–midnight. Closed Friday. 100F.

Philosophical thoughts are painted on the windows of this busy former delicatessen, which has blossomed into a restaurant. There are two dining rooms, but the main one is more atmospheric. A blend of stylish Marais inhabitants and gnarled workers tuck into *taramasalata*, *tzatziki*, falafels and the like. You can opt for a mixed plate for your choice; the price varies from 60F–80F, depending on what you order. Service can be a bit sullen.

CHINESE, VIETNAMESE AND THAI

Nïoullaville
32–4 rue de l'Orillon, 75011, tel. 43 38 30 44. Metro Belleville. Open noon–3:30 p.m.; 6:30 p.m.–1 a.m. Monday–Saturday, noon–1 a.m. Sunday. 100F.

Immense restaurant serving reasonable Chinese, Vietnamese and Thai food. The sixteen-page menu and space for 500 customers mean you need feel no compunction about dropping in here to order soup and Tsingtao beer, and there's plenty to watch. However, Belleville isn't a wealthy area and some may feel nervous alone, especially at night, though the restaurant is close to the Metro.

SCANDINAVIAN

Comptoir du Saumon et Cie
60 rue François Miron, 75004, tel. 42 77 23 08. Metro St-Paul. Open noon–3 p.m.; 6:30–11 p.m. 150F.

This new restaurant is an interesting change. Fish is the main event in the bright blue and turquoise interior, accompanied by wine by the glass or chilled vodka. You can choose marinated herrings or caviar, but the speciality is salmon of all types, from Scottish to Norwegian.

LATIN AMERICAN

Anahi
49 rue Volta, 75003, tel. 48 87 88 24. Metro Arts et Métiers. Open 8 p.m.– midnight daily. 150F.

This restaurant, formerly a butcher's shop, has retained the white tiled walls and marble slabs in the window. Young photographers and journalists rub shoulders with families, in a relaxed atmosphere, to the tune of soft panpipes. The margaritas here wake your mouth up, the guacamole comes with strips of soft, warm bread, and meat dishes like spicy Argentinian *merguez* (sausage) are served on a wooden board.

VEGETARIAN

Guenmaï
2bis rue de l'Abbaye, 75006, tel. 43 26 03 24. Metro St-Germain-des-Prés. Restaurant open noon–3:30 p.m.; closed Sunday (cold snacks available after 3:30 p.m.). Shop open 9 a.m.–8:30 p.m.; closed Sunday. 60F.

Macrobiotic salads, quiches and pasties are served in a rather clinical green and white room attached to a health-food shop.

Grand Appétit
9 rue de la Cerisaie, 75004, tel. 40 27 04 95. Metro Bastille. Open noon– 7 p.m. Monday–Thursday, noon–2 p.m. Friday, Sunday. Closed Saturday. 70F.

Comfortable café tucked away at the back of a cramped shop selling everything from clogs to spices and organic vegetables. You can start with miso soup, move

to a salad of *céréales, légumes et algues* (grains, vegeta
round things off with fruit compote. Jade beer and *sake* ar

Le Grenier de Notre-Dame
18 rue de la Bûcherie, 75005, tel. 43 29 98 29. Metro Mau
noon–2:30 p.m.; 7–11 p.m. daily. 150F, formule économiq
70F.

Popular vegetarian/macrobiotic restaurant, where you can
bright space downstairs or up the spiral staircase in more
the sound of jazz. The menu is quite varied, featuring some in
tails. Seaweed, olive oil and other foods are available for sale.

Aquarius
54 rue Ste-Croix de la Bretonnerie, 75004, tel. 48 87 48 71. Metro Hotel de
Ville/Rambuteau. Open noon–9:45 p.m. daily. (Also at 40 rue de Gergovie,
75014, tel. 45 41 36 88). 80F.

Rather austere restaurant serving reliable, if unspectacular, vegetarian fare.
Customers sit at long wooden tables, served by grave waiters bringing soup, salad
or quiche. Also sells books on topics such as "TV and Health."

No smoking zone.

LIGHT MEALS AND BRUNCH

Le Comptoir
14 rue Vauvilliers, 75001, tel. 40 26 26 66. Metro Les Halles.
Open noon–1 a.m. daily. 100F.

Former Les Halles bistro, now a tapas bar frequented by a young crowd. The
designer decor is beginning to look a bit shabby, but Le Comptoir is convenient
for an informal snack. Brunch on Sundays.

Les Fous de l'Ile
33 rue des Deux-Ponts, 75004, tel. 43 25 76 67. Metro Pont Marie.
Open noon–3 p.m.; 7–11 p.m. daily. 90F.

A relaxed and welcome change from some of the overpriced and overdecorated
places on l'Ile Saint-Louis. Here you'll find papers and magazines to read, quiet
jazz, and chess and checkers to play. The salads and *plats du jour*, such as
estouffade québécoise (beef stew), are good. Or choose a mixed plate of cheese
and a glass of red wine.

Le Petit Fer à Cheval
30 rue Vieille-du-Temple, 75004, tel. 42 72 47 47. Metro Hotel de Ville/St-Paul.
Open 9 a.m.–2 a.m. Monday-Friday, 11 a.m.–2 a.m. Saturday and Sunday; for
hot food noon–1:30 a.m. 150F.

One of the few places left in Paris to have a counter in the shape of a horseshoe.
A confident, cosmopolitan crowd packs in, so don't come for a quiet meal with
your book. Seated on wooden benches at the back, choose from six or seven simple main courses chalked up on the board. The salmon pasta is good. Finish with
a huge slab of cheesecake or rich chocolate mousse, and enjoy the boisterous
banter kept up by the staff.

...rmi Ailée
...du Fouarre, 75005, tel. 43 29 40 99. Metro Maubert-Mutualité.
...en noon–7 p.m. Closed Tuesday. 80F.

This tearoom at the back of a women's bookshop is an oasis of tranquillity. Good simple food is served in a friendly, unhurried atmosphere making a perfect antidote to battling through crowds or lining up in museums. What's more, their *tarte au fromage blanc* is delicious.

L'Arbre à la Canelle
57 passage des Panoramas, 75002, tel. 45 08 55 87. Metro rue Montmartre.
Open 10 a.m.–6 p.m. Monday-Friday, 11:30 a.m.–6:30 p.m. Saturday. Closed Sunday. 70F.

If you're exploring the passages off rue Vivienne, chances are the charming Napoleon III decor of this tearoom will catch your eye. The arching windows and carved wood interior recall the nineteenth-century heyday of these covered shopping streets. Quiches and salads are accompanied by revitalizing fruit cocktails.

Marais Plus
20 rue des Francs-Bourgeois, 75003, tel. 48 87 01 40. Metro St-Paul.
Open 9 a.m.–midnight; Sunday 9 a.m.–8 p.m. 70F.

Although this is primarily a gift shop selling cards, novelty teapots and children's toys, there's a café at the back. Vegetarian pies, tarts and salads are served on colorful crockery by young men in jeans.

Le Loir dans la Théière
3 rue des Rosiers, 75004, tel. 42 72 90 61. Metro St-Paul.
Open noon–11 p.m. daily. 90F.

Comfortable, welcoming tearoom where you can either slump in the battered armchairs or sit at a polished wooden table. "The dormouse in the teapot" is decorated with a Lewis Carroll theme mural and fresh flowers. This is a popular spot, and there's always a hum of conversation. Opt for salad with toast and warm goat's cheese, or *truite fumée* (smoked trout).

Tea Follies
6 place Gustave-Toudouze, 75009, tel. 42 80 08 44. Metro St-Georges.
Open 9 a.m.–9 p.m.; Sun 9 a.m.–7 p.m. 90F; brunch 110F.

Place Gustave-Toudouze is one of the more pleasant corners of Pigalle, and a good place to stop for brunch or a snack. Local families, mothers with children and young Pigalle residents crowd into this tearoom, decorated in spare, contemporary style, or sit out on the square. Dishes include *salade Tea Follies au foie gras* and *terrine de légumes*. It's best to make reservations for Sunday brunch.

Les Enfants Gâtés
43 rue des Francs-Bourgeois, 75004, tel. 42 77 07 63.
Metro St-Paul/Rambuteau. Open noon–7 p.m. daily;
brunch Saturday, Sunday noon–4 p.m. 90F; brunch 100F–200F.

"The spoilt children" welcomes chic Marais regulars who flop down in low, battered leather armchairs to order snacks or a huge brunch. Ceiling fans, green plants and photos of movie stars created a semi-colonial-club atmosphere.

Paradis du Fruit
27–9 quai des Grands-Augustins, 75006, tel. 43 54 51 42. Metro St-Michel.
28bis rue Louis-le-Grand, 75002, tel. 42 65 33 23. Metro Opéra. 1 rue des
Tournelles, 75004, tel. 40 27 94 79. Metro Bastille. Open 11:30 a.m.–1 a.m.
daily. 90F.

Fresh fruit cocktails, yogurts and ices are a speciality. Also salads, fruit pastries and tarts for lunch.

Brocco
180 rue du Temple, 75003, tel. 42 72 19 81. Metro Temple.
Open 8 a.m.–7 p.m. daily. 50F.

Breakfast on light, flaky croissants and *pain au chocolat* in luxurious nineteenth-century surroundings. The mirrors, sculpted moldings and wispy painted cherubs recall the optimistic days when Monsieur Brocco opened his *patisserie* under the Third Republic. Prices, fortunately are far from grand. You can also order dishes like *quiche aux oignons/poireaux* (onion/leek quiche) or *bouchée à la reine* (small vol-au-vents). Worth a trip up to place de la République.

Café Mouffetard
118 rue Mouffetard, 75005, tel. 43 31 42 50. Metro Censier d'Aubenton.
Open 7 a.m.–9 p.m. (–noon Sunday). Closed Monday. 40F.

Down rue Mouffetard, where a busy market fills the street with shoppers and street performers, you'll find this tiny, smoky café where they make their own excellent croissants. Take one or two from the basket on the bar, and order a coffee to go with them.

TAKEOUT

Chez Marianne
2 rue des Hospitalières-Saint-Gervais, 75004, tel. 42 72 18 86. Metro St-Paul.
Open 11 a.m.–5 p.m.; 5:30 p.m.–midnight. Closed Friday.

A range of central European/Jewish produce to takeout.

Le Mezel
1 rue Ferdinand-Duval, 75004. Metro St-Paul. Open 7:30 a.m.–8:30 p.m.
Closed Friday.

Boulangerie–patisserie selling *falafel maison* for 18F.

Restaurant-traiteur Yahalom
22 rue des Rosiers, 75004, tel. 42 77 12 35. Metro St-Paul. Open 11 a.m.–
3 p.m. daily.

Takeout falafel for 20F.

Così
54 rue de Seine, 75006, tel. 46 33 35 36. Metro Mabillon. 53 avenue des Ternes,
75017, tel. 43 80 86 70. Metro Place des Ternes. Open noon–11 p.m. daily.

Choose your filling (e.g., blue cheese, celery and carrot salad) or devise your own at the counter of this upscale sandwich shop. The soft bread is baked on the premises, and the sandwiches are huge and well stuffed. If you want to, you can eat here to the sound of the day's opera (the name is written on a board by the counter). Wine is available. Sandwiches 20–50F depending on filling; cakes 30F.

Phinéas

99 rue de l'Ouest, 75014, tel. 45 41 33 50. Metro Pernety.
Open 9 a.m.–11 p.m. Closed Sunday, Monday.

Tucked away in the streets south of Montparnasse station, Phinéas sells tarts and quiches of all description, both savory and sweet. Choose a slice from the menu or order a whole tart with your chosen ingredients. Unusual fillings such as *noix de coco* (coconut), *pavot* (poppy seeds) and *griottes* (morello cherries) tempt the imagination. Tart portion 30F–40F, sit-down menu 70F.

Mexi and Co.

10 rue Dante, 75005, tel. 46 33 04 89. Metro Maubert-Mutualité.
Open 11 a.m.–9 p.m. 60F.

Mexican deli with spices, tequila and the like on sale around a counter where you can eat a range of South American specialities or order a snack to take out.

Gargantua

284 rue Saint-Honoré, 75001, tel. 42 60 63 38. Metro Tuileries.
Open 8:30 a.m.–7:30 p.m. Closed Sunday.

Perfect for stocking up for a picnic in the Tuileries gardens. Choose from a tempting range of sandwiches on chewy *pain poilâne*, or *baguettes*. Portions of *foie gras* and *barquettes* (plastic container) of salad, patisserie and ices are also on sale. Sandwiches 20F–30F.

Flo Prestige

42 place du Marché Saint-Honoré, 75001, tel. 42 61 45 46. Metro Pyramides.
Open 8 a.m.–11 p.m. daily. 36 avenue de la Motte-Picquet 75007, tel. 45 55 71 25. Open 9 a.m.–9:30 p.m. daily.

With eight branches in Paris and one in Tokyo, the Flo Prestige chain is doing well out of upscale takeouts. Ready meals with all the trimmings can be delivered, or you can pick up everything you might need for a celebration picnic.

Fauchon

26 place de la Madeleine, 75008, tel. 47 42 60 11. Metro Madeleine.
Open 9:40 a.m.–7 p.m. Closed Sunday.

Gourmet food for confident shoppers makes up the lavish window displays in place de la Madeleine. Here you can buy everything from stuffed snails to rare mushrooms or individually dressed duckling.

Hédiard

21 place de la Madeleine, 75008, tel. 42 66 44 36. Metro Madeleine.
Open 9:15 a.m. – 11 p.m. Closed Sunday.

Not so famous as Fauchon, but scarcely less exclusive, Hédiard sells prepared dishes, exquisite *patisseries* and the like.

CAFÉ-BARS

Café Costes

4–6 rue Berger, 75001, tel. 45 08 54 39. Metro Les Halles.
Open 8 a.m.–2 a.m. daily.

Philippe Starck's design may be starting to look dated, but the large café terrace opposite the beautiful Renaissance Fontaine des Innocents remains a popular spot for people-watching. Inside, things tend to be quieter, and you may feel less on display. Drinks are expensive.

Café Beaubourg
100 rue Saint-Martin, 75004, tel. 48 87 89 98. Metro Les Halles.
Open 8 a.m.–2 a.m. daily.

Books sit on shelves, magazines are available and *pensées* adorn the walls of this café, next door to the Pompidou Center. Other than that, it's just as style-conscious as Café Costes, but the seats are more comfortable. From the terrace you get a good view of the street performers and jugglers outside the Pompidou.

La Pointe Saint-Eustache
1 rue Montorgueil, 75001, tel. 42 33 15 05. Metro Les Halles.
Open 8 a.m.–midnight daily.

This ordinary corner café is a good antidote to the expensive designer meccas nearby in Les Halles.

Café de Flore
172 boulevard St-Germain, 75006, tel. 45 48 55 26. Metro St-Germain-des-Prés.
Open 7:30 a.m.–1:30 a.m. daily.

A Saint-Germain legend, the Flore was frequented by some of the city's most illustrious women, among them Simone de Beauvoir, Juliette Greco and Simone Signoret. You can still spot young hopefuls discussing their latest novels.

Les Deux Magots
170 boulevard St-Germain, 75006, tel. 45 48 55 25. Metro St-Germain-des-Prés.
Open 7:30 a.m.–1:30 a.m. daily.

Another legendary focus for literary Paris, but more glitzy than the Flore, the Deux Magots is nowadays frequented by an adult, sophisticated crowd. Well-dressed shoppers with tiny dogs under their chairs sip chocolate and tuck into pastries, while publishing executives sample the malt whiskey. None of this comes cheap, which doesn't discourage the crowds jostling for a terrace table when the weather is fine.

Café de l'Industrie
16 rue Saint-Sabin, 75011. Metro Bréguet-Sabin.
Open 11 a.m.–1:30 a.m. Closed Saturday.

An ordinary local café from the outside. Once you're past the bar you go into a large back room furnished with plants, black-and-white photos of jazz musicians, and scuffed wooden chairs and tables. The atmosphere is easygoing. You can order wine by the pitcher, and food like *chili con carne* and *salade niçoise*.

Pause Café
41 rue de Charonne, 75011, tel. 48 06 80 33. Metro Charonne.
Open 9 a.m.–9 p.m. Closed Monday.

A 1950s atmosphere prevails among Formica tables and yellow and red chairs, where Bastille trendies meet for a snack of *tarte au chèvre* or a *pain poilâne* sandwich. Scrutinize the posters plastered up for the latest arts events, browse through the magazines, or simply sit on the terrace watching the street life.

Café de la Paix
12 boulevard des Capucines, 75009, tel. 42 68 12 13. Metro Opéra.
Open 10 a.m.–1:30 p.m.; 2:30 p.m.–midnight daily.

Lush Second Empire decor with frescoes of cherubs and sculpted molding attract holidaymakers who tend to pack the terrace, especially at cocktail hour. Matches Garnier's Opéra nearby.

Le Sélect
99 boulevard du Montparnasse, 75006, tel. 45 48 38 24. Metro Vavin.
Open 8:30 a.m.–2 a.m. daily.

The long list of bourbons and whiskies in this Montparnasse café recalls the days when characters like Hemingway rested here. It may have lost its former glamour, but the terrace is still a good spot for observing the goings-on on busy boulevard du Montparnasse.

Café Mouffetard
118 rue Mouffetard, 75005, tel. 43 31 42 50. Metro Censier Daubenton.
Open 7 a.m.–9 p.m., noon Sunday. Closed Monday.

Pop into this local workers' café for a coffee after visiting the market down rue Mouffetard.

Ma Bourgogne
19 place des Vosges, 75004, tel. 42 78 44 84. Metro St-Paul.
Open 7 a.m–1:30 a.m. daily.

Location makes this restaurant/café/bar popular to overflowing, but this doesn't detract from the pleasure of sitting under the arches of Paris's oldest square for morning coffee, serenaded by harp or violin players. Snacks are served at the bar, or you can get a full meal inside.

Le Flore en l'Ile
42 quai d'Orléans, Ile Saint-Louis, 75004, tel. 43 29 88 27. Metro Pont Marie.
Open 10 a.m.–1 a.m. daily.

The renovated, sparkling interior provides a marvelous view of Notre-Dame while you sip your beer or linger over one of Berthillon's excellent ices.

Au Vieux Colombier
65 rue de Rennes, 75006, tel. 45 48 53 81. Metro St-Sulpice.
Open 6:30 a.m.–midnight. Closed Sunday.

A corner café with nineteenth-century-style decor, popular with St-Germain shoppers who come for a glass of white wine after a hard day's work trawling the boutiques.

COCKTAIL BARS

La Closerie des Lilas
171 boulevard du Montparnasse, 75006, tel. 43 54 21 68. Metro Vavin.
Open 10 a.m.–1:30 a.m. daily.

Beyond the restaurant is a packed bar where tables carry brass plaques commemorating famous Montparnasse inhabitants of bygone days. A mixed crowd of *soixante-huitards,* literary and executive types keep up the tradition, choosing from a long list of spirits, cocktails and something for the morning after. Not the place to drink alone.

Le Bélier bar de l'Hôtel
13 rue des Beaux-Arts, 75006, tel. 43 25 27 22. Metro St-Germain-des-Prés.
Open 24 hours, seven days a week.

This luxurious little bar in the hotel where Oscar Wilde died beyond his means is the epitome of hedonism. Comfortable sofas, a tinkling fountain and lush green plants help you to unwind, and the attentive waiters promptly bring your choice of cocktail from the expensive menu. Well-heeled American visitors, photographers, and models and actors seem to be among the regulars.

La Mousson
9 rue de la Bastille, 75004, tel. 42 71 85 20. Metro Bastille.
Open 7 p.m.–1:30 a.m. daily.

Basket chairs, ceiling fans and jazz feature in this once very fashionable Bastille spot. Lots of space makes this a good place to sit over a cocktail without any embarrassment.

China Club
50 rue de Charenton, 75012, tel. 43 43 82 02. Metro Reuilly Diderot.
Open 9 p.m.–1:30 a.m. daily.

A sophisticated cocktail bar with a small dining area attached, decorated in red and black with Art Deco lamps and leather sofas. Not cheap.

Les Portes
15 rue de Charonne, 75011, tel. 40 21 70 61. Metro Charonne.
Open 6:30 p.m.–2 a.m. daily.

Push open the doors of Les Portes, and you're in an intimate little spot where chic Bastille *habitués* prop up the bar. The furniture – a low mirror-topped table here, a tigerskin-covered armchair there – is interesting, and the low-beamed ceiling and dim lighting create a moody but unsleazy atmosphere. Further attractions include jazz-funk, and large shots for the price.

Le Bar Sans Nom
49 rue de Lappe, 75011, tel. 48 05 59 36. Metro Bastille.
Open 8 p.m. –1 a.m. daily.

The "bar without a name" is recognizable from the outside by its red paintwork and the crowds of young people chatting animatedly over long tables in the shabby interior. Off-beat music and cheap drinks are among the attractions.

La Buvette
4 rue des Panoyaux, 75020, tel. 46 36 81 79. Metro Ménilmontant.
Open 9 p.m.–2 a.m.

Arty regulars crowd into this bar in Ménilmontant to enjoy cheap punch and tequila and the eclectic music – anything from modern classical to African beats. Best avoided alone, as it's on a rather dark, dilapidated street.

La Perla
26 rue François Miron, 75004, tel. 42 77 59 40. Metro St-Paul.
Open noon–2 a.m. daily.

A crowded Mexican bar in the Marais serving a range of national beers and cocktails – also Mexican food, in tapas-size portions. The chatty bar staff speak English, and the atmosphere is generally cheerful and welcoming.

BARS À VIN

La Tartine
24 rue de Rivoli, 75004, tel. 42 72 76 85. Metro Châtelet. Open 8 a.m.–10 p.m. Monday, Thursday, Friday, Saturday, Sunday; noon–10 p.m. Wednesday. Closed Tuesday.

A good place to go for reasonably priced wines in an authentic Parisian setting. Laconic waitresses fill your glass from the marble bar, and you pay at the counter when you've finished. They also do lovely chewy *pain poilâne* sandwiches.

La Cloche des Halles
28 rue Coquillière, 75001, tel. 42 36 93 89. Metro Les Halles. Open 8 a.m.–9 p.m. Monday-Friday; 9:30 a.m.–6 p.m. Saturday. Closed Sunday.

Recognizable by the bell sign outside, this café is one of the least pretentious lunch spots in the area. It gets very crowded so if it's warm enough, sit outside to enjoy *une charcuterie* (a plate of cured meats) and *un rouge* (a glass of house red).

Jacques Mélac
42 rue Léon-Frot, 75011, tel. 43 70 59 27. Metro Charonne. Open 9 a.m.–7:30 p.m. Friday, Saturday; 9 a.m.–10 p.m. Tuesday, Wednesday, Thursday. Closed Sunday, Monday, mid-July–mid-August.

A convivial wine bar where locals gather to imbibe their choice from the large selection chalked up on boards. It's a rustic place with sawdust on the floor, rough stone walls and a beamed ceiling festooned with hams and sausages. You can accompany your wine with cheese or charcuterie, or one of the tasty *plats du jour.* Nonsmoking room at the back.

L'Ecluse
15 quai des Grands-Augustins, 75006, tel. 46 33 58 74. Metro St-Michel. Open noon–1:30 a.m. daily.

Possibly a bit commercialized for some tastes, this spruce wine bar with red velvet *banquettes* caters specially to Bordeaux enthusiasts. Expensive.

Willi's Wine Bar
13 rue des Petits-Champs, 75001, tel. 42 61 05 09. Metro Pyramides. Open 11 a.m.–11 p.m. Closed Sunday.

Upscale bar beloved of the expatriate British, which can be a haven if you want to chat to someone in English. English owner Mark Williamson stocks a good Côtes-du-Rhône.

Juvenile's
47 rue de Richelieu, 75001, tel. 42 97 46 49. Metro Palais-Royal. Open 11 a.m.–11. p.m. Closed Sunday.

A younger version of Willi's under the same ownership, Juvenile's is more relaxed, with tapas-style food to accompany the wine. The front tables are best, so arrive early at lunch or dinnertime to avoid being stuck at the back behind the coatstand.

Chez Georges
11 rue des Canettes, 75006, Metro Mabillon.
Open 11:30 a.m.–2 a.m. Closed Sunday, Monday, mid-July–mid-August.

Small, scruffy wine bar popular with St-Germain locals and students. The floor is littered with cigarette butts, while yellowing posters of sixties protest singers decorate the walls.

PUBS

Pub St-Germain
17 rue de l'Ancienne-Comédie, 75006, tel. 43 29 38 70. Metro Odéon.
Open 24 hours daily.

Walk through the touristy restaurant to the comfy low-ceilinged bar at the back, settle in one of the curving booths, and try and choose from over 400 beers. If you're alone, separate tables allow you to avoid hassle, although things can get rowdy at night.

Kitty O'Shea's
10 rue des Capucines, 75002, tel. 40 15 00 30. Metro Opéra.
Open noon–1:30 a.m. daily.

A famous, friendly Irish pub packed with English, Irish and French drinkers. Order in English, but don't expect pub prices. Expect some good-natured come-ons.

ENTERTAINMENT

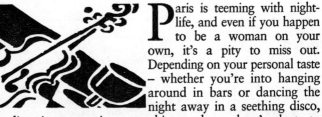

Paris is teeming with night-life, and even if you happen to be a woman on your own, it's a pity to miss out. Depending on your personal taste – whether you're into hanging around in bars or dancing the night away in a seething disco, or prefer listening to music or watching a play – there's plenty to choose from. Any lone woman opting for the first category is bound to feel conspicuous. In most straight clubs the unattached men tend to outnumber the women by three to one, and a foreign woman alone is seen as fair game. But as long as you're feeling in a confident, partying mood, you'll probably have fun.

Obtaining tickets, especially for opera and big concerts, can be a problem. Try to make reservations before you arrive, or on your first day in Paris go to a ticket office like the FNAC Musique (4 place de la Bastille, 75012. Metro Bastille. Open Monday, Tuesday, Thursday, Saturday 10 a.m.–8 p.m.; Wednesday, Friday 10 a.m.–10 p.m.) or Virgin Megastore (56–60 avenue des Champs Elysées, 75008. Metro Franklin D. Roosevelt Open Monday-Thursday 10 a.m.–midnight; Friday, Saturday 10 a.m.–1 a.m.; Sunday 2 p.m.–midnight) and reserve a seat in advance. Although any successful touring band will pass through Paris, the French rock music scene is generally abysmal with few, if any, good live shows to choose from. On the other hand, jazz and world music enthusiasts should be well satisfied. Paris has some of the best jazz clubs in Europe, and the African music scene boasts many exciting musicians. Classical music lovers should check out church concerts, which are more frequent, less expensive and more accessible than major performances. St-Germain-des-Prés is especially recommended. The only drawback is discomfort: churches are renowned for poor heating and hard chairs.

The appeal of theater obviously depends on how good your French is. Ballet is clearly more accessible, and a good excuse for visiting the Opéra Garnier, largely devoted to dance since it was usurped in its role as the capital's opera house by the Opéra Bastille. Film is hugely popular, as you can see by the enormous number of movie theaters dotted all over the place – from the tiny independents showing obscure reruns of little-known classics to the plush multiscreen UGC or Gaumont chains, which show a wide variety of up-to-the-minute films from any nation that boasts a film industry. All major British and American films will be on somewhere (especially on the Champs Elysées and around Odéon) in the original English-language version.

B A R S

Where you start your evening depends largely on where you plan to end it: whether you're aiming for a brief *digestif* in a small, crowded, lively bar a quick walk from your hotel, or feel like getting dolled up to mix with the glitterati. You may plan to sip a whisky whilst making notes about your fellow-drinkers *à la* Hemingway, or perhaps you prefer to finish the evening crammed in a cellar inhaling stale smoke and cheap aftershave, drinking an unidentifiable liquid that the barman has sold to you as Sangria. Whatever you fancy, one thing is certain: Paris has the bar for it. There must be at least as many bars as there are people in Paris, which makes you wonder why they are all so crowded, but this small selection aims to cater to most tastes.

Juvenile's
47 rue de Richelieu, 75001. Open 11 a.m.–11 p.m. Closed Sunday.
More of a wine bar, English-owned and run. Wines by the glass, and delicious tapas in a totally unintimidating environment.

The James Joyce
5 rue du Jour, 75001.
Noisy, packed and typically Irish. Not a place to go if you want to be alone.

Le Crocodile
6 rue Royer-Collard, 75005. Open until 2 a.m.
Old-fashioned bar, small, cozy, with a background of baby-boomer music.

La Closerie des Lilas
171 boulevard du Montparnasse, 75006. Open 11 a.m.–2 a.m.
Good cocktails and live piano in a classy environment. Frequented by media and literary types in the footsteps of Hemingway.

Pub St-Germain
17 rue de l'Ancienne-Comédie, 75006. Open 24 hours a day (including food).
A young crowd drinks from the huge selection of excellent beers. Tends to get hot in the dark smoky interior. Live music downstairs.

Le Fouquet's
99 avenue des Champs Elysées, 75008.
Cocktails strictly for lottery winners, and a chance to rub shoulders with the rich and the famous.

Le Dépanneur
27 rue Fontaine, 75009.
Drown your sorrows in tequila in this trendy monochrome atmosphere.

Le Péniche
1 avenue du Président Kennedy, 75016.
For 270F you can dine and watch the cabaret on this floating bar on a barge [*péniche*].

LIVE MUSIC

Live rock bands do exist, but can vary from mediocre, playing the latest French hits which you are unlikely to recognize, to downright awful, playing cover versions of English and American songs. By and large, much better quality and excitement is provided by some of the many African and Latin American musicians who have settled in Paris.

The two venues for full-blown rock concerts by international stars are Palais des Omnisports de Bercy (8 boulevard de Bercy, 75012, tel. 43 41 72 04), a huge stadium that attracts vast crowds for the big-name concerts, and Le Zenith (211 avenue Jean-Jaurès, 75019, tel. 42 08 60 00), a vast inflatable tent which, at a third of the capacity of Bercy (i.e., 6500) seems positively cozy in comparison. Tickets for both obtainable from FNAC.

The following small live music venues are recommended. Otherwise, for the best live music that Paris has to offer, head for the jazz clubs.

Les Trois Mailletz
58 rue Galande, 75003, tel. 43 54 00 79. Open 6 p.m.–4 a.m.
Varied program covering everything from rock to jazz, with a clientele made up mainly of students, piled in together in the cellar or having a bite to eat in the piano-bar upstairs.

New Moon
66 rue Pigalle, 75009, tel. 45 95 92 33. Open 11 p.m.–dawn.
Mainly French and German bands play to a 200-capacity audience of live rock *aficionados*. Good atmosphere.

Chapelle des Lombards
19 rue Lappe, 75011, tel. 43 57 24 24. Open 11:30 p.m.–dawn.
Friendly, sweaty club atmosphere in this former women's prison, where you can hear some of the best in African music, plus occasional salsa and samba.

JAZZ CLUBS

Paris is the jazz lover's dream. An endless choice of venues serves up every conceivable kind of jazz, in every conceivable sort of setting. Three pages of listings in *Pariscope*, featuring everything from someone playing their heart out in a smoky cellar to a full-blown concert, bear witness to the fact that jazz is very much alive and well and, indeed, enjoying greater and greater popularity with audiences of all ages. The following are among the best-known clubs but consult the listings for details of who is playing where, or simply locate the jazz club nearest to where you are staying.

Le Baiser Salé
58 rue des Lombards, 75001. Open until 4 a.m.

The "salty kiss" is located in one of the liveliest nighttime areas of Paris, and pumps out its own blend of Brazilian rock and contemporary jazz.

L'Eustache
37 rue Berger, 75001. Open 9 a.m.–4 a.m. Food served only till 10 p.m.

Typical Parisian bistro, regularly hailed as the purveyor of the cheapest good jazz in the capital. You could do worse.

Les Bouchons
19 rue des Halles, 75001. Open 8 p.m.–3 a.m.

Comfortable place where you can dine and listen to jazz without constantly being hassled to buy a drink. No cover; reasonably priced cocktails.

Le Caveau de la Huchette
5 rue de la Huchette, 75005. Open 9:30 p.m.–2:30 a.m.; 4 a.m. Saturday, Sunday.

Authentic cellar crammed with people listening and bopping to Dixieland jazz. A bit of a pick-up joint.

Le Bilboquet
13 rue St-Benoît, 75006.

One of the many jazz clubs in the sixth *arrondissement*, this one's of the dine-while-you-listen school. The comfortable bar/restaurant with Art Nouveau decor has live jazz every evening. Not cheap.

CLUBS AND DISCOS

The scariest thing about going out for a bop is not necessarily the prospect of going alone. Even in a group, you won't escape the ultimate arbiters of style, trend, fashion, and what makes a club into the sort of heaving mass other people want to cram themselves into: the doormen. One glance can reduce your carefully thought-out evening outfit to a bunch of outmoded rags, and your self-esteem to pulp. Don't be disheartened: it happens to everyone, and if your face doesn't happen to fit, comfort yourself that it is either senior citizens' night or a club for nubile nymphets, neither of which would probably have suited you. Clubbing gear can vary enormously, from your very own little black number to your very oldest pair of jeans. Only experience can tell; anyway you may happen to stumble on a theme night, in which case you couldn't possibly avoid being inappropriately dressed. Don't be put off. There are plenty of places with perfectly normally dressed people just out for a good time. Note that many clubs have a practice of letting women in free on off-peak nights. The reasoning behind this may be suspect, but at least you can take the advantage to check out a club that you might want to return to on a paying night. Most places don't start filling up till at least midnight.

Les Bains
7 rue Bourg-L'Abbé, 75003. Open 11:30 p.m.–5 a.m. Entrance 120F including drink.

If you feel that a trip to Paris wouldn't be complete without a chance to rub bony shoulders with top models, minor celebrities and the like, then this is the place to do it – always supposing the ferocious lady at the door allows you to. Set in what used to be Turkish baths, frequented by the illustrious – such as Proust – this is definitely a place to see and be seen.

Le Saint
7 rue St-Séverin, 75007. Open 11 p.m.–5 a.m. Entrance 70F including drink.

The other end of the scale from Les Bains, this small unpretentious disco, set underground, attracts a youngish student-type clientele, dancing unselfconsciously to an unidentifiable mishmash of "disco" hit records. No danger of being turned away here.

Ruby's Club
31 rue Dauphine, 75006. Open from 10 p.m. Entrance 80F.

Formerly a famous Latin Quarter cellar frequented by Sartre, Simone de Beauvoir and Juliette Greco.

Le Palace
8 rue du Faubourg Montmartre, 75009. Open 11 p.m.–6 a.m. Entrance 130F.

Set in a former theater and popular with everyone, this huge club (capacity 2000) boasts the latest in laser technology to illuminate the hordes bumping and grinding on the impressive dance floor. A good place to show off your best party gear.

El Globo
8 boulevard Strasbourg, 75010. Open 11 p.m.–4 a.m. Entrance 70F.

Unusual club in that it doesn't slavishly adhere to any one style in order to obtain a homogeneous clientele. A lively mixture of all sorts makes for a fun, exuberant sort of evening.

Le Balajo
9 rue de Lappe, 75011. Open 10 p.m.–5 a.m. Teatime dancing 3–5:30 p.m. Sunday. Entrance 100F.

Oozing with nostalgia, this club used to play host to the likes of Edith Piaf and Jean Gabin, and has kept the period decor intact. On Saturday nights it echoes to French popular songs and the strains of the accordion – more soberly in evidence on Sunday afternoons, when aged couples take their turn around the dance floor. You have to wait until Monday for some more conventional bop music.

La Locomotive
90 boulevard de Clichy, 75018. Open 11 p.m.–6 a.m. Entrance 100F. including drink. Women free on Sundays.

Vast nightclub spread out over three floors, popular with the young and trendy without being snooty or uptight.

LESBIAN CLUBS

Not nearly as numerous as gay men's clubs. If you're looking for an all-female atmosphere, you may be disappointed, since several places let men in so long as they behave themselves.

Entre Nous
17 rue Laferrière, 75009. Open from 11 p.m.

Small, intimate club, exclusively for women.

Studio A
51 rue de Ponthieu, 75008. Entrance 100F including drink.

Lesbian every night except Wednesday.

Le Privilège
9 Cité Bergère, 75009. Open 11 p.m.–dawn. Entrance 100F.

Well-known club under the same ownership as the famous Katmandou, which burnt down in mysterious circumstances.

Chez Moune
54 rue Pigalle, 75018. Open from 10 p.m.

Cabaret, made up mostly of women, is not for the faint-hearted feminist; it includes a striptease by women for women. For the more sedate, there's a women-only tea dance on Sunday afternoons, 4:30–8 p.m.

THE ARTS

If you're looking for more classical entertainment, you'll be equally spoilt for choice. Advertisements in the paper, posters in the Metro, and handbills stuck up in cafés or on church railings carry details of concerts for every night of the week, 365 days a year. Despite hiccups in the programming of the brand-new opera house at Bastille, the high standard of opera in Paris attracts international stars though, as anywhere, tickets for the best performances can be hard to come by.

Paris is the home of ballet, invented by Louis XIV, and France boasts a number of very fine provincial companies, notably in Montpellier and Marseilles. The Opéra Garnier has its own resident company, directed by former dancer Patrick Dupond, who took over the position from Rudolf Nureyev. Visiting companies include the Bolshoi, Kirov and New York City Ballet, while the highlight of the dance calendar is the Festival of International Dance of Paris every autumn. Last, but not least, a rich selection of theaters offers a constant and varied program of plays – from the farcical to the classical; from the polished professionalism of the Comédie Française to the fumbling, sometimes excruciating amateurishness of the Café Théâtre. Only suitable for those with fairly fluent French, unless you've always had a yen to see your schoolgirl Molière performed in the flesh – in that case of course, this is your chance.

CONCERTS

Théâtre Musical de Paris Châtelet
1 place du Châtelet, 75001, tel. 40 28 28 40.
Also opera and dance.

Centre Georges Pompidou/IRCAM
rue St-Martin, 75004, tel. 42 77 12 33.

Salle Pleyel
252 rue du Faubourg St-Honoré, 75008, tel. 45 63 88 73.

Théâtre des Champs Elysées
15 avenue Montaigne, 75008, tel. 47 20 36 37.
Also dance.

Maison de la Radio-France
116 avenue du Président Kennedy, tel. 42 30 23 08.

CHURCHES

Eglise Saint-Eustache, 2 rue du Jour, 75001.
Eglise Saint-Roch, 296 rue St-Honoré.
Saint-Chapelle, 4 boulevard du Palais. Special candlelit concerts.
St-Germain-des-Prés, 3 place St-Germain-des-Prés, 75006.
St-Sulpice, place St-Sulpice, 75006. Exceptional organ.
La Madeleine, place de la Madeleine, 75008.

OPERA

Opéra Comique, 5 rue Favart, 75002, tel. 42 96 12 20 (also dance).
Opéra Paris Bastille, 2 place de la Bastille, 75012, tel. 40 01 16 16.

DANCE

Théâtre de la Ville, 2 place du Châtelet, 75006, tel. 42 74 22 77.
Opéra de Paris Garnier, place de l'Opéra, 75009, tel. 47 42 53 71.
Théâtre de la Bastille, 79 rue de la Roquette, 75011, tel. 43 57 42 14.

THEATER

Comédie Française, 2 rue de Richelieu, 75001, tel. 40 15 00 15.
Palais-Royal, 38 rue Montpensier, 75001, tel. 42 97 59 81.
Théâtre National de l'Odéon, 1 place Paul Claudel, 75006, tel. 43 25 70 32.
Théâtre National de Chaillot, 1 place du Trocadéro, 75016, tel. 47 27 81 15.

FILM

France hasn't yet fallen victim to video culture in the way that the States have. The French still prefer to go out to the movies than watch them on a 21-inch screen at home. There's something about the sense of anticipation as the long line forms outside, the big plush fold-down seats once you get in, and the size of the screen that sucks you bodily into an imaginary world to provide the purest form of escapism. Both *Pariscope* and *Officiel des Spectacles* carry complete listings, broken down by cinema and divided helpfully into *arrondissements*. Note that "V.O." indicates that the film will be shown in the original language with French subtitles, while "V.F." means it will be dubbed into French. Most theaters offer reduced ticket prices on Monday and Wednesday nights.

Action Rive Gauche and Action Ecoles
5 and 23 rue des Ecoles, 75005, tel. 43 25 72 07/43 29 44 40.
Two of a small independent chain specializing in old movie classics.

Le Grand Rex
1 boulevard Poissoniere, 75002, tel. 42 36 83 93.
The largest screen in Europe with seating for 2800 and its own line in kitsch decor. Identifiable for its Art Deco-style tower, which itself looks like something straight off a Thirties film set.

Lucernaire Forum
53 rue Notre-Dame-des-Champs, 75006, tel. 45 44 57 34.
Temple of art film, set in an arty complex comprising three screens, plus two theaters, a bar and a restaurant.

La Pagode
57bis rue de Babylone, 75007, tel. 47 05 12 15.

Despite showing the latest blockbusters, often in English, the setting of this remarkable theater is pure Japanese. The *grande salle* is sumptuously decorated with elephants and dragons, and a small tearoom serves delicious cakes and tarts while you wait for the film to start. One of the nicest and most original places to spend a wet Sunday afternoon.

SHOWS AND CABARETS

For many visitors, Parisian nightlife is synonymous with names like the Folies Bergère and the Moulin Rouge, but it's hard to imagine why women who come to Paris alone or in groups would want to watch a lot of other women, bare-breasted and expressionless, giving a glitzy, well-choreographed performance, featuring slick routines and no soul. In case you're still curious, these are probably the most popular, and unlikely to offend even your grandmother.

Folies Bergère
32 rue de Richer, 75009, tel. 42 46 77 11.

The oldest venue, opened in 1869. From 9 p.m. Show only 360F. Phone for details of a pre-revue dinner.

Moulin Rouge
82 boulevard de Clichy, 75011, tel. 46 06 00 19.
Shows at 8 p.m., 10 p.m., midnight. Dinner and show 530F.

Once the haunt of Toulouse-Lautrec's model, Jane Avril, and home to the cancan.

Paradis Latin
28 rue Cardinal-Lemoine, 75005, tel. 43 25 28 08.
From 8:30 p.m. Entrance and dinner 510F.

Set in a theater built by Gustave Eiffel, this is supposedly the best review in town.

CAFÉ-THÉÂTRE

This is something else that Paris is known for. The format consists of a handful of people crammed into a pint-sized theater to watch, more often than not, a humorous one-man show. Your French would have to be pretty good to enjoy it.

Blancs-Manteaux
15 rue des Blancs-Manteaux, 75004, tel. 48 87 15 84.

Two separate theaters attract a young lively crowd.

Café de la Gare
41 rue du Temple, 75004, tel. 42 78 52 51.

Miou-Miou and Gérard Depardieu once tested their talents here.

CHANSONS

An alternative to other forms of live music, this is for those who dig out their old Piaf records to get them in the mood for Paris. For a nostalgic listen to live performances of old French favorites over a glass of wine, try:

Le Caveau de la Bolée

25 rue de l'Hirondelle, 75006, tel. 43 54 62 20. Open 9:30 p.m.–6:30 a.m.

Former haunt of Baudelaire.

Le Caveau des Oubliettes

11 rue St. Julien le Pauvre, 75005, tel. 45 83 41 77.
Open 9 p.m.–2 a.m.

SHOPPING

From department stores to street markets or designer boutiques, Paris is a great place for shopping. The big chain stores like Printemps and Galeries Lafayette sell almost anything and tend to have the best bargains, especially for foreigners, while food markets are a special treat for anyone who revels in the sight and smell of fresh produce. The pricier clothes shops, especially those allied to names such as Chanel or Yves St. Laurent, are predictably intimidating, and you'll feel better if you already look smart before you walk in. At the slightly more affordable end, shops such as Joseph and Agnès B tend to be a bit cheaper, with more choice, than their London branches.

MARKETS

France is justly renowned for its food markets, and Paris is no exception. For many residents, the Sunday-morning treat is to go out to the local market and pick up basketloads of goodies before returning to bed with fresh croissants and the papers. Few can resist feasting their eyes on the ten varieties of olives, glistening black and green in their oil, burying their noses in fresh basil or drooling over the selection of chalky white cheeses while everyone else around sniffs, pinches and squeezes the produce before that vital moment of making their choice.

Other kinds of market may be equally fascinating, but none is held in the reverence with which the French regard their food markets. Also Parisian flea markets, while fun to visit, rarely yield unexpected bargains these days.

THINGS TO TAKE HOME

A Hermès silk scarf

Genuine Moutarde de Dijon in its gray earthenware pot

Hédiard's fruit jellies [*pâtés de fruits*]

A bottle of Sauternes to be enjoyed with Fauchon's *foie gras*

A poster from a Beaubourg exhibition

Cheeses (if you carry them in an airtight container and eat them as soon as you get home)

A scented candle from Dyptique (boulevard St-Germain)

Your favorite French perfume

Lingerie by Christian Dior

Children's clothes from department stores

FOOD MARKETS

Most start at around 8 a.m. either stopping definitively at lunchtime or taking a pause before they reopen in the afternoon. Markets vary considerably, so it is best to go in the morning.

Rue Cler, 75001.
Metro Ecole Militaire.
Quality foods.

Rue Mouffetard, 75005.
Metro Censier Daubenton/Monge.
One of the oldest, it's all you could want from a typical Parisian market.

Rue de Seine/Buci, 75006.
Metro Odéon.
Extremely lively and popular, with an excellent cheese shop that spills out into the market.

Marché d'Aligré, 75012.
Metro Ledru-Rollin.
An unusual mix of more exotic produce.

FLEA MARKETS [MARCHÉS AUX PUCES]

These sell mostly a mixture of clothes, bric-a-brac, old records, "antiques," and every kind of junk. You need to be there very early to beat the dealers, but it's still fun to rummage.

Porte de St-Ouen/Porte de Clignancourt, 75018.
Metro Porte de Clignancourt/Porte de St-Ouen.
Open 7:30 a.m.–7 p.m. Saturday, Sunday, Monday.
The biggest in Paris, some say the world, this is the most well-known, and therefore the most touristy, flea market. Different sections deal in antiques, clothing, jewelry, records, books, lamps, and all manner of bric-a-brac. Watch your bag when you're walking in the very busy aisles. Deep into the market, you might still find furniture from the 1930s.

Porte de Montreuil, 75020.
Metro Porte de Montreuil.
The best bet for secondhand clothes; not as brash and touristy as Clignancourt.

SHOPPING HOURS
Most shops are open all day Monday to Saturday from 10 a.m. to 7 p.m. Food shops are closed Sunday afternoons and Mondays. Some clothes shops, especially in the Marais, open on Sundays.

Marché d'Aligre, place d'Aligre, 75012.
Metro Ledru-Rollin. Open 9:30 a.m.–1 p.m. Closed Monday.

Essentially a food market, it has now ceded some of its space to silverware, bric-a-brac, jewelry and clothes.

Porte de Vanves, 75014.
Metro Porte-de-Vanves. Open 7 a.m.–7 p.m. Saturday, Sunday.

A junk market – and junk is the operative word. A mish mash of every conceivable type of object offered by amateurs and professionals alike.

Special antiques fairs are held in and around Paris, especially in the autumn. Look out for posters indicating a "Foire aux antiquaires" or "Brocante." Twice a year (early spring, early autumn) the famous "Foire à la brocante de Chatou" – one of the most interesting fairs – takes place in the west of the capital. (Take the RER in the direction of Saint-Germain-en-Laye.)

FLOWERS AND ANIMALS

The flowers are beautiful, but the animals in cages present a bit of a sorry sight. The quai de la Megisserie near Châtelet is traditionally the place to find birds and animals.

Place Louis-Lépine, 75001.
Metro Cité. Open 8 a.m.–7:30 p.m.

Saturday for flowers and plants; Sunday for birds and pets.

Place de la Madeleine, 75008.
Metro Madeleine. Open Tuesday–Sunday 8 a.m.–7:30 p.m.

Flowers and plants.

Place des Ternes, 75008.
Metro Ternes Open Tuesday–Sunday 8 a.m.–7:30 p.m.

Flowers and plants.

BOOKS, STAMPS AND POSTCARDS

For books, it is worth remembering the *bouquinistes* who line, among others, the quais des Grands Augustins, Conti and Malaquais, on the Left Bank, displaying their selections of second hand books, postcards and prints in green wooden boxes that can be conveniently padlocked at the end of the day to be left suspended from the parapet of the river walls.

Marché aux Timbres (Stamp market)
Cour Marigny, 75008. Metro Champs Elysées.
Open 10 a.m.–sunset, Thursday, Saturday, Sunday, public holidays.

A stamp collector's paradise.

Marché aux Cartes Postales Anciennes
3 rue Mabillon, Marché St-Germain, 75006. Metro Mabillon.
Open 11 a.m.– 6 p.m. Wednesday.

Nothing but old postcards.

Marché aux Livre
Pavillon Baltard, Parc Georges-Brassens, rue Brancion, 75015. Metro Porte de Vanves. Open 9 a.m.–6 p.m. Saturday, Sunday.

Antique and secondhand books.

DEPARTMENT STORES

Paris is famous worldwide for its department stores, the most famous being Galeries Lafayette and Le Printemps. You'll find *everything* in these stores at a wide range of prices, as well as top-floor restaurants and tearooms where you can rest weary feet as you gaze over panoramic views of the city.

It was Aristide Boucicaut who, in 1852, "invented" the *grand magasin* concept by creating Le Bon Marché. Others followed shortly after him: Le Louvre in 1855 (since disappeared), Le Printemps in 1865 and, in 1869, La Samaritaine. The Galeries Lafayette were the last to open, in 1912.

Galeries Lafayette
40 boulevard Haussmann, 75009. Metro Chaussée d'Antin.
Open 9:30 a.m.–6:45 p.m. Monday-Saturday.

Be sure not to miss the central glass dome [*la coupole*] of the Galeries Lafayette building, and notice the circular shape of the entire interior space. The ground floor, as in all department stores, is almost entirely dedicated to women's cosmetics and perfumes. The scent as you enter is almost overwhelming. Bags, leather belts, jewelry, hats, scarves, and a wide range of tights, stockings, socks, and the like, are also stocked on this level. The first floor houses designer fashion and shoes; the second floor is dedicated to coordinates for businesswomen (Cerrutti, Max-Mara, Georges Rech) and to famous *couturiers* – Lacroix, Chanel, Castelbajac, and Yves Saint-Laurent. The third floor offers a wide selection of children's clothes and accessories, while the top floor includes furniture, household goods and books. The rooftop restaurant is worth stopping for, especially in summer when you can eat outside and enjoy the beautiful view over Paris rooftops. You'll find a vast range of kitchenware in the basement, which has direct access to the Metro.

Le Printemps
64 boulevard Haussmann, 75009. Metro Havre-Caumartin.
Open 9:35 a.m.–7 p.m. Monday–Saturday.

Being in direct competition with the Galeries, this store has recently opened a new section called Printemps de la Beauté, which presents the widest range of cosmetics in Paris (and maybe in the world) spread over the entire ground floor. The designer fashions on the first and second floors are similar to that stocked by Galeries Lafayette, so if you can't find your size in one, it's always worth trying the other. Printemps is also known for designer furniture; French designers include Philippe Starck and Andrée Putnam.

Marks & Spencer

35 boulevard Haussmann, 75009. Metro Auber. Open 9:30 a.m.–7 p.m.

A British chain that offers a good range of clothes, cosmetics, and household items. There's also a café that makes Brits feel at home.

Le Bon Marché

Rue de Sèvres/rue du Bac, 75007. Metro Sèvres-Babylone. Open 9:30 a.m.–6:30 p.m. Monday-Friday; 7 p.m. Saturday.

This department store, also called *le Grand Magasin de la Rive Gauche* (because it is the Left Bank's only department store), is much smaller than Galeries Lafayette or Printemps, but well-known for fine lingerie. Everything is very tasteful.

La Samaritaine

19 rue de la Monnaie, 75001. Metro Pont Neuf.
Open 9:30 a.m.–7 p.m.; 8:30 p.m. Tuesday, Friday.

"On trouve tout à la Samaritaine" (You'll find everything at the Samaritaine) is this store's famous slogan. It was started in 1870 by Ernest Cognacq and his wife Louise Jay; the name comes from a hydraulic pump on the Pont Neuf, which, from 1609 to 1813 fed water into the *quartiers* of the Louvre and the Tuileries. On the front of this "castle-shaped" pump, at the level of the bridge, stood a gilded representation of the Samaritan conversing with Jesus. It is almost certain that Ernest Cognacq named his first small shop, and later his department stores, after this *Samaritaine*, which he could see every day while he sold goods on the Pont Neuf as a young man.

CLOTHES: DESIGNER

Chanel

42 avenue Montaigne, 75008.

Very expensive.

Jean-Paul Gaultier

6 rue Vivienne, 75002.

More and more outlandish. A favorite with Madonna!

Hermès

24 faubourg Saint-Honoré, 75008.

Men's ties are among the most beautiful. Bring back one of their famous *carrés* (square silk scarf).

Christian Lacroix

73 rue du Faubourg Saint-Honoré, 75008.

The newcomer to the *haute couture* world whose reputation is already firmly established. His brightly colored designs, inspired by Provence and Spain, are astonishing.

Claude Montana

3 rue des Petits Champs, 75001.

Less way-out, but expensive.

Thierry Mugler
10 place des Victoires, 75002.
Futurist shapes.

Yohji Yamamoto
25 rue du Louvre, 75001.
Japanese design: bizarre, avant-garde shapes and fabrics.

Yves Saint Laurent Rive Gauche
6 place Saint-Sulpice, 75006.
Classic luxury clothing.

LESS EXPENSIVE DESIGNER FASHION

Agnès B
6 rue du Jour, 75001.
Famous for her jackets made of sweatshirt fabric and mother-of-pearl press studs available in all colors. Simple, trendy shapes at affordable prices. Great striped T-shirts.

Barbara Bui
23 rue Etienne Marcel, 75001.
Beautiful soft-tailored blouses, trousers and jackets.

Cacharel
5 place des Victoires, 75001.
Liberty shirts and classic coordinates.

Joseph
44 rue Etienne Marcel, 75002.
Superb knitwear. Expensive.

Kenzo
3 place des Victoires, 75001.
Bright, extremely colorful clothes for women and men. Original styles that never go out of fashion.

Max-Mara
37 rue du Four, 75006.
Italian classics.

Claudie Pierlot
23 rue du Vieux Colombier, 75006; 4 rue du Jour, 75001.
Very Parisian. Lovely knitwear.

Sonia Rykiel,
175 boulevard St-Germain, 75006.

Famous for beautifully cut, simple knitwear, she now sells bags, berets, shoes and luggage as well as other clothes.

Olivier Strelli
55 rue Bonaparte, 75006.
Beautiful clothes from Belgium.

Ventilo
27 bis rue du Louvre, 75002.
Beautifully cut skirts, among many other things.

FASHION AT REASONABLE PRICES

Kookaï
49 rue de Rivoli, 75001.
Trendy tops and dresses. Inexpensive – you can tell by the quality.

Monoprix and Prisunic
Chain stores where you can sometimes pick up some budget imitation designer clothes.

SHOES

André
80 rue Saint-Antoine, 75004.
Range of low-priced shoes.

Eram
12 rue de Rivoli, 75004.
Another unremarkable shop, but with quite a variety of styles at low prices.

Bally
3 boulevard St-Michel, 75005.
Reasonable prices.

Sacha
rue de Renne, 75006.
Try their ankle-high boots.

La Chausseria
rue du Vieux Colombier, 75006; Forum des Halles, 75001.
Reasonable prices for very fashionable shoes.

FAMOUS FRENCH SHOE-DESIGNERS

Robert Clergerie
46 rue Croix des Petits Champs, 75001.
One of the best.

Stéphane Kélian
Place des Victoires, 75008.
Trendy, expensive shoes. Superb quality.

Charles Jourdan
39 rue de Grenelle, 75007.
Reliable quality and good colors.

Michel Perry
42 rue de Grenelle, 75007.
Very original and expensive.

LEATHER AND LUGGAGE

La Bagagerie
41 rue du Four, 75006.
Trendy bags.

Céline
58 rue de Rennes, 75006.
Classic bags and accessories.

Lancel
43 rue de Rennes, 75006.
Excellent sturdy luggage.

Hermès
24 rue du Faubourg-Saint-Honoré.
The best there is – for those who can afford it.

JEWELRY

Cartier
13 rue de la Paix, 75002.
The real thing.

Boucheron
26 place Vendôme, 75001.
Classic, quality jewelry.

Agatha
97 rue de Rennes, and rue Bonaparte, 75006.
Real and imitation at reasonable prices. Lovely designs.

Réminiscence
22 rue du Four, 75006.
Original designs.

COSMETICS

Parfumerie Luxembourg
3 rue Gay Lussac, 75005.
Duty-free shop.

Body Shop
7 rue de l'Ancienne Comédie, 75006.
Full range of Body Shop products, but no beauty parlor.

Guerlain
2 place Vendôme, 75001.
One of the most famous *parfumeurs* in the world. Try their new range of cosmetics.

Silver Moon
8 rue du Vieux Colombier, 75006.
Range of cosmetics and perfumes at discount prices.

BOOKS AND MUSIC

Brentano's
37 avenue de l'Opéra, 75002.
French and American books.

Fnac
Forum des Halles, 75001.
Major French book and record shop chain, with a foreign-language section.

Joseph Gibert
26 30 boulevard St-Michel, 75006.
Vast bookstore with a large section catering to schools and universities. Also good for maps and travel guides. English books on the fourth floor.

Librairie des Femmes
74 rue de Seine, 75006.
Paris's only remaining women's bookstore. Wide range of feminist magazines and books.

Shakespeare & Company
37 rue de la Bucherie, 75006.
The original store started by Sylvia Beach is still going strong.

Village Voice
6 rue Princesse, 75006.
Cozy shop of Anglo-American books.

W.H. Smith
248 rue de Rivoli, 75001.
Good range of English books, including a comprehensive guide section.

POSTERS AND STATIONERY

Papier Plus
rue du Pont Louis-Philippe, 75004.
Great photo albums, stationery by weight, and lovely color pencils.

Marie Papier
rue Vavin, 75014.
Office accessories covered with their exclusive paper. Stationery, pens and pencils.

La Banque de l'Image
13 rue de la Cossonnerie, 75001.
Posters and postcards.

Librairie du Centre Georges Pompidou
place Pompidou, 75004.
Great range of posters of famous and less famous works of art. Also large choice of fine arts books; good postcards and T-shirts.

Galerie Maeght
12 rue St-Merri, 75004.
Art books, magazines, original lithographs and posters.

KITCHENWARE

Geneviève Lethu
95 rue de Rennes, 75006.
Everything you need for the kitchen and diningroom in nice, classic patterns.

Habitat
Forum des Halles, 75001.
Reasonable prices.

Christofle
Galeries Lafayette and 95 rue de Passy, 75016.
Silver cutlery at its best. Popular for Parisian wedding presents.

Kitchen Bazaar
6 ave du Maine, 75015.
Original utensils for the modern kitchen.

FOOD AND DRINK

Dalloyau
2 place Edmond Rostand, 75006.
Delicious cakes. One of the oldest and most famous shops in Paris.

Fauchon
26 place de la Madeleine, 75008.
As famous as Dalloyau and London's Fortnum and Mason. Mouthwatering but expensive.

Ladurée
16 rue Royale, 75008.
Pastry shop known for its macaroons. Cozy tearoom.

Hédiard
21 place de la Madeleine, 75008.
Quality French products.

Mariage Frères
rue du Bourg-Tibourg, 75004.
Teas from all over the world, with a lovely tearoom at the back.

Nicolas
35 rue Rambuteau, 75004.
Recommended wine shop.

La Maison du Chocolat
225 rue du Faubourg Saint-Honoré, 75008.
Chocaholics' heaven, selling some of the best fresh homemade chocolates and plain slabs of varying degrees of richness.

CHILDREN AND BUSINESSWOMEN

CHILDREN

Paris may seem very much an adults' city, but children are generally welcomed everywhere, provided they behave. Let them run rampant, and you'll soon find yourself in for a lecture on the benefits of discipline. Together with eating, children figure high among the main preoccupations of the French, who firmly believe in combining the two without any fuss. To this end it's not unusual to see a Parisian family in a seriously gastronomic restaurant sitting down with two small children solemnly plowing their way through the set menu in a sort of initiation process.

If this doesn't sound much fun, don't worry. There are plenty of bars and restaurants that accept children in a relaxed atmosphere, and in summer there are lots of places to picnic. Compared to the English, French people tend to adore children, and even most Parisians – who are not renowned for their warmth – will be accommodating. Indeed, walking around with a small child can be a positive asset, as even the most forbidding-looking French woman waitress, and especially a *boulanger* (baker), is likely to melt as you approach.

That said, negotiating Paris with a stroller is undoubtedly a struggle. Streets are often narrow, with pavements blocked either by scaffolding, workmen, or appallingly badly parked cars. Down in the Metro it's even worse, mostly because of the stairs, the very stiff doors and the dreadful turnstiles which give access to the platforms. The best advice – if your child is really too tiny to walk, and you cannot afford or don't want to opt for a babysitter – is to use a very light weight stroller that folds up easily or a backpack carrier. Be prepared, too, for a sad lack of changing facilities and the fact that the average restroom is cramped and not very clean. On a more positive note, breastfeeding in public though not common, is not a problem, and most bar and hotel staff will be helpful about warming up milk or baby food.

CHILDREN AND BUSINESSWOMEN

Traveling with babies and toddlers has undoubted drawbacks, but provided you're not set on full-time sightseeing, other age groups shouldn't be hard to entertain. Rather than simply dragging them round your chosen itinerary, try to get older ones involved in planning each day. Carry sketchbooks and a notepad so that they can record their own impressions, and encourage them to practice their French by letting them order in cafés or ask for things in shops. Tempt budding French readers with the huge array of comics for sale in virtually any news kiosk or popular bookshop [*librairie*]. (Pom d'Api titles, published by Bayard Presse, are excellent and cater to all ages.) Paris may not be great on green spaces, but younger children can also enjoy a variety of entertainment – from donkey rides, puppet shows and playgrounds to special workshops in museums and exhibitions. To let off steam, follow the lead of most Parisian families and head for the Bois de Boulogne, where you can hire bikes or go boating when you're tired of playing ball games or running around.

GENERAL INFORMATION

Inter-Service Parents
tel. 43 48 28 28. Open 9:30 a.m.–12:30 p.m.; 1:30–5 p.m. Monday–Tuesday, Friday; 9:30 a.m.–12:30 p.m. Wednesday; 1:30–5 p.m. Thursday.

Free service giving details of childminding services and activities for children, as well as all sorts of advice for concerned parents. Not aimed at visitors, but staff try to help with all inquiries in any language.

Départment d'Affaires Culturelles
Hôtel d'Albret, 31 rue des Francs-Bourgeois, 75004, tel. 42 76 40 40. Open 9 a.m.–6 p.m. Monday–Friday.

This office, situated in the Marais, provides information on all sorts of cultural activities for children, divided by age group.

For a weekly rundown of what's available for children, consult the appropriate section of *Pariscope*. In addition, French readers staying in the capital for more than just a few days might find it worth buying a copy of *Le Paris des Tout-Petits* (99F), a 500-page paperback on Paris for the under-twelves, published by Les Editions d'Annabelle and revised every year. It's widely available, and though much of the information – for instance, on antenatal classes and education – may be superfluous, you'll also find a wealth of relevant details.

Most of the following listings are designed to be read by children. For full addresses, including Metro stops, see under individual sites in the main section of this book.

MUSEUMS AND CATACOMBS

Each of these museums has special exhibitions, workshops [*ateliers*] or other attractions for children. Workshop staff are usually kind and friendly, but you'll feel better if you know a little French.

Atelier des enfants du Centre Georges Pompidou
tel. 42 77 12 33.

Free art workshops for six-to-twelve-year-olds, where you paint and make things out of interesting materials.

Other art workshops occasionally take place in the Musée des Arts Décoratifs; Musée de la Mode et du Costume; Musée du Petit Palais; and Musée d'Art Moderne de la Ville de Paris. Ask when you visit, or get your parents to phone for details.

Musée d'Orsay
tel. 45 49 48 14.

Ask for the special printed sheets (in English) that suggest parts of paintings, sculptures and other exhibits to look out for.

Musée des Arts Africains et Océaniens
tel. 43 43 14 54.

Unmissable tropical aquarium and crocodile pit.

La Cité des Sciences et de l'Industrie
tel. 46 42 13 13.

Two special sections, for 3–6-year-olds and 6–12-year-olds, offer a chance for you (and your parents) to touch, smell, feel and play with things, push buttons on computers, and generally learn and discover some of the secrets of the universe for yourself!

Musée de La Poste
34 boulevard de Vaugirard, 75015. Metro Montparnasse. tel. 43 20 15 30. Open 10 a.m.–5 p.m. Monday–Saturday.

Follow the history of the post office, starting with how letters were sent in Roman times and coming right up to the present day.

Catacombs
1 place Denfert-Rochereau, 75014. Metro Denfert-Rochereau, tel. 43 22 47 63. Open 2–4 p.m. Tuesday–Friday, 9 a.m.–11 a.m. and 2–4 p.m. Saturday, Sunday.

Get your own back after a morning in the Louvre: drag your parents down ninety steep steps into a maze of dimly lit passageways where rows of skulls and bones line the walls, neatly arranged in geometric designs.

The catacombs date back to 1785; they were created out of old underground stone quarries as a place to dump the contents of various Parisian cemeteries after the locals complained of the unsanitary effects of living close to diseased and rotting corpses. It's interesting to imagine that in the nineteenth century, when visits were first allowed, people would be given a candle to light their way. Presumably a gust of air would have been enough to blow out the flame and spread mass panic. Perhaps the ghosts of forgotten visitors still haunt the place.

PARKS, ZOOS AND THEME PARKS

Parc de la Villette

This park next to the Cité des Sciences et de l'Industrie has a great playground for children of all ages, including a huge dragon-shaped slide, a pirate ship to climb on and quite a few rocking horses and objects to explore.

Jardin d'Acclimatation

Open 10 a.m.–6 p.m. daily. Entrance 8F.

A combination of park, zoo and amusement park with bumper cars, pony rides, camel rides, puppet shows, a short boat trip on an enchanted river, go-karts and various species of birds and animals to gaze at. There's also a little train you can ride on, or you can rent a bike to explore the woods' cycle trails. Finally, the park includes two museums: La Grande Maison des Poupées, with a big collection of antique dolls, and the Musée en Herbe – especially for children.

Jardin des Plantes

Open 9 a.m.–6 p.m. daily.

If you're not interested in medicinal plants, the Natural History Museum (closed on Tuesdays) includes dinosaur skeletons and a fantastic insect collection. There's also a small zoo (getting a bit old, unfortunately), a vivarium, and one of the few adventure playgrounds in Paris.

Jardin du Luxembourg

Unlike most public gardens, where signs tell you to "Keep Off the Grass," this park at least has an area of green grass specially reserved for children. You can also play around the big round pond – even rent a model yacht. Or there's a puppet theater, go-karting and donkey rides as well as playground attractions.

Parc Floral and Zoo de Vincennes

Great playground with slides, swings, table tennis, mini-golf, and an electric car circuit.

The zoo opposite the Parc Floral is much bigger and better than the little one in the Jardin des Plantes.

Parc des Buttes-Chaumont

Rue Botzaris, 75020. Metro Buttes-Chaumont.

This pretty park, complete with folly, grotto, waterfall and a very big lake, was created at the request of Napoleon III, who wanted to provide greenery and fresh air for people who were too poor to have their own gardens. It should definitely appeal to parents, and there's lots for you to do too, from boating or riding on the merry-go-round to puppet theater and donkey-cart rides.

Parents of younger children who just want a sandpit in an attractive setting could do worse than spend a few hours in the place Vendôme, contemplating the façades of probably the most beautiful seventeenth-century square in Paris while your children bury each other in the sand. Otherwise, the Parc Monceau is an especially pretty park in which to have a family picnic in the 17th *arrondissement* before wandering around.

AWAY FROM THE CITY

Parc Astérix
61028 Plailly, tel. (16) 44 62 31 31. RER B3 Roissy-Aéroport Charles de Gaulle, then bus Couriers Ile-de-France. Open 10 a.m.–6 p.m. Monday–Friday; 7 p.m. Saturday, Sunday. Entrance 150F adults; 100F 3–12-year-olds.

Animated theme park based on the famous comic-strip character, whom you'll find in the Gaulish village with his friends Getafix and Obélix. Most of the actors speak some English, and when you're tired of them there are always gladiators, chariots and comic battles to watch, as well as plenty of rides, parades and sideshows.

EuroDisney Resort
Marne-la Vallée, tel. 64 74 30 00. RER A4 Parc EuroDisney stop. Entrance to all attractions 200F adults; 150F children.

Not as big as the real thing, but some great rides. Probably a must if you won't get the chance to go to Florida.

France Miniature
25 route du Mesnil, 78990 Elancourt, tel. 30 51 51 51. RER C7 St. Quentin-en-Yvelines.

Over 20 little villages and 150 historical monuments in miniature give an entertaining overall view of the rest of France.

Zoo de Thoiry
78770 Thoiry-en-Yvelines, tel. 3 87 52 25. By train: Gare Montparnasse, Monfort-l'Amaury stop, then bus.

Gigantic safari park with over 800 species living in conditions close to their natural environment.

CIRCUSES

The French take circuses very seriously. Seasonal shows take place all the year round (check under *Cirques* in *Pariscope*) and a permanent circus, the *Cirque d'Hiver Bouglione*, runs from October to January. For details, tel. 47 00 12 25.

PUPPET THEATERS

The younger children are, the less likely they'll be bothered by the language barrier. Puppet shows, known as *guignols* – another strong French tradition – are generally visual enough to give the gist of a story, and the atmosphere of intense concentration punctuated by bursts of laughter does much to persuade the audience that they're having a good time. The list below covers the main locations, scattered throughout the city's principal parks.

Marionnettes du Luxembourg
Jardin du Luxembourg. Metro Notre-Dame-des-Champs/Vavin. Shows from 3 p.m. Wednesday, Saturday, Sunday.

Marionnettes du Parc Montsouris
Avenue Reille, close to the lake. Metro Glacière or Cité Universitaire.
Shows 2:30, 3:30, 4:30 p.m. Wednesday, Sunday.; 2:30, 3:30 p.m. Saturday.

Rond-Point des Champs Elysées
Metro Champs Elysées-Clemenceau. Shows 2 p.m., 3 p.m., 4 p.m. Wednesday,
Saturday, Sunday.

Théâtre de la Petite Ourse
Jardin des Tuileries. Metro Concorde. Shows 3:30, 4:30 p.m. Wednesday,
Saturday, Sunday. Every day during the holidays.

FOOD

French children are generally expected to enjoy the same food as their parents, though no waiter will be surprised if you order just a plate of fries [*frites*]. Most restaurants are happy to provide children's portions, but highchairs and special menus are more of a rarity. One place where they're available is a French fast food chain called Hippopotamus, which serves the predictable range of burgers and fries plus salads with menus you can color in with the crayons provided. Branches include:

> 29 rue Berger, 75001, tel. 45 08 00 29
> 1 boulevard des Capucines, 75002, tel. 47 42 75 70
> 1 boulevard Beaumarchais, 75004, tel. 42 72 50 07/93 87
> 119 boulevard Montparnasse, 75006, tel. 43 20 37 05
> 66 avenue de Wagram, 75008, tel. 47 63 65 40
> 42 avenue des Champs Elysées, 75008, tel. 45 63 41 93
> 4 rue Louis-Armand, 75015, tel. 40 60 10 00.

Alternatively, there are always the ubiquitous McDonald's or Burger King, or the Chicago Pizza Pie Factory, 5 rue de Berri, 75008, tel. 45 62 50 23.

SHOPS

Paris is packed with tempting children's "boutiques" selling wonderful clothes at staggering prices. If you don't want to empty your purse, your best bet is to look in the major department stores, all of which have good children's line. Look out especially for tights, good corduroy pants, and interesting hair accessories.

Almost every major designer, from Pierre Cardin to Sonia Rykiel, seems to have introduced a children's range (there's even a Baby Dior); one of the best is Agnès B. For slightly less rarefied clothes, try:

Clayeux
Branches include: 8 rue Vavin 75006; 60 rue du Commerce, 75015;
C.C. Les 3-Quartiers, boulevard de la Madeleine, 75001.
Good-quality classics in lively colors.

Du Pareil au Même
*Branches include: 7 rue St-Placide, 75008; 24 rue du Mogador, 75009;
135 avenue Emile Zola, 75015; 97 avenue Victor Hugo, 75016.*
Wide range of clothes in bright colors for 0–14-year-olds.

Jacadi
You're unlikely to miss one of these shops, since there must be almost 100.
Classic clothes for 0–16-year-olds.

Petit Bâteau
*Branches include: 81 rue de Sèvres, 75006; 13 rue Tronchet, 75008;
72 avenue Victor Hugo, 75016.*
Especially good for cotton T-shirts and underwear.

Pom d'Api
13 rue du Jour, 75001.
Great shoe shop specializing in small versions of fashionable shoes such as
cowboy boots and Doc Martens.

TOYS AND BOOKS

Chantelivre
13 rue de Sèvres, 75006.
Wonderful bookshop including games, audio-cassettes and videos, and some
books in English.

Au Nain Bleu
406–10 rue Saint-Honoré, 75008.
Paris's oldest and most prestigious toystore, with prices to match.

Il Etait Une Fois
1 rue Cassette, 75006.
Real treasure trove, including some clothes.

Jouets & Cie
11 boulevard Sebastopol, 75001.
Huge toystore on two floors, unmissable from the giant baby doll in the
window.

BABYSITTING
The main babysitting agencies are:

Ababa
*8 rue du Maine, 75015, tel. 45 49 46 46. Open 8 a.m.–9 p.m.
Monday–Saturday. Rates around 30F an hour, plus 50F booking fee.*
Minimum two hours' notice needed. Many sitters speak English.

CHILDREN

Kid's Service

159 rue du Rome, 75017, tel. 47 66 00 52. Open 8 a.m.–8 p.m. Monday–Friday, 10 a.m.–8 p.m. Saturday. Reduced hours August. Rates around 30F an hour, plus 55F booking fee.

Excellent, well-established agency. English-speakers on request.

Zabou

351 rue des Pyrénées, 75020, tel. 46 36 03 76. Open 10 a.m.–7 p.m. Monday–Saturday. Rates around 25F an hour, plus 30F booking fee.

Sitters perhaps less experienced, but this is the only agency to guarantee finding someone within the hour, 24 hours a day.

Allo Maman Poule (tel. 47 47 78 78) also has English-speaking babysitters.

BUSINESSWOMEN

Traditionally, women heading companies tended to have inherited them from their fathers or brothers, and were expected to pass them on to their sons as soon as possible. This remains true of most leading businesswomen, the difference being that they no longer seem to be in a hurry to relinquish control!

France has a huge public sector, and many women, attracted by the power held by top-ranking civil servants, have managed to gain prominence in jobs as museum curators, television executives, top-ranking financial and judicial advisers. In the wake of Françoise Giroud, for many years director of the weekly *Express*, there are also quite a few top-level women journalists. Among the best-known businesswomen are Francine Gomez, president of Waterman (the pen manufacturer) and a member of the European Council; Annette Roux, head of Bénéteau, the pleasure cruise manufacturers; and Véronique Morot, who runs a leading fireworks company.

Other – perhaps more predictable – areas for leading business-women are *haute couture* (although the majority of designers are men) and cosmetics. A very successful example is Hélène Rochas, who stepped into her husband's shoes when he died fairly young, and has seen the perfume "Madame Rochas" achieve equal renown with Coco Chanel's No. 5, Jeanne Lanvin, and Nina Ricci's "L'Air du Temps." On the other hand, clothes designer Agnès B, who has several shops in Paris and two in London, started at the age of nineteen as a young fashion editor for *Elle* magazine and became one of the most respected purveyors of classic street style outside the realms of *haute couture*.

Doing business as a woman in France is much the same as it is in other Latin countries. It's principally a man's world, but being female can have its advantages. Men tend to be less suspicious of a businesswoman, they enjoy the inevitable play of seduction that goes on, and they believe all too easily in female gullibility – which, unless you really are naïve, can be used to your advantage. And of course they enjoy "helping" a woman – it's part of their education. According to many French businesswomen, this "help" should not be dismissed; having prominent "protectors" in a tough, aggressive world very much dominated by personal relationships can be invaluable.

Long business lunches in chic or brasserie-style restaurants are terribly important in France, for this is where most contractual and creative decisions are made. French businessmen (and women) can appear stiff, cold and even bad-mannered from the other side of their desk in some sumptuous office, but put the same person in front of a dozen oysters accompanied by a bottle of wine, chosen especially "for you," and he or she is likely to become totally charming. Remember; food makes the French relax.

USEFUL ADDRESSES

Faxing

Most hotels have fax machines which guests can use. Otherwise you can send one from any major post office. Receiving faxes is clearly more difficult. Main post office open 24 hours:

La Poste, 52 rue du Louvre, 75001, tel. 40 28 20 00.

Photocopying

Post offices also tend to have photocopiers. They're okay for the odd copy, but extremely unsophisticated. If you have a lot to do, go to a photocopy shop such as:

Rep 11, 24 rue du Regard, 75006, tel. 42 22 12 48; or Copie 2000, 46 rue de Provence, 75009; tel. 42 81 11 12.

Translation and Interpreting

Contact Europe Paris, 39 rue de Tourenne, 75003, tel. 40 27 87 37.
Abadec, 80 rue Blanche, 75009, tel. 48 78 52 52.
Adam Aspin, 73 rue Bichat, 75010, tel. 42 06 78 04.

Temporary Offices

Multiburo, 34 boulevard Haussmann, 75009, tel. 48 01 48 01.
Carlton, 32 rue de la Bienfaisance, 75008, tel. 42 94 60 00, fax 42 94 60 01.

Car Rental/Chauffeur-Driven

Avis Chauffeur France
tel. 45 54 33 65 (special business day rate inclusive of bilingual chauffeur from 2583F).
Budget
4 Avenue du Président Roosevelt, 75008, tel. 42 25 79 89 (one of the best values).
Europcar
Charles de Gaulle Airport: Terminal 1, tel. 48 62 33 33; Terminal 2, tel. 48 62 56 47.
Orly Sud: Terminal A, tel. 49 75 47 48.

BACKGROUND

CHRONOLOGY
OF KEY HISTORICAL DATES

BC
3rd century   The Parisii, a Gallic tribe, settle in the area and take Île de la Cité as their capital.

AD

52	Caesar's armies arrived, the area became a Roman colony, Lutetia.
418–751	The Merovingians
451	Merovius, King of the Salian Franks (from Belgium) defeats Attila the Hun. Origin of the word France.
476	Fall of the Roman Empire in the west.
508	King Clovis of the Franks declares Paris the capital.
751–986	The Carolingians
800	Charlemagne crowned Emperor of the Holy Roman Empire.
843	Treaty of Verdun, Carolingian Empire divided, present-day France given to Charles the Bald, son of Louis I.
987–1328	The Capetians
987	Hugh Capet elected King of France.
1066	Battle of Hastings, Normans conquer Britain, William Duke of Normandy crowns himself King of England.
1137	Louis VII married Eleanor of Aquitaine.
1270	Louis IX St. Louis dies on his way to the Crusades.
1337–1475	The Hundred Years War. Battle between the Capetians and Plantagenets for the throne.
1348	The Black Death
1422	Marie d'Anjou marries Charles VII.
1429	Joan of Arc recaptures Orléans. Charles VII crowned at Rheims.
1431	Henry VI of England crowned King of France in Notre Dame.
1436	Charles VII recaptures Paris, Marie d'Ecosse at the age of 15 marries the future Louis XI, then 13.
1461	Louis XI on the throne.
1514	Claude de France marries the future François I.
1515	François I

1562–98	Wars of Religion, Catholics versus Protestants
1547	Henry II comes to the throne, his wife Catherine de' Medici becomes regent on his death in 1559.
1570	St. Bartholomew's Day massacre of 20,000 Protestants.
1589	Henry of Navarre becomes Henry IV and renounces his Protestant faith.
1598	Edict of Nantes, in favor of religious tolerance.
1600	Henri IV marries Maria de' Medici.
1610	Louis XIII becomes King.
1615	Louis XIII marries Anne of Austria.
1643	Louis XIV becomes King at the age of five. Anne of Austria nominates Mazarin first minister. The Sun King reigns for 72 years.
1660	Louis XIV marries Marie-Thérèse of Austria.
1670	Court transfers to Versailles.
1684	Madame de Maintenon becomes the morganatic wife of Louis XIV.
1685	Revocation of the Edict of Nantes.
1715	Louis XV succeeds to the throne.
1725	Louis XV marries Marie Leszczynska.
1769	Corsica becomes part of France.
1771	The future Louis XVIII marries Marie-Josèphe Louise de Savoie.
1773	The future Charles X marries Marie-Thérèse de Savoie.
1774	The future Louis XVI marries Marie-Antoinette of Austria.
1774	Louis XVI crowned King.
1783	Treaty of Versailles marks the end of the American War of Independence.

The French Revolution (1789–99)

1789	Creation of the National Assembly and storming of the Bastille.
1792	Proclamation of the Republic.
1793	Louis XVI and Marie-Antoinette guillotined.
1794	Execution of Robespierre.
1796	Napoleon marries Joséphine Beauharnais.
1799	Napoleon declares himself First Consul of the Republic.
1804	Napoleon crowns himself Emperor of the French in Notre Dame.
1813	Napoleon loses the Battle of Leipzig and abdicates. Farewell at Fontainebleau.

The Restoration (1815–48)

1815   Napoleon loses the Battle of Waterloo, restoration of the monarchy. Louis XVIII back on the throne.

1821   Napoleon dies on St. Helena.

1830   Charles X violates the constitution and a revolution puts Louis-Philippe on the throne.

Second Republic and Second Empire (1848–70)

1848   Louis Napoleon elected President of the Republic.

1852   Proclamation of the Second Empire under Napoleon III.

1870   End of Second Empire, proclamation of the Third Republic.

1870   The Fourth Republic

1914   First World War German armies repulsed in the Battle of the Marne.

1919   Signing of the Treaty of Versailles marks the end of the First World War.

1940–44   German Occupation during the Second World War.

1958   De Gaulle elected President of the Fifth Republic after the downfall of the Fourth following the Algerian crisis. Algerians obtain their independence in 1962.

1959   EEC founded.

1968   May student uprisings.

1981   Mitterrand elected president.

1989   Celebrations of the Bicenntenial of the French Revolution.
               Opéra Bastille, Grande Arche and Pyramid unveiled.

1991   Edit Cresson elected first female Prime Minister of France.

B A C K G R O U N D

RECOMMENDED BOOKS

The novels, short stories and nonfiction works that feature Paris are endless – something to suit every reader's interests whether it be the seductive delights of Colette in *Chéri*, Janet Flanner's *An American in Paris*, or Claire Duchen's more taxing but fascinating *Feminism in France*.

The following is just a *soupçon* to guide you towards your own discoveries.

Fiction

Djuna Barnes – *Nightwood, Ladies' Almanac*
Colette – *Chéri, The Last of Chéri, Gigi, The Pure and the Impure*, and many more
Simone de Beauvoir – *The Mandarins, A Woman Destroyed*
Elaine Dundy – *The Dud Avocado*
Marguerite Dura – *The Lover*
Janet Flanner – *An American in Paris*
Nancy Mitford – *The Pursuit of Love, The Blessing*
Anaïs Nin – *The Four-Chambered Heart, Henry and June*
Jean Rhys – *Quartet, After Leaving Mr. Mackenzie*
Françoise Sagan – *Bonjour Tristèsse*
Marguerite Yourcenar – *Memoirs of Hadrian*

Autobiography/Biography/Journals/Letters

Deirdre Bair – *Simone de Beauvoir: A Biography*
Djuna Barnes – *I Could Never Be Lonely Without a Husband*
Sylvia Beach – *Shakespeare and Company*
Janet Flanner – *Darlinghissima*
Madame de Lafayette – *The Princesse de Cleves*
Brenda Maddox – *The Biography of Nora Joyce*
Hilary Mantel – *Theroigne de Méricourt*
Anaïs Nin – *The Journals*
Judith Okely – *Simone de Beauvoir*
Edith Piaf – *My Life*
George Sand – *Lettres d'un Voyageur*
Diana Souhami – *Gertrude and Alice*
Gertrude Stein – *The Autobiography of Alice B. Toklas, Everybody's Autobiography*
Fanny Trollope – *Paris and the Parisians*

History/Politics/Society
Shari Benstock – *Women of the Left Bank*
Simone de Beauvoir – *The Second Sex*
Claire Duchen – *Feminism in France*
Linda Kelly – *Women of the French Revolution*
Elaine Marks – *New French Feminisms*
Nancy Mitford – *The Sun King*
Marina Warner – *Monuments and Maidens*
Elizabeth Wilson – *The Sphinx in the City*

INDEX

BACKGROUND

HIDDEN GUIDES

Adventure travel or a relaxing vacation? "Hidden" guidebooks are the only travel books in the business to provide detailed information on both. Aimed at environmentally aware travelers, our motto is "Adventure Travel Plus." These books combine details on unique hotels, restaurants and sightseeing with information on camping, sports and hiking for the outdoor enthusiast.

HIDDEN BOSTON AND CAPE COD *228 pages. $7.95*
HIDDEN COAST OF CALIFORNIA *480 pages. $14.95*
HIDDEN FLORIDA *492 pages. $14.95*
HIDDEN FLORIDA KEYS & EVERGLADES *156 pages. $7.95*
HIDDEN HAWAII *468 pages. $14.95*
HIDDEN MEXICO *444 pages. $13.95*
HIDDEN NEW ENGLAND *564 pages. $14.95*
HIDDEN PACIFIC NORTHWEST *528 pages. $14.95*
HIDDEN SAN FRANCISCO
  AND NORTHERN CALIFORNIA *456 pages. $14.95*
HIDDEN SOUTHERN CALIFORNIA *516 pages. $14.95*
HIDDEN SOUTHWEST *504 pages. $14.95*

ULTIMATE GUIDES

These innovative guides present the best and most unique features of a destination. Quality is the keynote. They are as likely to cover a mom 'n pop café as a gourmet restaurant, a quaint bed and breakfast as a five-star tennis resort. In addition to thoroughly covering each destination, they feature short articles and one-line "teasers" that are both fun and informative.

ULTIMATE ARIZONA *328 pages. $11.95*
ULTIMATE CALIFORNIA *528 pages. $14.95*
ULTIMATE WASHINGTON *312 pages. $11.95*
DISNEY WORLD AND BEYOND:
  The Ultimate Family Guidebook *300 pages. $9.95*
DISNEY WORLD AND BEYOND:
  Family Fun Cards *90 cards. $7.95*
DISNEYLAND AND BEYOND:
  The Ultimate Family Guidebook *240 pages. $9.95*
FLORIDA'S GOLD COAST:
  The Ultimate Guidebook *192 pages. $8.95*
LAS VEGAS: The Ultimate Guidebook *240 pages. $9.95*
THE MAYA ROUTE:
  The Ultimate Guidebook *432 pages. $14.95*

An alert, adventurous reader is as important as a travel writer in keeping a guidebook up–to–date and accurate. So if you happen upon a great restaurant, discover an intriguing locale or (heaven forbid) find an error in the text, we'd appreciate hearing from you. Practical details such as opening hours, telephone numbers, transportation details, prices, the standards in hotels and restaurants and popularity of certain bars and clubs are all liable to change. The guide will be constantly updated over the coming years, so please keep us informed.

Ulysses Press
3286 Adeline Street, Suite 1
Berkeley, CA 94703

VIRAGO WOMAN'S TRAVEL GUIDES

Written through a woman's eye and steeped in the grand tradition of travel literature, these guides speak directly to the special interests of solo female travelers, businesswomen and women traveling with children. Each title offers a fascinating blend of practical information and cultural insights. History, art and contemporary society are examined from a woman's point of view with fascinating results.

NEW YORK   *350 pages. $13.95*
ROME   *360 pages. $13.95*

OTHER ULYSSES PRESS TRAVEL TITLES

Critically acclaimed as the best resource to Costa Rica in print, *The New Key to Costa Rica* has captured the imagination of travelers everywhere. This edition is completely updated with hundreds of details on tropical rain forests, endangered species and awesome volcanoes.

THE NEW KEY TO COSTA RICA   *312 pages. $13.95*

FOR A FREE CATALOG OR TO ORDER DIRECT For each book send an additional $2 postage and handling (California residents include 8% sales tax) to Ulysses Press, 3286 Adeline Street, Suite 1, Berkeley, CA 94703. Or call 800-377-2542 or 510-601-8301 and charge your order.

BOOKS FROM ULYSSES PRESS